GOOD READING FOR THE DISADVANTAGED READER

MULTI-ETHNIC RESOURCES

George D. Spache, Ph.D.
Professor Emeritus
University of Florida

GARRARD PUBLISHING COMPANY
CHAMPAIGN, ILLINOIS

371.97
S 732g

COPYRIGHT © 1970 BY GEORGE D. SPACHE

MANUFACTURED IN THE UNITED STATES OF AMERICA
STANDARD BOOK NUMBER: 8116-6009-5

Table Of Contents

Introduction

Our CONCERN IS WITH WAYS of improving reading instruction among the disadvantaged minority groups in our population. As reading specialists, we choose to make our small contribution by leading teachers of such children to new approaches in reading instruction which we believe will lead to easier mastery of this foundational ability.

It is our hope that this book will alert teachers to the need to help pupils to find books with which they can identify—books in which they can find positive images of their race or ethnic type. How can we expect reading success among economically-deprived pupils when we feed them a constant diet of fantasy material dealing with a way of life they have never known (and may never experience)?

Oh, yes, we now have the multi-racial, the integrated, socially-conscious basal reader—in some cases by pasting a few black or brown faces into the upper middle-class pictures. But the Negroes portrayed in some of our "new" basal readers, for example, must be drawn from that minute group of millionaires in the suburbs of Atlanta, for the average Negro does not live in the style depicted in some of these books.

On the other hand, some publishers are producing fine, realistic, integrated stories. We must offer our minority children these realistic stories—with central characters whom they can admire and imitate. At the very beginnings of reading instruction, the paucity of simple materials available implies that we, or the children themselves, may have to write these stories. But we must have stories about the Puerto Rican family, the Negro policeman, the Oriental shopkeeper, the Indian farmer, and the like, to channel our pupils' interest and strengthen their motivation for reading. If this means that we substitute the language experience approach for the basal method, we see only superior advantages.

Daily experience with teachers of underprivileged primary children for the past five years has convinced us that the language experience is the most realistic and profitable approach to "children without"—without language development, standard English, or middle-class background. Limited as these children may be, their own language and their own perceptions of life around them, as expressed in dictated or self-written stories, offer the greatest chance for success for most of these pupils, in our opinion.

As the author of one such study, we are well aware that the large-scale First Grade Studies, as they are called, failed to show any major advantage for the language experience or the basal method (or any other

approach) for minority groups *when results were measured by test scores.*
(1) Using the child's own language and experiences as the bases for teaching him to read does not, we agree, accelerate his progress in levels of reading materials. In the first place, his limited background and language development would militate against accelerated progress. But our personal experiences in classrooms in segregated schools, as well as what we have learned from statistical data, support these observations. First, the range of end-of-year reading scores is distinctly greater when underprivileged (or even overprivileged) children are taught by the language experience approach rather than by the basal. Freed to progress at the rate made possible by their abilities, very capable disadvantaged children make more progress than expected under the basal program. Second, the realization that reading is really talking written down, and that children can learn to read as well as write what they think and what they say, is reached earlier. It is manifested in more fluent, natural reading that parallels their own speech in rate, inflection, and intonation. The monotone of word-calling, characteristic of beginners under other methods, is largely absent, for the child is constantly aided by his auditory memories for the phrases and sentences he himself has composed. Third, using the child's own experiences and language as the bases of his reading materials keeps the language model within his easy comprehension. He is not subjected to the often highly artificial sentences of the pre-primer and primer (that resemble no known spoken language patterns); nor is he expected to deal with a style of English foreign to his home and his culture. Since he creates the reading matter, it is couched in familiar phrases and patterns and deals with familiar subject matter.

Finally, the language experience approach fosters more frequent and more varied teacher-pupil contacts, with the inherent possibilities of greater mutual understanding of each other and of the cultures each represents. Often the teacher's middle-class attitudes and values conflict with those of the lower socioeconomic background of the child. Or, cultural ideals of pupil and teacher clash when the child comes from a subculture different than that of the community. By avoiding the imposition of the stereotyped, middle-class values offered in the average basal reader, and substituting the perceptions of life as the child projects them in his own stories, there is the opportunity, at least, for the teacher to begin to understand and, perhaps, to appreciate the child's cultural background. True, she may wish to modify the child's perceptions, but she must first know and understand them in order to plan the experiences which may result in their modification.

Perhaps we have sufficiently defended our own biases regarding primary reading instruction for the disadvantaged child to continue our explanation of the rationale of this book. As soon as the child's power of reading, and the supply of appropriate materials permit, we would move toward the use of books dealing with people and events identified with the child's own cultural group. It is immaterial, in our opinion, whether this instruction in ethnically-oriented stories is conducted in individualized or in small-group fashion. Personally, we prefer a real effort toward pupil self-selection and self-pacing in order to provide a wide gamut of reading experiences. But, in working with some two hundred primary teachers in the past three years, we have learned that this approach is highly dependent upon teacher planning and classroom organizational abilities—not upon the strength of our belief in its values.

No matter what our instructional pattern (excepting, of course, a whole-class arrangement which would be self-defeating), our goal is to provide reading materials to enhance the child's sense of ethnic identity. We want him to meet outstanding and respected members of his group, to learn more about their cultural and political contributions to America, to become familiar, in a word, with himself as a member of an important segment of our population.

We are not suggesting that the child of any ethnic group should be limited in his reading to books dealing only with his group. He must also read stories about other groups (such as those represented in his class-room) for comparison and mutual understanding. A diet of reading limited to books dealing only with his own group would strengthen his ego and sense of identity, but it might just as readily leave him socially ignorant and bigoted. As the reader inspects our lists of resources in later chapters, he will note the inclusion of many books for fostering intergroup relation-ships both by their content and dual language presentations.

Our selection will be seen to include the gamut of attitudes on race and human relations, from the extreme left to the far right. Some authors recognize the equality of all men, while others perpetuate the stereotypes believed in by the average White-Anglo-Saxon-Protestant. Defamatory as well as flattering portraits of various groups are present. Appeals to the humane feelings of readers, as well as incitements to riot and revolution, are all deliberately included. These contrasting materials are offered for those teachers who will attempt to promote insightful, critical reading among their pupils. If, again, an opinion is warranted, we feel that the goals we have outlined can only be achieved by the free and frank dis-cussion of these more provocative materials we have included. It is as im-portant for children and young adults to understand the falsities and biases in some stories of their own and other ethnic groups as it is to find them-selves a worthy member of a respectable group.

REFERENCES

1. Harris, Albert J. et al., "Comparing Reading Approaches in First Grade Teaching with Disadvantaged Children-Extended into Second Grade," *Reading Teacher*, 20 (1967) 698-703.

CHAPTER I

The Self-Concept

T HE SELF-CONCEPT HAS BECOME a subject of intensive research by psychologists and sociologists only within the past decade. Today
these investigators are exploring definitions of the self-concept, measures of
it that are appropriate among children and youth, and ways and means of
modifying this introspective feeling about self. In the past, educators and
others simply accepted the fact that almost everyone, child or adult, has a
self-concept. We just naturally knew that each individual thinks he sees
certain characteristic traits in himself, has ideas about the ways in which
he relates to others, and even thinks he knows what other persons see in
him. We accepted the fact that each individual has, in effect, a number of
mental pictures of himself as a physical being and as a social being and
makes some more or less conscious comparisions of his characteristics
with those of the persons around him. These are common-sense definitions
of the self-concept that almost all of us accept.

But these common-sense definitions do not satisfy the scientific in-
vestigator. He feels it essential to trace the development of this self-
view and the forces or factors which control its development. He would
study the efforts of the individual to maintain the integrity of his self-
concept, or the ways in which the child or adult more or less consciously
controls his behavior in an effort to be consistent with his view of himself.
The scientific study of the self-concept is also concerned with the role of the
family, the school, the teacher, and others in influencing the development of
each child's concept. In particular, the psychologist is anxious to learn how
events, persons, and the individual's own behavior which conflict with his
self-concept disturb his personal and mental adjustment. The researcher
wants to discover why some persons develop chronic feelings of guilt, inadequacy, depression, or pessimism. It is essential to find out, if we can,
why, to some the world is threatening, unfriendly, angry, or overdemand-
ing; while to others it is a happy, considerate, friendly, and tolerant world.

DEFINITIONS OF THE SELF-CONCEPT

Scientific efforts to describe or define the self-concept result in statements such as:

> Paul C. Berg of the University of South Carolina describes the self-
> concept as 1) the individual's understanding of the expectations of
> society and his peers and 2) the kinds of behavior which the individual
> selects as a "style of life." (2)

Dr. Berg is appropriately emphasizing that each person tries to be the

1

kind of person that he *thinks* his environment expects him to be. If his parents or his teacher show him that they think he is bright, he tries to meet this expectation, and he accordingly tends to achieve academically (even though he may not be very bright). Conversely, if the adults indicate by their remarks and their attitudes that they expect him to do poorly, he performs at a level in keeping with the adults' estimates of his ability almost regardless of his true ability.

Middle-class parents whose children fail to do well in school often find it very difficult to see this relationship between their attitudes toward the child and his scholastic underachievement. They would insist that they have never openly disparaged the child's abilities to his face; that they have always maintained that he has real ability. But the fact remains that because of their expectation of high school achievements which their child has not met in every respect, the child often becomes convinced that he cannot possibly do well, in general, as his parents expect him to. He has failed to meet his parents' expectations so often (perhaps because the combination of his abilities and weaknesses is never really recognized) that eventually he hopelessly ceases trying to excel in any school area. He comes to believe that he just hasn't got what it takes to make good grades in certain academic areas, and, of course, he usually fails in those subjects.

As Dr. Berg points out, in each and every aspect of life and in every type of physical and social activity, the individual tends to behave (and to achieve or succeed) in a fashion that is highly consistent with the picture he has of himself and that which he believes society has of him.

Dr. Arthur W. Combs expresses his view of the self-concept as:

> People discover who they are and what they are from the ways in which they have been treated by those who surround them in the process of growing up. (5)

In effect, Combs is saying that the self-concept begins to emerge from the first contacts the child has with his family. These experiences in infancy lead gradually to an awareness of self, as maturational forces and environmental experiences shape this self-view. Early childhood research certainly confirms this viewpoint of the effects of environmental pressures upon the child's self-view and outlook upon life. We know, for example, that children who are hospitalized or institutionalized in infancy fail to show normal reactions to the world about them in social behavior and even in language development. Children who are abandoned or for other reasons fail to receive an adequate amount of "mothering" in the first years of life, appear stunted in intellectual, emotional, and social growth. When parents are strict, quick to punish (and slow to reward), lacking in affection and physical love gestures, their children tend to lack emotional response, to appear dull and unresponsive, and perhaps, eventually, to feel angry toward and resistant to any authority.

Dr. Combs is telling us that one's family conveys its judgments of the child to him in verbal and nonverbal ways. In consequence, the child builds images of himself from the pictures held up to him by the parents' actions and words. He sees himself as others lead him to understand what they think they see. Furthermore, this same pressure toward a self-view is moulded by the culture of the group (the family, relatives, peers) — in manners, speech, religion, ethical and moral values, and in prejudices toward other individuals.

As life goes on, we learn to project to the environment the feelings it has taught us; we reflect back and ascribe to others the same feelings we think the world has about us. We like or dislike, love or hate, tolerate or despise others as they have shown us that they feel about us. Or we respond with the kinds of behavior that appear to be appropriate for the ways in which the world seems to treat us—anger against unfair pressures, violence against intolerable domination, or affection toward the love we feel others give us. Sometimes our responses are not so obvious and, rather than fight back against a threatening world, we turn our feeling inward against ourselves or retreat into a fantasy life and present an almost blank exterior to the world. In a word, we tend to answer or behave toward the world around us in the ways that the world has made *us* feel, or in ways that seems to protect us or defend us from the world.

SELF-CONCEPT AND MINORITY GROUPS

Those children and adults who don't quite fit into the mainstream of middle-class, white American life because of color, speech, physical appearance, education, or even religion, present unique problems for those of us who are concerned. These "deviates" just don't fit neatly into the life patterns of the White-Anglo-Saxon-Protestant way of life. They don't use their knives and forks properly; they don't bathe often enough; they wear dirty or worn work clothes; they don't live in the nicer parts of the community. They talk too loudly, or ungrammatically; their speech inflections are wrong; they aren't fluent in their efforts to communicate; they just don't seem to have the vocabulary to express their ideas. They have too many children; they discipline them too loudly or too rigorously; they don't wash or dress the children in fresh clothes often enough, etc. "They just don't know any better" or "They're just too lazy to lift themselves out of their present conditions" or "What can you expect from those————?"

Our middle-class children are quick to learn the differences between themselves and these minority-group individuals from conversations at the breakfast and dinner table. It helps their own self-concept of superiority, their feelings of belonging to their own society, to learn to use such terms as: wop, guinea, spik, nigger, polack, kike, mick, white trash, jigaboo, nigra.

The non-White-Anglo-Saxon-Protestant child learns very early in life that he is different—inferior, distasteful, and despised. He learns that in his birth he has committed an unforgivable sin against the majority of society—by differing in some fashion from the average middle-class white. He discovers that it is very difficult to erase, hide, or overcome this difference and to become a fully accepted member of the group that appears to matter in our society.

No matter how the minority parents feel or how hard some of them may try to build a positive self-concept for their children, their efforts are constantly being contradicted, if not even defeated, by the majority of society. The older members of his ethnic group, his older brothers and sisters, help to convey to the minority child all the nasty feelings they now have about others—and about themselves. The ambitions of his parents may be high for the minority child, but as is obvious from our statistics in higher education and employment, these aspirations can hardly be achieved. Only a small proportion of Negro, Puerto Rican, Mexican, or Indian children persist in school or enter institutions of higher education. This number is far less than the proportion of such groups in our total population. The same failure exists in vocational pursuits, for these groups find it very difficult to secure quality education to fit them for higher level jobs. In fact, most of them have even been excluded from the skilled trades or other positions controlled by labor unions until very recently, when the federal government has begun to exert pressure in this area.

Despite the parental aspirations, the minority child will almost always lack the background characteristics of middle-class society. The traits of self-denial, prolonged striving toward long-range goals, thrift, and stimulating intellectual family activities are often missing in this child's background. There is also a tendency toward language deprivation because of the lack of communication within the family, often composed of members who themselves have limited education and therefore limited language facility and intellectual interests.

The absence of these typical middle-class family traits are real handicaps for the minority children in the environment of the middle-class school, and practically all schools are devoted to achieving the goal of producing middle-class citizens. Children of minority groups just don't have the facility with words to compete in the highly verbal setting of the school. Nor is the school that attempts to overcome the language deprivation often very successful in its efforts. The periods of rapid language development that are, in a sense, foundational for the rest of life tend to occur during preschool years and the early school years. Expansion of auditory and speaking vocabularies is not as rapid at later periods of life and, hence, the opportunity for early stimulation has been almost irretrievably lost shortly after the child enters school.

The minority child tends to learn more about responding nonverbally to life than he does about communicating with words. In fact, he often amazes his teacher by the fact that he can become involved in violent interaction with another child—without ever having exchanged a word! The teacher, of course, isn't familiar with the provocative or insulting meanings that are conveyed by gestures and bodily movements.

For all these reasons, verbal communication between the minority child and the minions of the school, and understanding of each other's demands and needs, is very poor. Nor is this problem quickly solved, in this writer's opinion, by a program of study in sentence patterns, structural linguistics, programmed vocabulary study, or any other program offered for this purpose. A total handicap in meeting the middle-class demands of the school is not cured by practice with middle-class patterns of speech or word study or the like. As we have tried to point out, the minority child is not ready to assume the mores, customs, and niceties of middle-class life just because he is exposed to a few months or years of trying to talk like his teachers. Inherent in all such programs (and the minority child is quite well aware of this) is the rejection of his own speech and ideas as unfit or improper. Even if such programs are successful in stimulating better speech, and some seem to be, what does this training really do for the child? Does it supply content for more ideas or the experiences which, after all, are the foundation (words) upon which thinking and ideas are based? Does the training give him ideas and experiences to think with, or does it simply make him a bit more fluent in speech, more facile in using various sentence patterns, and give him a few more words to memorize?

If, as one group of linguists, the semanticists, tell us, our language is a reflection of us—our background, the depth and variety of our experiences, our aspirations, our fears—how does a program in manipulation of arrangements of words change the basic "us" to a middle-class person? If we project our self-concept in our use of language, and we certainly do, can we really expect to change this self-concept by learning more about word order, inflection, word usage, and the like? As we shall point out later, a much greater active involvement of the child, his feelings, and his attitudes in the training is essential.

As much research shows, there are other negative factors which may be present in the minority child's background. These factors tend to make it even more difficult for such children who experience them to meet the school's demands. Some minority parents have negative attitudes toward school success and see little value for education in their own or their children's lives. When parents in certain industries, such as shrimpfishing, workers in the oil fields, and others, can earn much more money than teachers, almost regardless of their education, they see few reasons for their children to persist in school.

Some uneducated parents tend to restrict the normal freedom of childhood experiences and thus, again, handicap the child for school success. Parents who conceive of themselves as educational, marital, or vocational failures tend to transmit their feelings of frustration and hopelessness to their children. Furthermore, several studies show that boys learn from the behavior of their fathers that success in reading is not often part of the male sex role they are trying to emulate. (18).

Of course, there are positive influences toward school success in the homes of some minority children. For example, in a study of library usage in low-income families, Peil (14) found no constant cultural or socioeconomic factors. Despite lower income, Negro mothers in this study tended to read more books and magazines than white mothers, even when the elements of age and education were controlled. Mothers who used the library bought more books for their children, and the use of the library by their first-grade children was related to its use by their mothers. We shall discuss these more positive factors in a later chapter which will consider their relationship to reading instruction for the disadvantaged child.

THE TEACHER'S SELF-CONCEPT

Like everyone else, teachers too have a self-concept which reflects their family background, their school experiences, their personal and social goals. This self-concept determines, of course, their understanding of the role of a teacher, which they may see as a combination of a social worker—a character builder—or a contributor to social progress by imparting the benefits of education to young people. Some see it as a temporary job, or a steppingstone to higher vocational levels. The teacher's self-concept of herself and her ultimate function delimits her relationships with her pupils—as a leader or a guide toward learning, as a moulder of our youth, as an imparter of information to undeveloped minds, or as baby-sitter.

Let us consider a description of the hypothetical average teacher and the implications of her background and training.* It is said that the average American teacher is a white, Protestant, married woman between the ages of 46 and 55 who was born in a lower middle-class family in a rural or small-town setting. She attended a relatively small college or university of second- or third-class quality, and achieved C+ to B grades, an average or slightly above average college performance in what many consider an easy curriculum. She selected the college largely for financial reasons and the fact that she could meet its entrance requirements. A large propor-tion of teachers who attended universities did not plan for an education major at entrance to the institution but rather gravitated toward it, per-haps as more feasible second or third choice. (16)

Teachers tend to see themselves as relatively well-educated, well-organized, and well-informed. Some observers note that teachers are quick to share their informational background, when the opportunity presents it-self, even in casual conversation (a habit to which this author is also ad-dicted). At the same time, the average teacher is socially conscious and concerned about the people around her. She shows this concern frequently by active participation in school and community affairs mainly of non-political nature. She contributes time and money to fund collections, school bond drives, community betterment projects, and the like. She probably secures more collegiate post-graduate training in her professional field and spends more time at workshops, seminars, and demonstrations of new ma-terials and techniques,as well as committee and staff meetings, than any other type of professional worker. The average teacher, it is said, also shows her social motif by contributing to indigent relations to a unique degree.

As the teacher may view them, her pupils are perhaps savages to be tamed and ruled, or developing intellects to be nurtured and directed, or they possess empty minds upon which, a la Rousseau, facts are to be permanently imprinted. They need strict rules and constant supervision, or simply the opportunities to work with ideas and materials which will evoke their creative powers. They need only open ears, and eyes, to absorb the constant flow of facts that the teacher and books will pour into them.

TEACHER SELF-CONCEPT AND READING INSTRUCTION

If our views of the average teacher are not completely astigmatic, the effects of teacher self-concept upon classroom procedures are obvious. As exemplified in the field of reading, some teachers need the carefully structured guidelines of the basal reader program to maintain their direc-tive, authoritarian role. Others see great merit in the detailistic operations of programmed reading materials, because, perhaps, these help in con-

---

*For the benefit of those teachers who resent this unglamorous potrait, let me admit frankly that most of the details cannot be proved statistically but represent this author's observations over a 30-year period.

trolling children's activities and keeping them busy (and, presumably, learning). A few choose the path of individualized reading because of their great concern about differences among pupil needs, rates of progress, and their strong desires to help each child to develop to his ultimate capacities. Other teachers flutter from one approach to the next, from basal to i.t.a., from language experience to a "total language arts program," from machines to kits, from reading as thinking to some ultra-phonic system, from encoding to decoding and back again—seeking that sweet nectar of success found in higher reading scores (that regularly appear with each change of method or material). The feelings of guilt that some teachers experience when they apparently fail to teach all or most of their pupils to read well must be assuaged somehow, it would seem.

In part, some of this vacillating is undoubtedly due to the sketchy nature of the actual preservice professional training in the field of reading. Almost two-thirds of the institutions that train teachers offer no real college course in reading methodology, for any such content is only a minor part of the general methods bloc. In other words, the teacher's familiarity with approaches, materials, and the nature of the reading-learning process is often encompassed in a total of six or eight clock hours of class discussions or lectures or staged demonstrations of reading lessons (delivered in third-grade style to the college class). To the best of our knowledge, only about 20 per cent of the states require a complete course in reading for certification of an elementary teacher. In fact, several states require a total of only nine college credits in the field of education to admit to the teaching profession those college graduates who are unemployed, or anxious to avoid the draft, or confused in vocational goals, or awaiting pregnancy. For hundreds of college graduates, the teacher's job presents a temporary, moderately-paid haven from the realities of life. For some, their first class represents their initial and only opportunity to observe, participate with, or relate to a group of children of any age. What sort of self-concepts as professionals can such pseudo-teachers bring to the classroom?

Failure of a child or even of a group of slow learners to show expected progress, or of ghetto children to achieve some level near the "national norm," is a frustrating, irritating, and guilt-provoking experience for many sincere teachers. This experience certainly disturbs administrators, parents, and the professional writers who make a good living belaboring schools and school people. Publication of the reading test results of a large school system such as New York City or Los Angeles is a signal for these critics to attack the current instructional program in reading (no matter what its nature). The focus of such attacks often is the classroom teacher and her new-fangled, unbusinesslike, ineffectual methods. The readers of these statistics become irate either about the discrimination against minority groups which produced their inferior scores, or the unproductiveness of the "expensive" school system, or its lack of "discipline," etc., etc. The ultimate scapegoat is the teacher, and another round of guilt feelings to be calmed by fluttering to still another method or approach is precipitated, even among professional teachers.

TEACHER SELF-CONCEPT AND PUPIL-TEACHER RELATIONSHIPS

If challenged, the average teacher is likely to defend her views as liberal, tolerant, and unprejudiced toward other racial, ethnic, or religious groups. She claims to give equal opportunity to all the members of her multi-ethnic class, boys as well as girls, rich as well as poor. She thinks of herself as fair and just, impartially giving out rewards and punishments as deserved, a veritable Solomon in judgment (and what child can successfully challenge her decisions?).

But research does not yield quite precisely a mirror image of the teacher's self-concept. If, like the great majority, she is white, Protestant, and socially-upward mobile, she has had almost no social experiences with individuals of other racial or ethnic groups, or the poor, or the dirty ones of our society. After all, who invites such people into their homes? Like all of us, she absorbed the prejudices of her parents as these were displayed, in the breakfast conversations and in the unconscious social exclusion of those of different race, religion, or socioeconomic status from the parents' home. Although the changes in home sites might have brought new church affiliations to the family, this hardly extended to visits to the church services of other religions, or to any major change in the types of family friends. Early in life she observed the assignment of only menial jobs and poor housing, etc. in the community to those who did not belong to the White-Anglo-Saxon-Protestant sect, and she probably saw no injustice in this arrangement, for it was an order based, presumably, on worth and ability.

Doesn't she readily accept the term "culturally-deprived" as an accurate description of these other groups, for, by her standards, they do indeed lack any recognizable culture?

Studies of the interviews of typical middle-class teachers with the parents of their pupils show revealing facets of teacher-pupil-parent relationships. Such teachers devote most of their parent interviews with middle-class parents to a discussion of ways and means of motivating greater school achievement by their children (despite the fact that such children are not, in general, poor achievers). When dealing with lower-class parents, the emphasis is on school behavior, character, and social traits, even though these children are indeed the low achievers and are failing to meet the school's primary goal for them. When teachers' oral comments to children are taped and classified, it is apparent that the majority of the positive remarks are addressed to the smartest pupils, or to the middle-class pupils, or to the girls. The gold stars, the pats on the head, the scholarships, and other rewards somehow or other seem to go only to these acceptable children.

Class discrimination against pupils is often present even when both teacher and pupils are of the same race, or both are of lower-class origin. Paradoxical as it may seem, some teachers are intolerant of the efforts of the duller pupils even of their own race or ethnic group. As one of the author's black teachers phrased it quite frankly and loudly, "They ain't never gonna amount to nothin'," (as she stood directly in front of the small group being given an intensive readiness program intended to overcome some of their handicaps). A white teacher publicly dubbed another such group "The Impossibles," and used this term constantly in calling them to her for small group work. Teachers of any race who have struggled upward to the recognized status of a "professional" may show "hinktiness" (superciliousness) toward those they have left behind on a lower social step. The high self-concept of these teachers has aided their upward mobility, and it is not surprising that they deny the identification with the less capable children of their former peers (for in all probability they never did identify themselves with their original group).

How can we expect any teacher to comprehend the problems of groups about whom she knows literally nothing, and with whom she has so few experiences in common? How can we expect a teacher to recognize the influence upon learning and school behavior when:*

One's sole real meal each day is the school lunch (all others are catch-as-catch-can).

One is constantly tired from sleeping in a bed shared with four or five siblings (and used by a second family in the daytime).

One's irritability is high because of a constant lack of calcium in the diet (coffee, wine, or soft drinks are substitutes for milk).

One's stamina or endurance (or attention span, if you prefer) is poor because of a low protein diet (cheap cuts of pork and lots of greens, no eggs or cheese).

One is afraid or unwilling to go home because of a violent, alcoholic father (who can be avoided only by slipping in late at night).

One hates to go home at any hour to meet the pawing and pinching of an unfamiliar new "uncle" who is sleeping with one's mother today.

One doesn't know the name of or have any mental memory of one's father (and consequently isn't even sure of one's own last name, and must use one given him by his mother).

One faces the pointlessness of going home, for there isn't any food or any mother, or anyone else there, until the evening.

One hears and speaks (if indeed anyone speaks more than a few words) only some other language or dialect than that accepted by the teacher who sees her role as that of constantly correcting (and hence squelching) one's version of English.

One hears little but vulgar or obscene terms from one's parents (and soon learns to communicate, in return, in this style).

One has learned, in self-protection, to tune out the loud voices and reverberating noises of crowded living (and also to tune out selectively the remarks of one's teachers).

One's sense of personal appearance is so poor (for lack of a mirror in the home) that one can't even draw a recognizable self-portrait or profile.

One has never owned a toy, a ball, or blocks which might have fostered form perception or experiences with objects in space or in movement.

One hates and despises the local bullies of the school or community (and hence all members of his group) who blackmail one almost daily for one's lunch money, in lieu of beating one up, (and helped one to learn that in this world only strength and violence count in getting things).

One's experiences with the police who seem to delight in breaking

_____
*These are true incidents personally familiar to the author.

up one's street games or interfering with the fun of throwing rocks or kicking over garbage cans—have left one with a distrust and dislike for all authority figures, particularly those who threaten or actually do push, kick, or slap one around.

One's earlier experiences with teachers from the kindergarten on have been filled with frustration, threats, and punishments because of one's inability to meet or understand their demands.

How well indeed does the middle-class teacher understand and adjust her procedures to combat these influences? How does she decide which problem children can profit most from a phonic or a non-phonic approach to reading, from a language experience basis for reading, from the structured, paced learning rate of a basal series, or from the security of the constant reinforcement present in a programmed system? Are these decisions irrelevant to the child's visual, auditory, language, or emotional experiences?

In her efforts to relate to these children and meet their individual needs, how much self-analysis has the teacher done to enable her to recognize and deal with her own feelings and attitudes, when (as she views them) :

A pupil is obviously unwashed, and his clothes and he smell offensively.

A pupil, who has never owned a handkerchief, solves the problem by letting mucus from his nose dry on his upper lip.

A pupil responds to mild correction with a stream of gutter expressions directed right at us.

Any physical contact is strongly spurned and the child turns away every time we approach him.

The child constantly ignores or doesn't hear directions, and spends his time in playing or teasing his neighbor.

A pupil constantly disrupts the class by loud, irrelevant remarks or by physical activity unrelated to the assigned task.

A child ignores all directions or tasks and does literally nothing but sit passively, but, when pressured, responds with outbursts of obvious hatred and even violence.

The pupil never seems to finish any task, although his initial efforts are fairly good.

No activity in the classroom interests this child to the point that he really enters into it, and we cannot discover any interests whatever by questioning.

The child's native language isn't ours, nor do we speak his, and for lack of understanding he cannot follow any directions except a few gestures.

He speaks in a horrible, uneducated dialect which hardly resembles normal English, and half of the time we can barely translate his remarks.

The pupil continually drops endings on words, as well as auxiliary verbs, and makes many errors in usage both in speech and writing. The child shows all the aggressiveness, wheeler-dealer, non-Christian traits of his group and continually pushes himself forward in an attempt to assume leadership.

How does the middle-class White-Anglo-Saxon-Protestant teacher deal with these distasteful incidents? How does she learn to accept and work with children who violate most of her standards for what is right and proper, clean and good? Does she continually strive to pull these children up out of their level in the naive belief that, after all, the main purpose of a public school education is to fit pupils into her kind of society?

What are some of the basic beliefs of the middle-class teacher that she may have to deny, if she is to help her pupils?

To succeed in life, people must:

a. be bodily clean, and cleanly dressed
b. use correct English
c. live in quiet, clean, and attractive surroundings
d. be thrifty, and able to work toward long-range goals
e. show good social and table manners
f. be careful with their own property and that of others
g. believe wholeheartedly in the ultimate values of education
h. aspire to ever higher vocational and social goals
i. be attentive, quiet, and industrious in school

San-su C. Lin has raised the question of whether it is the teacher or the pupil whom we should term "disadvantaged," for surely the middle-class teacher is greatly handicapped by her background and her self-concept in dealing with such children. As this author points out, she tends to apply her value judgments to her pupils—to confuse their language retardation with mental retardation, to regard their persistent use of dialect as due to inferior intellect. Middle-class teachers (and some linguists, too) think that one can't think efficiently or logically in nonstandard dialect, and they can't comprehend how such language could function adequately for the child's needs. They tend to interpret the lack of inflection in nouns and verbs as evidence of laziness or slovenliness in thinking, thus making the mistake of equating quality of language with quality of character.

In a recent research study of the communication barriers between the races, the average white could not distinguish between middle-class or lower-class Negro speech. (11) In this same study any Southern pronunciation heard on the tapes was Negro, rural, and uneducated to most middle-class whites. It is obvious that value judgments, or racial discrimination if you prefer, dictated the observations of the white listeners.

Let us look at this belief that language portrays the social value of a person from another viewpoint. Have you ever asked a plumber or a garage mechanic to explain the details of the repair job he has just done successfully? Does his ability to verbalize his actions, his use of vague terms such as "the whatsit," "the thingamajig," "the whosit" interfere with his mechanical effectiveness? Is he unable to think because he really can't verbalize the steps of the repair job?

"To attack his dialect, whether directly or by implication, is to attack his loyalty to his group, his identity, his worth," says Lin (10) in dismissing the traditional attempts to change minority-group children into the middle-class mold. Later in this chapter we will discuss alternate, more positive approaches to this language problem.

Edward Hall, (6) an anthropologist, has made very pertinent observations of the behavior of certain minority groups that confuse the middle-class teacher. He points out that Navaho Indians scrupulously avoid open-faced looks into the teacher's eyes. "Does the frustrated teacher, trying to secure the 'attention' of such children, ever realize that the Navaho culture believes that to look directly into the eyes of another is to show anger toward him? Does the white teacher," asks Hall, "realize that a black assumes you are listening to him if you are in the same room, without expecting you to give any indication with your eyes or body position that you are listening? And that he listens to the teacher in the same 'inattentive' fashion? Does the white teacher recognize that the Negro child looks down as a mark of respect when speaking to an adult, rather than meeting him eye to eye? And that this behavior is not, as most white teachers seem to think, evidence of extreme shyness, diffidence, fear, or evasion?"

The Self-concept and School Success

Many research studies have shown the tremendous significance of the child's self-concept for school success. A recent doctoral dissertation lists a dozen or more such studies (15), the details of which need not be repeated here. The self-concept has been shown to be more closely related to reading performance than intelligence itself. (20) Furthermore, many studies of good readers show that they possess feelings of personal worth, belongingness, personal freedom, and self-reliance. In contrast, poor readers often feel discouraged and hopeless in their efforts to succeed in school. (23) School dropouts are often found to show no specific learning disability but rather a broad educational failure. They themselves interpreted their withdrawal from school as an escape or turning away from an intolerable situation. (19) Ketcham (8) found that self-concept components such as grades, the satisfaction of the student and his parents with his grades, the students' aspirations, and the family's encouragement were all positively related to reading achievement. A negative influence upon reading was present when students believed that reading is feminine, that only eggheads like to read, or that college is only for those who can afford it.

These facts make Dr. Paul C. Berg's question one that every teacher of reading must face: "Does the minority child see himself as having a need for reading, or see reading as part of his way of life?" (2)

Several other careful research studies show in even greater detail the relationships between the child's self-concept and his reading successes. Using his own nine-part Reading Skills Diagnostic Test, Bloomer (3) found significant inferiority in certain reading skills for rejected children. Rejection was measured by sociometric choices of playmates. A child rejected by 50 per cent of his peers and accepted by only 10 per cent was considered "rejected." Rejected children did well only in tests involving memory, according to Bloomer, such as letter identification and reading of nonphonetic words and phrases. In tests requiring analysis or synthesis, such as reading phonetically consistent words and phrases, letter and word cloze (supplying a missing letter in a word or word in a context), rejected children did much more poorly.

These studies make it obvious that feelings of anxiety, rejection, or a negative self-concept seriously affect pupil success. Moreover, these negative influences upon achievement operate without regard to the child's intelligence or social class status. Economically-advantaged children as well as the disadvantaged are subject to these handicaps, affirming again the importance of the child's self-concept.

As the dissertation of Dr. Nancy Prows (15) shows, teachers who want to help children succeed can modify their behavior toward these children. The effects upon academic success may not be immediate, but the pupils' self-concepts are improved as teachers take positive, supportive steps.

TEACHER EXPECTATION AND READING SUCCESS

Weintraub (21) and Polardy (13) have reviewed at great length the interaction between teacher expectations and their pupils' academic success. Weintraub recounts the direct effects of the experimenter's expectation of results upon rat-maze experiments, indicating how implicit this interaction is in every situation involving an authority figure and subjects that are expected to learn. In his own classroom experiments, this author told certain teachers that a few of their children were unusually intelligent (although this was really untrue). In keeping with the consequent teacher expectations, these children did show more gain in repeated tests of intelligence than their classmates. Teachers described these children as more curious and happier (?) than their other pupils. Other children who made significant gains in intelligence were not viewed so favorably by their teachers, particularly if they had been grouped in slow-track classes. Weintraub concludes his survey of the interaction of teacher expectation and child success by describing a number of other studies. Several of these show that the teacher's verbal behavior and the types of questions she asks definitely delimit children's thinking. Higher types of thinking were manifested by the children only when questions emphasized evaluation, interpretation, analysis, and synthesis of ideas. Other studies mentioned by Weintraub indicate that teachers contribute to the development of children's self-concept by nonverbal as well as verbal behavior. The teacher's touch, posture, tone of voice, facial expressions, and the like convey her approval and disapproval just as effectively as her words.

The teacher's nonverbal behavior is as significant, if not more so, than her verbal behavior in communicating with children. The tone of the voice conveys meaning as readily as the words spoken—and sometimes these have contradictory meanings—when the verbalisms are routine or habitual. The facial expression is an integral part of each spoken word and supports or contradicts the intended communication. Obviously, verbal praise or encouragement should not be given without appropriate inflection of the voice and related facial expressions, and yet how often we hear these encouraging clichés fall from unpursed lips in an expressionless face.

Even the hands of the teacher convey messages to children, for they can be used to calm an excited child, squeeze or hug in approval, pat in encouragement or, by their simple touch, impart a feeling of friendliness. The opposite feelings and emotions can be evoked by our hands, for everyone knows the meaning of a clenched hand, a pointed finger, a flip or shrug of the hands, or a push. But teachers tend to ignore or forget the impact of their nonverbal behavior upon children. They tend to fail to reinforce messages with their hands, face, or even tone of voice. Is it any wonder that they experience difficulty in "motivating" children to further effort?

Recognizing this nonverbal interaction and the potency of its effect upon children, Dr. Gabriel Della-Piana of the University of Utah employs video tapes of teachers so that they may be helped to recognize their own modes of nonverbal communication and evaluate the consistency, if any, between such behavior and their accompanying remarks to the child. Certainly most teachers would benefit from this sensitization training.

Palardy's study of teacher expectation and pupil reading success was conducted in a number of first grades, a critical stage in the child's development of a concept of himself as a reader. (13) Teachers with high expectations for their boy pupils were matched with low expectation teachers. Instructional materials, methods, grouping, teacher experience, and pupil readiness were likewise matched. As might be expected, although there were no real differences in the reading achievement of boys and girls in the total groups, boys with low expectation teachers were significantly poorer in paragraph meaning and word skills (phonics) tests. As in Bloomer's study mentioned earlier, these rejected boys were not handicapped in a memory type of test, namely that of sight vocabulary.

Collectively, these research studies strongly attest the effect of teacher expectation upon success in reading. The evidence is but a further manifestation of the fact that children tend to perform in the manner in which their self-concepts are influenced by teacher behavior.

CHAPTER II

Building the Self-Concept

The Teacher's Role

Efforts to strengthen or modify the child's self-concept must take three or four avenues of approach. First and foremost among these is the teacher's behavior, both verbal and nonverbal, toward the child. Simply telling a child he is worthy and able is not enough, for the teacher must believe and behave as though the child is worthy and able. In other words, both by actions and words she shows that she trusts the child, respects his judgments, expects him to succeed (and insures such an outcome by careful selection of the tasks chosen), believes he is interested in making progress in school and life, and that he wants to relate to (get along) with her. She must convey these impressions by word and actions, even when the child's behavior may seem to contradict them. This is not a hypocritical posture that she assumes, projecting false mirror images of the child. We believe that every child wants to be accepted, to succeed, to belong, even when a facade of bitterness or negativism or indolence seems to tell us otherwise. Perhaps only the psychotic, psychopathic, or severely emotionally disturbed child may lack these normal strivings for identification and acceptance. The teacher must assume that these basic needs are present or can be brought into the open from behind the pupil's surface behavior.

In every conceivable way, the child with a poor self-concept, or a weak ego, as the psychoanalyst terms it, must be given opportunities to feel secure, important to the classroom life, and increasingly successful in reading. It doesn't matter whether reading teachers promote these feelings by carefully programming the reading tasks to insure obvious success step by step, by frequent praise (when justified) or encouragement in the presence of temporary failure, by involving the pupil in selecting his reading and exercise materials, or by permitting him to pace himself in these materials rather than completing them at a speed in keeping with the teacher's urging. The perceptive teacher will probably include all of these techniques and many others she realizes are appropriate.

A recent research study of teacher-pupil interaction in three types of classroom reading situations adds a number of supportive facts to this argument for a program emphasizing individualization. Virginia B. Morrison (12) found significantly less participation, less assistance to pupils, less positive verbal, physical, and covert behaviors, and more self-restriction among pupils when the same reader was used for all children. When multi-level texts were employed there was more positive assistance to pupils, more individualization of activities, more positive statements, and significantly less punitive teacher behaviors. When enriched or individual-ized programs were present, teachers and pupils employed more demon-strations and interactions, and revealed more positive covert actions and less negative covert behaviors (and more mobility and noise, of course, which are unacceptable behavior in many classrooms).

Sooner or later teachers and curriculum specialists will recognize that programs intended to help children build self-confidence and other positive elements into their self-concepts should be an integral part of the school day. Some suggestions of this sort are already available in the pro-gram outlined by Bessell,* who offers practical daily experiences to be woven into the curriculum. These satisfactory experiences may begin, Bessell suggests, as early as kindergarten.

Other supportive steps by the teacher would include providing oppor-tunity for the child to present or share his work publicly with his group or class. He must often be helped to make this presentation interesting, varied, and even colorful. Teachers will find the list of fifty ways of sharing books, suggested by Jensen (7), of great help.

Of far greater impact upon the child, however, are the more subtle influences present in the teacher's daily behavior toward children. The best organized and most knowledgeable reading teacher in the world will not help her minority pupils to succeed in reading if her social class feelings are permitted to guide her actions. She must examine herself (and her teaching techniques and materials) critically and constantly to determine whether they are motivated by social class values and standards. Specifically, she must ask herself how she can possibly justify the use of readers which portray a way of life that is foreign or vastly different from life as the child knows it. She must seek materials that permit the pupil to identify with them—racially, ethnically, and culturally. He must find book characters whose customs he fully understands, whose manner of speech he recognizes, and whose behavior he would want to identify with. In other words, the child, be he black, white, red, brown, or yellow must have ample opportunity to read the literature dealing with people like himself. The teacher of developmental classroom instruction, or remedial work, should supply a heavy diet of racially- or ethnically-oriented books, suited in readability levels to the child's performance level. We are not referring here to the "multi-ethnic" readers offered by a number of pub-lishers. Most of these present a strong flavor of middle-class life, or are so organized that they perpetuate the teacher-selected, teacher-paced proced-ures to which we strongly object. To be perfectly frank, this author's im-pression of many of these special materials is that they offer black and brown faces pasted on the figures of characters in an upper middle-class setting.

We strongly urge that the teacher examine critically her role of imparting one reading skill after another. There is the fact that these skills, and particularly those emphasized in comprehension training, may only be verbalisms or labels we apply to the questions we ask. This myriad of labels often means literally nothing, for they do not describe specific

---

*Bessell, Harold, "The Content Is the Medium: The Confidence Is the Message," *Psychology Today* (January 1968) 32-35.

reading behaviors. For example, what actual behavioral differences exist when the pupil is said to be reading for main ideas or reading to form conclusions? Does his reading or his thinking or anything else measurable differ from one to the other? In our judgment, many so-called comprehension skills, except perhaps those involving library work and study techniques, exist only as labels given to outcomes of the reading act. Practice in one comprehension skill after another in separate units, as though they were distinctly different, is really often just repetitive drill in answering questions of varied structure, but demanding virtually only one type of thinking—recall of details.

We would certainly hope that children learn to think in various ways while reading, but this ability is best imparted by emphasizing evaluation and interpretation in the teacher's questions, and this training can be conducted just as effectively in trade books as in readers or workbooks.* If comprehension training is individualized to the material the pupil is reading and measured by face-to-face questioning, we provide another significant interaction between pupil and teacher. Avoiding the impersonal nature of worksheets and workbooks, and substituting individual and small group conferences, strengthens mutual understanding of teacher and pupil to a degree no other teaching procedure provides.

The reading teacher should be conscious of the middle-class standards she is applying in judging pupil progress in expecting at-grade test scores and the like. Our standardized tests have been established largely on middle-class populations, and they tend to reflect the performances of white urban or small-town pupils, not those of minority groups. Very few tests are free of cultural bias in their pictorial illustrations, vocabulary items, and content of the test selections. Moreover, the use of time limits in such tests again introduces a middle-class standard. Minority-group children are not speed-conscious and tend to do poorly on timed tests. Their way of life does not reward the effort to complete as many tasks as possible in a limited time. The tasks of daily living for the minority groups are not stimulating and challenging; rather, they are apt to be dull and routine. The habits of the middle-class family in which each member has certain tasks to do, and for rapid completion of which various rewards are given—praise, affectionate gestures, allowance, presents, and the like—are missing in the minority home life.

Reading tests are constantly used as measures of progress of the pupil as a result of the training given him. The scores are usually interpreted as indicating the grade level of the reading materials that the pupil can deal with in comprehension or the level of performance in a certain skill. That test scores cannot represent performance in a variety of content fields or even in different types of literature, but that they are almost meaningless averages of all the reading abilities, as a fact that is usually ignored. If the child moves from 4.5 to 5.5 after training in a survey test, can he now handle mid-fifth grade materials of all types? We forget also that the expected gain—the degree of change in scores—is that found among middle-class children whose motivations differ markedly from the minority

---

*See *Reading in the Elementary School* by Evelyn B. and George D. Spache (Allyn and Bacon, 1969) for extended illustration of this approach.

groups. Moreover, a simple difference between a pre-training and a post-training test score is not necessarily a valid measure of progress. The reliability of the test, as well as a tendency for scores to regress toward the mean (to rise closer to the expected average), effects the size of the gain. But few research studies and hardly any reading teachers pay any attention to these influences in interpreting test scores. It is easier and more reassuring to the guilt-ridden teacher to believe that the difference in the scores is real and reflects only her instructional efforts. We don't have the space to offer the training in statistics needed to make these realistic corrections of gains in test scores, and ample explanation is available elsewhere. (18) The really significant point to be remembered is that most reading tests reflect middle-class expectations which are hardly applicable to minority pupils.

Theron Jacobson, a primary teacher in the Washington School of Decatur, Illinois, has movingly expressed the feelings of a Negro child toward school and life in these words:

WHO AM I?

by Theron Jacobson, Primary Teacher
Washington School

I am Negro—
    I am bad.
I am poor white trash—
    I am bad.
My mother whips me to make me good—
    I am bad.
My preacher says the devil will get me—
    I am bad.
Jesus don't love me—
    I am bad.
I don't know what the teacher says—
    I am bad.
I don't understand her so I don't listen—
    I am bad.
I don't know them funny black marks in my book—
    I am bad.
I can't make them marks stay on the lines—
    I am bad.
My teacher puts a paper on my desk—
I don't know what to do—
I do nothin'—
    I am bad.
I make pretty colored marks on the paper
(I like my crayons)—
It makes me feel good—
I want to show it to the kid next to me and tell him about it—
I talked—
I marked up my paper—
    I am very, very bad.

That kid next to me—he is good—
The teacher likes his paper—
He went to play with some trucks and blocks—
I want to play with blocks and trucks—
    No! I am bad.
I marked up my paper—
Blocks and trucks are for good kids—
Bad boys put their heads on their desks—
    I am very bad.
I don't feel good—
I made marks on that kid's paper and threw it on the floor—
It made me feel good—
    Now I am very, very bad.
The bell rings—
    I can go!

THE ROLE OF CLASSROOM ACTIVITIES

We have already mentioned the importance of types of reading instruction and activities upon pupil-teacher interaction. But this understanding that the realia and the pupil activities of the average classroom day enter into building the child's self-concept may be broadened considerably. Carlton and Moore experimented with self-directive dramatization in a low socioeconomic, largely black population. Children read together in spontaneous groups formed for the specific purpose of mutually enjoying a particular story or book. Upon completion of the material, each child attempted to give an extemporaneous interpretation or dramatization of a book character. After two experimental periods of three and one-half months each, gains in reading achievement were large and significantly greater than in control groups. Changes toward more positive self-concepts were also present as a result of this experience. Certainly this was a gratifying experience for children in self-selection of the story, in immediate application of their understanding of the behavior and feelings of the characters, and in the opportunity to share their projection of the character with their peers. (4)

Role-playing may take a number of other forms in activities intended to clarify the self-concept and the "other-concept."* It may be employed with puppets, cutout figures, doll-play, and mock telephone conversations. Open-end stories composed by teacher or pupils, or both, may be completed in various ways enacted by the children. Simple plays planned jointly by teacher and pupils may be used to provide the experience of being an isolate, a member of an in-group, the subject of discrimination or prejudice, and the like. This dramatization may serve to convey something of the suffering endured and the defensiveness engendered by discrimination to pupils who are unaware of their impact upon others. Or, the plays may help bring to the surface some of the deep feelings of minority children who are all too familiar with the attitudes toward them. By airing these feelings and by expressing them out loud (and sometimes violently), such

---

*See references by Black, by Shafter, and others for role-playing activities in the later chapter on Reading Improvement materials.

youngsters are relieved of some of their inner tensions and thus helped to live with prejudice in a less resentful and bitter manner.

Progressing in the use of the role-playing techniques in realistically portraying life situations may be made quite slowly in some groups who find it difficult to express themselves or to enact unpleasant scenes. In other groups, the players may well go far beyond the script in releasing their pent-up feelings, once they have warmed up to the action. But with teacher help, these children must learn to express their feelings without physical violence to one another, to bring their deeper emotions to a verbal level where they may be expressed and discussed.

Most of the common audio-visual aids can be adapted to this inter-group education program. We have listed many of those of particular value in the later bibliographies on instructional materials and audio-visual resources, as well as a group of guides to assist the teacher in such activities in the list of professional resources.

Some teachers and psychologists would attempt to point out that the changing of attitudes and feelings is a very difficult, almost impossible task. But reports from many school systems belie this pessimism. We know that with some individuals attitudes change as information concerning social reality is acquired. Repeated experiences of the types we have outlined, supported by ample classroom and teacher comment, can affect such individuals.

Other persons are low in realism and may fail to respond to this exposure to the feelings and actions of their peers. Their attitudes are rigid, self-serving, even neurotic, and hardly amenable to facts or the feelings of others. Such individuals may not be touched by all our efforts.

A third type of ethnic attitude is present in others, in that their beliefs and behavior are ambivalent. Rather than having strong prejudices or likes, they are swayed by the pressure of the situation or the actions of the group. Sufficient experiences in tolerance and acceptance may help to crystallize their attitudes in the mode we wish to impart in many of these undecided individuals. There is also the favorable fact that for the most part we are dealing with young people whose attitudes have not yet hardened into logic-tight compartments. Most of them are inclined to respond to and imitate the thinking of the group, and that of the omnipotent teacher (when they recognize its honesty and sincerity).

Lest the reader think that we are naively optimistic in our hopes for the effectiveness of education in tolerance and understanding of others, we point out that such efforts are constantly under way in most of the countries of the world. In a UNESCO report, activities in a number of countries are mentioned, such as: (19)

Basic studies and research sponsored by national and international organizations in techniques and methods of international dialogue

Studies of the impact upon Eastern countries of students educated in the West, and vice versa

The establishment of permanent centers for the study of other cultures

University programs showing a dynamic interest in the cultures of other peoples, as of Oriental culture in many Latin American colleges

Regional associations of countries to study the contacts and communication of the area with other parts of the world

Fellowships granted by UNESCO for research and study in the culture of other countries to be transmitted to their compatriots on their return home

Exchange, scrutiny and revision of textbooks and educational materials by joint action of experts of several countries

Associated Youth Enterprises—which include meetings, study-trips, youth camps, pen-friendships, and publications

Dissemination of translations of significant literature, art albums, and art books, recordings of music, and films.

The teacher can join the worldwide movement to relieve intergroup tensions, first by initiating the intra-class experiences we have outlined above. Extra-class activities may extend the experiences in field trips, area surveys, visits to clubs, churches, and museums. When the interest of the class has been aroused, they can plan all-school participation in exhibits, festivals, pageants, or plays centered around the customs of a particular minority group. It is psychologically true that "prejudice tends to diminish whenever members of different groups meet on terms of equal status in the pursuit of common objectives," as pointed out by Gordon W. Allport, the eminent specialist in group relations. (1)

For the dubious teacher who sees this intergroup education as irrelevant to her primary goal of imparting knowledge and school skills, we may point out that information-giving is one of the major techniques for changing attitudes. Many of the activities we have suggested may be incorporated in a learning unit in the areas of the study of literature, music, social sciences, and other school areas. To aid the teacher who feels insecure in approaching intercultural education through dynamic group activities, we have listed many materials and resources in the later bibliographies that are relevant to planning study units.

No teacher with any degree of professional identity in her self-concept can ignore or decline to participate in this worldwide effort, at the risk of losing all that she treasures and, perhaps, even her own life. Unless we mitigate the interracial strife in our cities and between nations, we face local and international conflict that may eventually destroy civilization as we now know it.

The Role of the Book

Books themselves are a major tool in modifying the self-concept and the other-concept. Some schools utilize reading units in studying the cultural differences in family life, daily economics, the contributions of different ethnic and racial groups, and the personal problems of acceptance and rejection. Study of this type may begin at primary grade levels as evidenced in the Indian units commonly used in our American classrooms. Another profitable attack upon prejudices may be made through the analytic study of stereotypes. One has to look no further than our common readers to discover these false characterizations of different peoples. There we find

Italians depicted as organ-grinders or vegetable peddlers, Germans as watch repairmen or doll makers, Frenchmen as volatile, excitable, Indian-lovers, and Englishmen as arrogant, dictatorial snobs. Negroes, Indians, Mexican-Americans, and other subgroups in American society have apparently just been discovered by our textbook authors and illustrators. Comparison of the stereotyped descriptions in various books with the information available in resources on art, music, language, literature, and the like can help dispel these false concepts of other groups. Reading and contrasting several biographies of the same person, noting their contradictions and inaccuracies, and reacting to each author's bias can be begun as early as the fourth grade.

Bibliotherapy, or the direct use of books related to personal problems, is another effective technique. For this process to be effective, several prerequisites are essential. The books offered to the child should present a character with whom he can identify and whose problems are obviously like the reader's. As we have said before, the process must progress from "He's like me" or "I'm like him" to "Gee, I feel the same as he does" to "I can do it just like he did" or "I can do it too." (17)

Freedom of choice for pupils is essential if bibliotherapy is to operate successfully. There must be no pressure to report artificially on the books read. Of course, the teacher plays a constructive role in this selection by providing a variety of suitable books from among which the pupil may choose. The first step in bibliotherapy is the identification of the reader with the book character. Although the parallelism may seem obvious to the teacher, the child may need to be helped to see the similarities by discussion with a group and/or the teacher. The child's self-concept may be so vague or ambivalent that he cannot see any resemblance. If he blocks identification because it increases his anxieties, or rejects the character because its problems remind him so strongly of his own unresolved conflicts, we must try again with another story.

The child may see the similarity in the character and yet be unable to empathize with its feelings, perhaps because he has suppressed the identical emotions so long, in self-defense. In this particular stage of bibliotherapy, called catharsis, the child may need to be led into role-playing— trying to enact realistically and emotionally scenes from the book. Again, the teacher must attempt to steer the discussion toward the motives and feelings of the characters portrayed.

The "I can do it too" stage, or insight, requires that the pupil recognize the solutions attempted by the character, discuss them, and evaluate their effectiveness. Finally, he must face the fact that by analogy or imitation he can consider similar courses of action which may enable him, too, to solve the common problem, or at least to live with it with less tension.

It is apparent that this entire process is not accomplished overnight, or as the result of reading one book. Different books may be variously effective with children who face the same basic problem. Some pupils will react dramatically to a certain story that has no impact upon others. Some may need many opportunities to see themselves in book characters before they begin to experience the therapeutic effects. Many will have difficulty in translating the character's solutions into action on their part.

Winner (22) illustrates the dramatic effects upon book reading which may come from flooding our pupils and the community with paperbacks. When these are treated as completely consumable, not library withdrawals, and when no formal reports are required and no censorship imposed on children's selections, the negative attitudes toward reading, so common among ghetto children, may gradually be overcome. One of the author's students found that a paperback bookstore offering these at rock-bottom prices to slum-area children met with tremendous response. Store sales have reached as high as $6000-$7000 a year in a community where a large proportion of the families are on welfare. These children will read if given freedom and opportunity.

The basic concepts we have tried to impart regarding the child's self-concept, the influences upon it in the teacher, the school, and the community, and the ways in which it may be positively strengthened are readily summed up. The identification of self, and the recognition of the underlying feelings, is not a brief development. Several films or books or dramatizations will have only slight effect. These experiences must be pyramided in a long campaign of repetitive yet varied approaches. Attitude changes and feelings about self and others tend to be slight and specific to the situation experienced. They even tend to slip backward sometimes toward the original views, but fortunately not all the way. In effect, we must conduct a positive campaign, constantly trying to modify feelings and beliefs and to allay tensions and anxieties, to build positive, wholesome views of life.

REFERENCES

1. Allport, Gordon W., *The Resolution of Intergroup Tensions*. New York: National Conference of Christians and Jews, 1952.
2. Berg, Paul C., "Reading: The Learner's Needs and Self-Concepts," *The Florida Reading Quarterly*, 4 (June 1968) 3-8.
3. Bloomer, Richard H., "Reading Patterns of the Rejected Child," *Reading Teacher*, 22 (January 1969) 320-24.
4. Carlton, Lessie, and Moore, Robert H., *Reading, Self-Directive Dramatization and Self-Concept*. Columbus: Merrill, 1968.
5. Combs, Arthur W., "New Horizons in Field Research: The Self-Concept," *Educational Leadership*, 15 (February 1958) 315-19.
6. Hall, Edward, "Listening Behavior: Some Cultural Behavior," *Phi Delta Kappan*, March 1969.
7. Jensen, Amy Elizabeth, "Attracting Children to Books," *Elementary English*, 33 (October 1956) 332-39.
8. Ketcham, C. A., "Factors in the Home Background and Reader Self-Concept Which Are Related to Reading Achievement," in *Proceedings of the College Reading Association*, 7 (1966) 66-68.
9. Lichter, Solomon O. et al., *The Drop-Outs*. New York: Free Press, 1962.
10. Lin, San-su C., "Disadvantaged Student or Disadvantaged Teacher?" *English Journal*, 56 (May 1967) 751-56.
11. McDavid, Raven I. and Austin, Wm. M., *Communication Barriers to the Culturally Deprived*. Coop Res Project No. 2107—U. S. Dep't. of Health, Education and Welfare, Office of Education, Washington, D.C.: Government Printing Office.
12. Morrison, Virginia B., "Teacher-Pupil Interaction in Three Types of Elementary Classroom Reading Situations," *Reading Teacher*, 22 (December 1968) 271-75.
13. Palardy, J. Michael, "What Teachers Believe—What Children Achieve," *Elementary School Journal*, 69 (April 1969) 370-74.
14. Peil, Margaret, "Library Use by Low-Income Chicago Families," *Library Quarterly*, 33 (October 1963) 329-33.
15. Prows, Nancy LeJeune, *An Attempt to Increase Reading Achievement by Organizing Instruction and Sensitizing the Teacher to Building Positive Self-Concepts*. Doctoral dissertation, University of Florida, 1967.

16. Spache, George D., "The Learner's Concept of Self" in *Education for the Preservation of Democracy*, American Council on Education Studies, Series I, vol. 13, April 1949, 97-99.
17. Spache, George D., *Good Reading for Poor Readers*. Champaign: Garrard, 1970. See Chapter III, "Using Books to Help Solve Children's Problems."
18. Spache, George D., *Toward Better Reading*. Champaign: Garrard, 1963.
19. UNESCO, *Appraisal of the Major Project on Mutual Appreciation of Eastern and Western Cultural Values*. Paris: United Nations Educational Scientific and Cultural Organization, 1968.
20. Wattenberg, W. W., and Clifford, C., "Relationships of Self-Concept to Beginning Achievement in Reading," *Childhood Education*, 43 (Sept. 1966) 58.
21. Weintraub, Samuel, "Research—Teacher Expectation and Reading Performance," *Reading Teacher*, 22 (March 1969) 555-59.
22. Winner, Edward G., "The Paperback Goes Home," *English Journal*, 56 (March 1967) 453-55, 489.
23. Zimmerman, E., and Allebrand, G. W., "Personality Characteristics and Attitudes Toward Achievement of Good and Poor Readers," *Journal of Educational Research*, 59 (Sept. 1965) 28-31.

CHAPTER III

Reading Instruction and the Disadvantaged

T HERE IS A GROWING BODY of information regarding the disadvantaged child and the educational process. Scientists of a number of disciplines—psychology, sociology, anthropology, and linguistics, to mention only a few—are offering significant viewpoints bearing on this problem. We could not attempt to summarize all this evidence, for it is much too voluminous. Nor would such a survey of the literature really be relevant to our purpose, which is simply to suggest ways and means of improving reading instruction for educationally-handicapped children. As best as we can, we will select from the different fields the facts and implications that should be significant for the teacher of reading. We shall discuss the studies which deal with various general programs intended to overcome the reading handicap present in this segment of our population. Other sections on language development, readiness, reading instruction, and the special problems of the bilingual group will also be offered.

LANGUAGE DEVELOPMENT

Many studies of disadvantaged children emphasize the ramifications of the handicap present in the area of language development. It is pointed out that these pupils are deficient in such aspects as range and level of vocabulary, use of syntactic variations within sentences, and facility in use of verbs. Their sentences employ fewer clauses, infinitives, and verbals, but there is not too great a difference in structural patterns of sentences, other than the lack of linking verbs and the use of incomplete sentences. They seem to understand more than they can speak about and are best in spontaneous, unstructured communication situations. They tend to use a restricted code—fast speech, articulatory clues reduced, meanings confused and specific to the situation. Some of these same observations have been made in England among socioeconomically deprived children. Other observers point out that some of these deficiencies vary geographically in our country, as in range and level of vocabulary. (19)

Language development tends to lag behind intellectual development in a cumulative fashion. One of the reasons offered for this lag is the lack of verbal interaction between disadvantaged adults and their children. Even the beginning speech sounds of disadvantaged children appear later. Many early studies show that lack of mothering retards vocalization and the mastery of speech sounds among the very young of the economically disadvantaged. The language models presented by the parents are often not only meager, restricted, and grammatically incorrect, but also punitive and threatening in a manner that tends to repress the child's own speech.

Studies of nonstandard English show it to be prolific in errors such as omission of possessives, plurals, present and past tense endings, and auxiliary verbs; faulty use of negatives; and fumbling in dealing with complex constructions or structural ambiguities. (23)

It is not difficult to read into these bare facts about the disadvantaged child's language development the obvious implications for reading teachers. Many of these children enter school linguistically unready to deal with the process of learning to read or with the communication demands of the classroom. Most specific details of the relationship between this language handicap and reading success will appear as our discussion continues.

READINESS

Disadvantaged children tend to show strength in visual-motor speech channels and weakness in auditory-vocal channels. In other words, they are poor in the ITPA in verbal analogies involving the properties of common objects; and stronger in matching pictures of commonly related objects. One study seemed to indicate that this type of retardation could at least be partly overcome by special training. Other studies indicate that perceptual training over a five-or six-month period resulted in significant improvements in I.Q. scores for both Negro and white in one study (3) and in improved reading in the first grade in another. (25) Enrichment programs as brief as six weeks involving both parents and children gave gains in both I.Q. and readiness tests, according to Brazziel and Terrell (4).

The backgrounds of disadvantaged children give them less access to books, fewer experiences in being read to or spoken to. The mother's language style tends to determine the child's ability to handle language abstractions more than does his or her I.Q., according to one observer. (17) And these children show fewer words per remark and greater incidence of poor articulation and retarded speech than do middle-class children. In fact, one group of Negro kindergarten children failed to use 20-50 per cent of the words common to beginning reading materials, in their own speech. (27)

Disadvantaged children show, in general, poorer auditory discrimination, poorer visual discrimination, and weaker time and number concepts. They have had much less opportunity for the development of cognitive or thinking skills because of lack of intellectual stimulation. They are more dependent upon their siblings and peers, perhaps because their parents are often absent or inaccessible. Finally, such children are accustomed to receiving immediate rewards and punishments, based largely on the parents' interpretation of the consequences of the child's action, not upon his intentions. These multiple deficiencies have obvious implications for the beginning reading program and its emphases upon phonics, oral reading, word knowledge, and word discrimination.

READING INSTRUCTION

Among disadvantaged children we find that oral reading is affected by their inability to use the standard English of the reader. They are rated lower (perhaps than their true functional or instructional level) by the oral reading errors that nonstandard English promotes. Often these judgments based on oral reading, as in the common Informal Reading Inventory, underestimate the child's actual levels by overemphasizing oral errors and ignoring comprehension.

The paucity of the child's experiences, intellectual or physical, leaves him poor in visual imagery and in abstract verbal concepts. Thus the child tends to be concrete and almost inflexible in his thinking. This deficit appears to be cumulative and to affect his ability to meet demands in comprehension, concept formation, and problem solving.

The weaker auditory discrimination, auditory responsiveness, and auditory comprehension should give reading teachers pause in seeking easy solutions in phonics-oriented reading programs. They seem to forget, however, that phonics is supposed to enable the reader to pronounce a word and in doing so recognize it by its familiarity to his auditory vocabulary. This is a tenuous assumption in the case of language-handicapped children whose auditory vocabularies, as we have seen, are limited. (6) Phonics programs, particularly those that emphasize isolated (and distorted) letter sounds, as "buh" for/b/, ignore the auditory discrimination handicap of these children. Teachers of reading forget, in their emphasis upon word recognition, that extensive experience with meanings and associated concepts is essential for word recognition. Simple repetitive matching of word and picture or discrimination only by visual cues, such as single letters within the word, is not sufficient.

Russman (20) and Taba (26) have strongly stressed the need for study of the different approaches to learning and the need for more research into cognitive styles so that we may relate teaching procedures in reading to children's thinking approaches and the avenues through which they will learn best. Since we cannot generalize the auditory difficulties of many children to all of them, it is essential to determine the sensory modality for which each shows preference. The technique of testing for ability to learn words by visual, auditory, kinesthetic, or combined approaches is well established (15) but seldom used. Rather, in keeping with the times, we see wide and indiscriminate use of multi-sensory approaches or VAKT methods adopted without any objective justification, and despite the research which implies that multiple approaches are not necessarily more efficient.

Goodman (10) suggests three alternatives in reading programs for language-handicapped children:

1. Materials based on their own dialect by rewriting standard materials.
2. Teaching the child standard dialect before introducing him to the formal English of the reader or textbook.
3. Accepting the pupils' language or dialect, making it the medium of instruction (through the language experience approach), and gradually leading them toward more acceptable language.

We feel that the first of Goodman's suggestions is obviously economically unfeasible. We would have to republish or create materials in perhaps a dozen dialects if these were to mirror the speech of the different ethnic groups or regional dialects. Such a publishing program would skyrocket the cost of school materials unless it was privately underwritten by teachers or school systems. Besides, how would the average teacher, who speaks standard English only, read these dialects or use them in teaching?

Goodman's other programs of English training prior to formal reading, or the use of the language experience approach, have insufficient research support to recommend them strongly. We prefer the third type of program but can offer little conclusive evidence of superior values for it (11).

A fourth alternative might be added to Goodman's programs, especially for those children whose native language is not English. This program would present reading instruction in the child's native language, shifting later to instruction in English. Some rural Puerto Rican schools and Philippine school systems have followed this plan. But judging from the results of a recent study in Texas (12) with Spanish-speaking children, there are no significant advantages to first-grade programs stressing intensive language instruction in English or in Spanish prior to formal reading. Other studies are more favorable to beginning programs in the child's native language, but further evidence would be desirable.

Other writers offer programs in reading centered around linguistics or around an oral English development theme. The Miami Linguistic Readers are one such series apparently developed to meet a specific dialectal problem, that of the immigrant Cuban population. No conclusive research has shown that this approach is more than a hypothesis, however. Reading skills, again, were not materially benefited in Morrison's study with a structural linguistic program for Puerto Rican children in New York City. (16) The Perry Preschool Project in Ypsilanti, Michigan achieved some gains in I.Q. and certain aspects of language by morning preschool sessions followed by afternoon home visits with parents. But these gains were not sustained at the same rate in the second year of the program. As Rosen and Ortega (21) point out, there is still no strong evidence in favor of preparatory programs prior to or shortly after school entrance that emphasize oral English development, or linguistics, or materials in the child's native language. These authors question whether these programs really prepare the nonstandard English child, or the non-English-speaking child to deal with the task of learning to read in standard English.

One of the nagging problems in these various attempts to meet the instructional needs of the language-handicapped child is the uncertainty of the effects of limited opportunity and the difficulty in separating these effects from those due to motivation. Cultural or economic deprivation has different effects in various ethnic groups. We note, for example, the relatively superior academic achievement among Oriental children as a group despite economic or cultural handicaps. Or, we see that the number of Jewish college students exceeds by far their proportion in the general population. Parental aspirations are much more significant in pupils' academc success than parental socioeconomic or cultural status. (13)

Racial or ethnic origin alone is not sufficient to allow valid generalizations about children's potential or their instructional needs. Negro children reflect the socioeconomic status and the education of their parents, just as white children do. Their I.Q.'s and achievement vary according to their parental background and parental aspirations, as members of all minority groups do. Differences within races or ethnic groups are far greater than apparent differences between groups of varying social strata or racial origin. Rural children differ from urban children, in general, in sophistication in taking tests and in tempo of life and, hence in response to time pressures. Perhaps all of this implies that teachers of reading should seek a variety of programs for disadvantaged children, according to their specific characteristics, instead of seeking "a" reading program for all types of such children.

SPECIAL PROBLEMS WITH BILINGUAL PUPILS

Rosen and Ortega (21,22) have published recent comprehensive reviews of the problems inherent in offering reading instruction to bilingual children. These are excellent summaries of many aspects of this task and are well worth careful reading. We can do no more than touch upon the highlights of their reviews in this section.

Definitions: Rosen and Ortega and Singer (24) point out that there is no point in classifying Spanish-speaking children, whether Mexican-American or Puerto Rican or Cuban or other, as bilingual en masse, for the literature doesn't even offer a satisfactory definition of this type of language handicap. To illustrate, a bilingual may be one who speaks two languages— one well, one poorly, both well, or both poorly; or a person who speaks one language other than English; or, finally, one whose parents are foreign-born and speak some language other than English to him. These types of bilinguals do not present, in any sense, the same language development problem for the teacher of reading. Furthermore, in our Southwest, even these descriptions don't quite apply, for the "bilingual" tends to mix his utterances, regardless of which language's syntactic structure is being used.

Timing Programs: After reviewing a number of the related experiments, Rosen and Ortega express strong doubts about the values of intensive early introduction to English for the bilingual. In their opinion, inadequate timing and handling of such a program may well contribute to feelings of inadequacy in English and in one's own language, and may slow up general language development. Programs in English for non-English-speaking children probably should not begin until long after the native language is established, perhaps as late as the intermediate grades, according to these authors.

Substituting practice in oral English for reading instruction for six months to a year in the first grade gave favorable results in a study by James G. Cooper. (8) Oral speech was much improved at the end of the first grade, and reading comprehension was significantly better three years later. Replications of studies like this should help to answer Rosen's and Ortega's questions regarding the proper time for the inception of this type of program.

Methodology: Teaching English as a second language is not solved by a simple methodology analogous to foreign language instruction, Rosen and Ortega affirm. In foreign language instruction, the second language is unknown; while in second dialect teaching, the child's daily language is undergoing a refining and developmental process. Too often, some observers point out, this distinction in goals and methodology is lacking in our schools. Furthermore, the training of teachers leaves much to be desired, in the opinion of Rosen and Ortega. Frequently it concentrates on somewhat superficial aspects of linguistics, while cultural differences present in the two languages and distinctions in the physiology of their production are almost ignored.

Goals: Goals for bilinguals are often unrealistic, for, according to Rosen and Ortega, complete correctness of articulation in the second language is almost impossible, as is equal facility in both languages. There is too much attention to "correct" English and too little to growth in communication (and these are *not* synonymous). Some teachers insist that accent and syntactical errors are serious social handicaps, when obviously this is true only when the listener chooses to make them so.

Rosen and Ortega reiterate a point we have made several times: correction of a child's language habits is, in effect, a rejection of him, his parents and his cultural heritage. Moreover, if any training program is to be successful, we have to assume that the learner wants to identify with the majority group in behavior as well as in language. Obviously, the learner's experiences with segregation, prejudice, and poverty condition his desire to identify with the majority group. Finally, Rosen and Ortega point out that these factors vary regionally and geographically (and perhaps from one ethnic group to another?) in their interaction with the success of the language program. For example, it is obvious from recent statements of representatives of the American Indian and the American black that they do *not* seek close identification with the white majority at the cost of losing their own cultural identity. The current student demands for "black and brown" curricula, studies emphasizing Afro-American and Mexican-American cultures, strongly point toward a desire for independent recognition, not assimilation. Language programs that naively try to teach all racial or ethnic groups to speak the standard English of the white majority need some rethinking. They need to examine their true motives and to recognize the resistance likely to be encountered.

OTHER APPROACHES AND PROGRAMS

There is a great variety in the programs and in the experts' recommendations regarding reading instruction for the disadvantaged. Space permits only a brief survey of these.

The Texas Education Agency introduced a program for migrant children involving an eight-hour school day for six months. Additional staff, supplementary transportation, and better-than-average teachers were included. There were some gains in the second to fourth grades, none in the fifth and sixth. None of the gains were probably really significant.

Multiracial reading materials devised in Detroit resulted in a tendency to superior scores in word recognition and fewer errors in oral reading. Multi-ethnic children showed a strong preference for these materials over other basal readers, according to their authors. On the other hand, Collier's study (7) of four such reading series in primary grades elicited a number of weaknesses. Each series, Collier notes, presented only one socioeconomic group, not a mixture. This was usually a lower-class urban neighborhood, and yet the representation of various ethnic groups in such a setting was spotty. Negroes were prominent in only a few stories; other ethnic groups were even less represented. One series persisted in presenting middle-class values and experiences (even in a lower-class neighborhood) and others varied equally in the realism of their presentation of nonwhites.

Other programs have emphasized organizational changes such as: ungraded primary, team teaching, junior first grade, pre-kindergarten, transitional kindergarten or first grade (extending these for a second year), and a divided day in which a small group comes earlier or leaves later. In some cities these various plans seem to have been helpful. In others, they have been tried and abandoned as showing no special merits for the disadvantaged population.

Innovations in staffing have had widespread trials, with mixed results. Among these are: special reading and language arts teachers (as in California), master teachers or teacher-trainers to aid inexperienced teachers (as in New York City), three teachers assigned to two classrooms to permit more small-group instruction (as in Oakland), summer school or library enrichment or remedial programs for selected children (as in Jacksonville, Florida), and the assignment of extra teachers or supervisors for a school to function in various supplementary and remedial programs. (14, 28)

Paraprofessionals or teacher aides of many kinds are being experimented with. We see parents as part-time teaching assistants in the classroom, as interpreters in bilingual situations, as teachers of bilingual programs in reading and readiness, and as teacher substitutes to provide released time for "preparation" or attendance at in-service meetings. Parents are also used as receptionists, interpreters, clerical assistants, and the like.

The purpose in some of these multi-staffing or differentiated staffing projects seems to be to saturate the school with a plethora of help. The results, as in New York City and in Philadelphia, appear equivocal because of a lack of adequate statistical controls in many examples; or, when these are present, of definitive favorable effects upon reading achievement.

Special programs affecting the disadvantaged child include: early identification projects to find pupils' abilities, talents, and problems early in school life (as in New York), or to begin "preventive" efforts with small groups of selected children (as in Miami). All-day neighborhood schools with group work programs extending until 5 P.M. or with a variety of parent-involving activities such as courses in English, vocational training, child care, and human relations have been attempted in several large cities. Preschool programs of a wide variety claim such goals as prevention of school failure, enrichment of life experiences, improvement of parent-child relationships, and stimulation of language development.

Even school and college pupils are involved in some projects for disadvantaged children. College students are enlisted to tutor other college students, or high school or elementary school pupils. Older elementary pupils who are themselves poor readers work with primary children experiencing difficulty, sometimes with mutually beneficial results. (28)

Some of these various programs date from the inception of Title I, ESEA legislation a few years ago. This federal subsidy permitted prolific efforts such as: school or school system reading clinics, intensive in-service training of classroom teachers, special training of remedial reading specialists and other special school personnel, and an increase in services to school children from many professional groups such as counselors, psychologists, psychiatrists, optometrists, and other medical specialists. Other benefits were sensitizing programs for teachers of the disadvantaged, self-analysis by micro-teaching or videotaping of brief teacher-pupil contacts in the classroom, television courses, closed-circuit observations, school visits, professional study at workshops and NDEA Institutes, and many other in-service training activities.

As Dr. Mary C. Austin has pointed out that in many instances the outcomes of these child-need-centered, teacher-education, parent-involvement and personnel experiments have undoubtedly been extremely worthwhile. Insights into the learning process, the teacher-pupil relationship, and the impact of parental aspirations and involvement have been widely developed. Statistical evaluations of achievement have not always been as positive as the more obscure measures of attitudes, self-perceptions, and group relationships. (1)

We have known for a number of years that American classroom teachers, as a general group, were in need of much postgraduate training, not only in methodology of reading instruction, but also in human relations and group dynamics. We knew that we could not expect the average middle-class-oriented teacher to understand and function effectively with disadvantaged children. But many of these programs have begun to engender a basic understanding by the teacher of some of the differences of the disadvantaged child.

Teachers have begun to learn the role of social reinforcers—of face, tone of voice, and touch, and of making rewards and punishments more concrete (and less verbal) and more obviously related to the situation. They are learning to avoid "neutral" statements or even voice tones which really convey nothing to the disadvantaged child, and to substitute short-range goals and token reinforcements for vague long-range hopes. Teachers are attempting to see their subject matter through the eyes of the vocationally-minded disadvantaged child, and adapt it pragmatically to future life as it may be for these children.

In accepting differentiated staffing, teachers are facing up to the problem of class differences in attention span, distractibility, tolerance for noise, auditory discrimination and comprehension, physical motility, family mobility, and the like. They are, perhaps, recognizing that these factors interfere with the operation of a classroom in the whole-class or large-group manner possible (and all too frequent) among middle-class pupils. More and more, the middle-class teacher is becoming convinced of the need for small group or individualized instruction keyed to the child's learning modality and thinking styles, as well as his language level.

Other concepts being realized by teachers of disadvantaged children are:

1. Give individual, positive attention.
2. Vary the learning environment by letting the child participate in selecting an activity.
3. Be affectionate—reward by physical support—patting, snuggling, hugging.
4. Gratify child's needs by manipulating the pace of activities as needed.
5. Encourage child exploitation of materials, of space.

6. Provide cultural experiences by visiting community workers, points of interest, or by providing a wide variety of vicarious experiences through pictures, books, and other media, as well as storytelling.
7. Vary the physical environment in terms of color, shape, texture, and sound patterns (and by rearranging furniture).
8. Provide stimulating toys and centers of interest, as homemaking, reading, music, art, and shop work. Recognize the contribution that group play makes to language development.
9. Permit and promote spontaneity of expression, verbal and physical. Encourage socialization of groups and a variety of group activities.
10. Help children to organize their thoughts and to express their ideas by positive comments, not by criticism of accent or diction.

REFERENCES

1. Berg, Paul C., and George, John E. (eds.), *Bold Action Programs for the Disadvantaged*. Highlights of the 1967 Pre-Convention Institutes. Newark: International Reading Assn., 1967.
2. Bloom, Benjamin S., Davis, Allison, and Hess, Robert, *Compensatory Education for Cultural Deprivation*. New York: Holt, Rinehart and Winston, 1965.
3. Boger, Jack H., "An Experimental Study of the Effects of Perceptual Training on Group I.Q. Scores of Elementary Pupils in Rural Upgraded Schools," *Journal of Educational Research*, 46 (Spring 1952) 43-52.
4. Brazziel, Wm. F. and Terrell, Mary, "An Experiment in the Development of Readiness in a Culturally Disadvantaged Group of First Grade Children," *Journal of Negro Education*, 31 (Winter 1962) 4-7.
5. Ching, Doris C., "Reading, Language Development and the Bilingual Child," *Elementary English*, 46 (May 1969) 622-28.
6. Cohen, S. Alan, "Some Conclusions about Teaching Reading to Disadvantaged Children," *Reading Teacher*, 20 (Feb. 1967) 433-38.
7. Collier, Marilyn, "An Evaluation of Multi-Ethnic Basal Readers," *Elementary English*, 44 (1967) 152-57.
8. Cooper, James G., "Effects of Different Amounts of First-Grade Oral English Instruction upon Later Reading Progress with Chamorro-Speaking Children," *Journal of Educational Research*, 58 (Nov. 1964) 123-27.
9. Deutsch, Cynthia P., "Auditory Discrimination and Learning: Social Factors," *Merrill-Palmer Quarterly*, 10 (July 1964) 277-96.
10. Goodman, Kenneth, "Dialect Barriers to Reading Comprehension," *Elementary English*, 42 (December 1965) 852-60.
11. Harris, Albert J., Serwer, Blanche L., and Gold, L., "Comparing Reading Approaches in First Grade Teaching with Disadvantaged Children—Extended into Second Grade," *Reading Teacher*, 20 (1967) 698-703.
12. Horn, Thomas D., "Three Methods of Developing Reading Readiness in Spanish-Speaking Children in First Grade," *Reading Teacher*, 20 (October 1966) 38-42.
13. Karp, Joan M. and Sigel, Irving, "Psychoeducational Appraisal of Disadvantaged Children," *Review of Educational Research*, 35 (December 1965) 401-12.
14. Mackintosh, Helen K., et al., *Disadvantaged Children Series*. U.S. Department of Health, Education and Welfare, Office of Education. Washington, D.C.: Government Printing Office, 1965.
15. Mills, Robert E., *The Teaching of Word Recognition*. Fort Lauderdale: The Author, 1964.
16. Morrison, J. Cayce, *The Puerto Rican Study, 1953-57*. New York: Board of Education, City of New York, 1958.
17. Olim, Ellis G., Hess, Robert D., and Shipman, Virginia C., "Relationship Between Mothers' Language Styles and Cognitive Styles of Urban Pre-School Children," *Urban Child Study Center*, Chicago, 1965.
18. Passow, A. Harry (ed.), *Education in Depressed Areas*. New York: Teachers College Press, Columbia University, 1963.
19. Raph, Jane Beasley, "Language Development in Socially Disadvantaged Children," in *Review of Educational Research*, 35 (December 1965) 389-400.

20. Riessman, Frank, *The Culturally Deprived Child.* New York: Harper, 1962.
21. Rosen, Carl L., and Ortega, Philip D., *Issues in Language and Reading Instruction of Spanish-Speaking Children: An Annotated Bibliography.* Newark: International Reading Assn., 1969.
22. Rosen, Carl L., and Ortega, Philip D., Language and Reading Problems of Spanish-Speaking Children in the Southwest," *Journal of Reading Behavior,* 1 (Winter 1969) 51-72.
23. Shuy, Roger W., "Some Considerations for Developing Beginning Reading Materials for Ghetto Children," *Journal of Reading Behavior,* 1 (Spring 1969) 33-44.
24. Singer, Harry, "Bilingualism and Elementary Education," *Modern Language Journal,* 40 (November 1956) 444-58.
25. Spache, George D., Andres, Micaela C., Curtis, H. A., et al., *A Longitudianal First Grade Reading Readiness Program.* Cooperative Research Project No. 2742. Florida State Department of Education, 1965.
26. Taba, Hilda, "Cultural Deprivation As a Factor in School Learning," *Merrill-Palmer Quarterly,* 10 (April 1964) 147-59.
27. Thomas, Dominic Richard, *Oral Language, Sentence Structure and Vocabulary of Kindergarten Children Living in Low Socio-Economic Urban Areas.* Doctoral dissertation, Wayne State University, 1962.
28. Whipple, Gertrude, and Black, Millard H., *Reading for Children Without—Our Disadvantaged Youth.* Reading Aids Series. Newark: International Reading Assn., 1966.
29. Wilkerson, Doxey A., "Programs and Practices in Compensatory Education for Disadvantaged Children," *Review of Educational Research,* 35 (December 1965) 426-40.

MATERIALS TO PROMOTE POSITIVE SELF-CONCEPT

The lists which follow are an attempt to supply teachers with books and other teaching materials which can be used to build a more positive self-concept for minority students. Some of the lists offer background or historical materials regarding a group, such as the American Black or the American Indian. Other listings combine both historical and contemporary literature, as in the case of the Eskimo, the Mexican-American and others. Following the ethnic or racial group materials are sections on instructional aids and devices to aid the teacher in conducting activities centered around some aspect of the culture of a minority group. In these sections, books related to the art, music, literature, history, etc. of each of the minority groups are recommended. Instructional materials for units in social science, science, and for reading improvement are gathered together in another chapter. Audio-visual resources and reference materials for teachers are brought together in two other chapters.

The closing chapters deal with the problem of adult literacy, an educational program which we feel is closely related to the teaching of minority groups. The list of materials is specifically selected to contain those for functional illiterates, e.g. individuals below a fifth grade level. Items that would normally be considered remedial are mentioned in many other sources, such as our *Good Reading for Poor Readers* (Garrard Publishing, 1970) and were not repeated here.

Most of the books mentioned were graded for readability by the Spache or the Dale-Chall formulas. The student's reading ability needed to profit from a book is noted in R. L. (Reading Level). The analysis of the books to obtain these readability estimates was made by some sixty teachers of the Jacksonville, Florida public schools under the direct supervision of the author and his closest colleague, his wife. These data were obtained in a project for the Follett Library Book Company for their Fall 1970 catalog in which most of these graded books are listed. The readability of some books was estimated by the author and are noted under R. L. by a figure such as 6-7, or 7-8.

CHAPTER IV

Heritage of the Black Americans—From Africa and Other Countries

(Primary Level)

Buckley, Peter, *Okolo of Nigeria*. New York: Simon, 1962. R. L. 3-4. Okolo wants to go to school but must overcome the opposition of the village tribesmen.

Donna, Natalie, *Boy of the Masai*. New York: Dodd, 1964. R.L. 3-4. A Masai boy revisits the village where he was born, after having lived in the city.

Elkin, Benjamin, *Such Is the Way of the World*. New York: Parents Magazine, 1968. R.L. 3-4. Simple, repetitive story of an African boy hunting for his monkey.

Fournier, Catharine, *The Coconut Thieves*. New York: Scribner, 1964. R.L. 3-4. West African folk tale; picture book format.

Peterson, Melba F., *Beya's Train Ride*. New York: Friendship, 1961. R.L. 2-3. Beya goes from her small African village to the city on the train.

Stuart, Morna, *Marassa and Midnight*. New York: McGraw-Hill, 1967. R.L. 3-4. Twin Negro boys are separated by a revolution and endure many dangers until they are united.

(Intermediate Level)

Aardema, Verna, *Tales from the Story Hat*. New York: Coward, 1960. R.L. 4-6. African folk tales and fanciful tales.

Aardema, Verna, *More Tales from the Story Hat*. New York: Coward, 1966. R.L. 4.6. African folk tales.

Abrahams, Peter, *Tell Freedom: Memories of Africa*. New York: Knopf, 1954. R.L. 7-8. The author, a young coloured South African, tells the story of his childhood in a land where segregation was the way of life.

Achebe, Chinua, *Things Fall Apart*. New York: Obolensky, 1959. R.L. 6-7. The arrival of the white men upsets the customs of the villagers and disturbs the Nigerian people.

Baker, Richard St. B., *Kamiti: A Forester's Dream*. Des Moines: Duell, 1960. R.L. 6-7. Although trained as a forester in Europe, when Kamiti returns to Kenya he finds that European forestry techniques aren't always appropriate in his homeland.

Bishop, Claire H., *Martin de Porres, Hero*. Boston: Houghton, 1954. R.L.

36

6-7. Martin, a Peruvian Negro, gave his life for the less fortunate, regardless of race or class.

Chandler, Edna W., *With Books on Her Head*. Des Moines: Meredith, 1967. R.L. 6-7. A Liberian girl insists on a chance to go to school.

Childs, Fay, *Wacheera—Child of Africa*. New York: Criterion, 1965. R.L. 4.2. Story of the daily life of an African child.

Clair, Andree, *Bemba: An African Adventure*. New York: Harcourt, 1962. R.L. 5-6. Bemba tries to reconcile the life in the forest with the complicated life in the world outside.

Conton, William, *The African*. New York: Crown, 1967. (Paperback). R.L. 6-7. Educated by the whites, Kisimi returns to help his own African people.

Courlander, Harold, *The Piece of Fire and Other Haitian Tales*. New York: Harcourt, 1964. R.L. 4-5. Folktales.

Darbois, Dominique, *Agossou, Boy of Africa*. Chicago: Follett, 1962. R.L. 4.5. Daily life in an African village.

Elliot, Geraldine, *The Long Grass Whispers: A Book of African Folktales*. New York: Schocken, 1969. R.L. 4-5. A collection of folk tales.

Graham, Lorenz, *I. Momolu*. New York: Crowell, 1966. R.L. 4-5. Momolu of Liberia compares the ways of village life with modern civilization.

Guillot, Rene, *Fofana*. New York: Criterion, 1962. R.L. 6-7. Friendship between a French and an African boy.

Hallin, Emily W. and Buell, Robert K., *Follow the Honey Bird*. New York: McKay, 1967. R.L. 4-5. Masai herdboys have adventures.

Keating, Bern, *Chaka, King of the Zulus*. New York: Putnam, 1968. R.L 5.0. Biography of an African monarch.

Mirsky, Reba P., *Seven Grandmothers*. Chicago: Follett, 1952. R.L. 4.9. An African folk tale.

Mirsky, Reba P., *Nomusa and the New Magic*. Chicago: Follett, 1962. R.L 5.2. African tales.

Mirsky, Reba P., *Thirty-One Brothers and Sisters*. Chicago: Follett, 1952. R.L. 4.5. Story of Nomusa, daughter of a Zulu chief. Nomusa has an adventure with a wild boar.

Palmer, C. E., *The Cloud with the Silver Lining*. New York: Pantheon, 1967. R.L. 4-5. Two enterprising Jamaican boys help their crippled grandfather.

Scherman, Katharine, *The Slave Who Freed Haiti*. New York: Random, 1954. R.L. 6.2. Biography of Toussaint Louverture.

Schloat, G.W., *Duee, A Boy of Liberia*. New York: Knopf, 1962. R.L. 4-5. In clear text and many photographs, the life in Liberia is illustrated.

Schloat, G. W., *Kwaku, A Boy of Ghana*. New York: Knopf, 1962. R.L. 4-5. Through many photographs, a boy's life in Ghana is presented.

Sheehan, Arthur and Odell, Elizabeth, *Pierre Toussaint—Pioneer in Brotherhood*. New York: Kenedy, 1963. R.L. 5-6. A revered Catholic Negro leader.

Sherlock, Philip, compiler, *West Indian Folktales*. New York: Walck, 1966. R.L. 4-5. Myths brought from South America to the West Indies.

Spencer, Cornelia, *Claim to Freedom*. New York: John Day, 1962. R.L 5-6. Through the story of an Indian boy in Nairobi, the author attempts to portray the progress toward freedom.

Syme, Ronald, *African Traveler, The Story of Mary Kingsley*. New York: Morrow, 1962. R.L. 5.7. A biography of a woman who devoted her life to social work in Africa.

Syme, Ronald, *Nigerian Pioneer—Mary Slessor*. New York: Morrow, 1964. R.L. 5.9. A biography of a missionary to Africa.

Van Stockum, Hilda, *Mogo's Flute*. New York: Viking, 1966. R.L 5-6. An East African boy learns that assuming responsibility can be gratifying.

Watson, Jane, *Ethiopia: Mountain Kingdom*. Champaign: Garrard, 1966. R.L. 4.0. The colorful history of this African nation.

Whitney, Phyllis A., *Secret of the Tiger's Eye*. Philadelphia: Westminster, 1961. R.L. 5.0. Teen-age mystery story laid in Capetown, South Africa. Touches on problems of American family in adjusting to customs of South Africa.

Wolfe, Louis, *Ifrikya*. New York: Putnam, 1964. R.L. 5.3. True stories of Africa and Africans.

Woodson, Carter G., *African Myths*. Washington: Associated Publishers, 1943. R.L 4-5. A collection.

(Jr.-Sr. H. S. Level)

Cain, Alfred E., editor, *Negro Heritage Reader for Young People*. Yonkers: Educational Heritage, 1965. R.L 8-9. A collection of articles and essays.

Courlander, Harold, *The African*. New York: Crown, 1967. R.L 8-10. A shocking novel about the slave trade.

Dannett, Sylvia G. L., *Profiles of Negro Womanhood—(1619-1900)*. Yonkers: Educational Heritage, 1965. R.L. 6-7. Biographical materials.

Evans, Lancelot, editor, *Emerging African Nations and Their Leaders*. Yonkers: Educational Heritage. Vol. I. (Burundi to Liberia) : Vol. II. (Malawi to Zambia). R.L. 8-9.

Joy, Charles R., *Young People of West Africa*. Des Moines: Duell, 1961. R.L. 7-8. Short stories of real young people who will help shape the future of their West African countries.

Kayira, Legson, *I Will Try*. New York: Doubleday, 1965. R.L. 6-7. True account of a boy who walked 2500 miles across Africa to get passage to an American school.

Kenworthy, Leonard and Ferrari, Erma, *Leaders of New Nations*. New York: Doubleday, 1967. R.L. 6-7. Candid biographies of leaders of African and Asian nations.

Kittler, Glenn D., *Equatorial Africa*. New York: Nelson, 1964. R.L 7-8. Leaders of the newly independent nations of Africa.

Luthuli, Albert, *Let My People Go*. New York: McGraw-Hill, 1962. R.L. 7-8. Luthuli writes and fights for his people against oppression in South Africa.

Mitchison, Naomi, *Friends and Enemies*. New York: John Day, 1968. R.L. 6-7. A black boy grows up in Bechuanaland to think like a man in a free country.

Montejo, Esteban, *The Autobiography of a Runaway Slave*. New York: Pantheon, 1968. R.L. 8-9. Told in the dialect of a Cuban slave, runaway, revolutionary character.

Nkrumah, Kwame, *Ghana: The Autobiography of Kwame Nkrumah*. New York: Nelson, 1957. R.L 7-8. Nkrumah's life was devoted to securing the independence of his country, until he was deposed as a dictator.

Nolen, Barbara, *Africa Is People*. New York: Dutton, 1967. R.L. 6-7. First-hand accounts from Africa of today.

Paton, Alan, *Cry, the Beloved Country*. New York: Scribner, 1961. (Paperback) R.L. 7-8. Apartheid in South Africa.

Paton, Alan, *Tales from a Troubled Land*. New York: Scribner, 1961. R.L. 7-8. Stories dealing with apartheid and other problems in South Africa.

Phillips, Norman, *The Tragedy of Apartheid: A Journalist's Experience in South Africa*. New York: McKay, 1960. R.L. 7-8. Phillips tells the story of the massacre in Sharpsville.

Plimpton, Ruth T., *Operation Crossroads Africa*. New York: Viking, 1962. R.L. 6-7. The work of a volunteer group in African countries sponsored by a New York church.

Turnbull, Colin M., *The Lovely African*. New York: Simon, 1962. (Paperback) R.L. 7-8. The story of the young people and new nations of Africa.

Van der Post, Laurens, *Flamingo Feather*. New York: Morrow, 1954. R.L. 6-7. The struggle between black and white in South Africa.

CHAPTER V

American Heritage of the Black American

THIS LIST CONTAINS MATERIALS ON the Black American from the time the first Negro landed in America as a member of a Spanish exploring party to about the end of the nineteenth century. It emphasizes the Black's history, his outstanding leaders, and his relations with other Americans during this period. The true story of the Black in America over a period of more than four centuries is reflected in both the factual and fictional literature included here. Perhaps the life and feelings of the Black American of today can be better understood, by both black and white people, through this background material.

(Primary Level)

Epstein, Sam and Beryl, *George Washington Carver: Negro Scientist.* Champaign: Garrard, 1960. R.L. 3.0. Good for introducing biography in the lower grades or for slow readers in the upper grades.

Keats, Ezra J., *John Henry—An American Legend.* New York: Pantheon, 1965. R.L. 3-4. Story of a favorite folk hero.

Patterson, Lillie, *Booker T. Washington: Leader of His People.* Champaign: Garrard, 1962. R.L. 3.0. Biography of the Negro leader and educator.

Patterson, Lillie, *Frederick Douglass: Freedom Fighter.* Champaign: Garrard, 1965. R.L. 3.0. Biography of an American Negro who devoted his life to fighting slavery.

(Intermediate Level)

Bacmeister, Rhoda W., *Voices in the Night.* Indianapolis: Bobbs, 1965. R.L. 5-6. Jeanie inadvertently becomes involved in the Underground Railroad.

Baker, Betty, *Walk the World's Rim.* New York: Harper, 1965. R.L. 5-6. Esteban, a Negro slave, survived an expedition into Florida in 1527. He joined the Indians and worked against slavery.

Bontemps, Arna, *The Story of the Negro.* New York: Knopf, 1958. R.L. 5-6. Through the contributions of many Negro leaders, the author presents a brief history of the Negro in America.

Bontemps, Arna, *George Washington Carver.* Chicago: Grosset, 1950. R.L. 5-6. A moving portrait and unsentimentalized biography of a great scientist.

Durham, Philip and Jones, Everett L., *The Adventures of the Negro Cowboys.* New York: Dodd, 1965. R.L. 3-4. Adapted from the adult book.

Epstein, Sam and Beryl, *Harriet Tubman: Guide to Freedom.* Champaign: Garrard, 1968. R.L. 4.0. A prominent Negro figure in the Underground Railroad.

Felton, Harold W., *Jim Beckworth*: *Negro Mountain Man*. New York: Dodd, 1966. R.L. 5-6. Account of an extraordinary man and his stories.

Finlayson, Ann, *Decathlon Men*: *Greatest Athletes in the World*. Champaign: Garrard, 1966. R.L. 4.0. Stories of the greatest of the Olympic Athletes.

Graham, Shirley, *Booker T. Washington*. New York: Messner, 1966. R.L. 5.9. Biography of the Negro educator.

Guy, Anne W., *William*. New York: Dial, 1961. R.L. 4-5. Eleven-year-old William must summon all his courage in a strange, new school.

Hennessy, Maurice and Sauter, Edwin W., Jr., *A Crown for Thomas Peters*. New York: Washburn, 1964. R.L. 6-7. Thomas Peters became a passionate leader of his people.

Hughes, Langston, *The First Book of Negroes*. New York: Watts, 1952. R.L. 4-5. In a fictional manner, the author provides historical data concerning the accomplishments of several famous American Negroes.

Hughes, Langston, *The First Book of Jazz*. New York: Watts, 1955. R.L. 5-6. A simple explanation of the evolution of jazz, plus a brief description of famous jazz musicians.

Kendall, Lace, *Rain Boat*. New York: Coward, 1965. R.L. 5-6. The heroic Negro Shem shelters three children from a terrible flood.

Kerr, James L., *The Boy Jacko*. New York: Watts, 1963. R.L. 6-7. Matt and Jacko are imprisoned aboard a slave ship, captured by pirates and jailed in Virginia before reaching their destination.

Meadowcroft, Enid L., *By Secret Railway*. New York: Crowell, 1948. R.L. 5-6. Jim, a freed slave, is kidnapped by slave traders. The story depicts the warm friendship of two fifteen-year-old boys.

Millender, Dharathula H., *Crispus Attucks, Boy of Valor*. Indianapolis: Bobbs, 1965. R.L. 4.5. Story of a Negro hero in Revolutionary times.

Montgomery, Elizabeth, *William C. Handy*: *Father of the Blues*. Champaign: Garrard, 1968. R.L. 4.0. Life history of the first blues musician.

Morsbach, Mabel, *The Negro in American Life*. New York: Harcourt, 1967. R.L. 5-6. Contributions and life history of over 300 prominent Negroes.

Orrmont, Arthur, *Fighter Against Slavery*: *Jehudi Ashmun*. New York: Messner, 1966. R.L. 5.5. Biography of a Congregational minister who devoted his life to fighting slavery.

Rollins, Charlemae H., *They Showed the Way*. New York: Crowell, 1964. R.L. 5-6. Forty brief biographies of Negro men and women who triumphed over great obstacles and achieved success in various fields.

Spangler, Earl, *The Negro in America*. New York: Lerner, 1966. R.L. 6.5. A brief history of the Negro in America.

Sterling, Dorothy and Quarles, B., *Lift Every Voice*. New York: Doubleday. (Paperback). R.L. 5-6. Biographies of four outstanding Negroes.

Sterling, Phillip and Logan, Raymond, *Four Took Freedom*. New York: Doubleday, 1967. R.L. 5-6. Biographies of four Negroes who escaped from slavery to build a new life.

Stevenson, Augusta, *Booker T. Washington*: *Ambitious Boy*. Indianapolis:

Bobbs, 1950. R.L. 4-5. A childhood biography of the great Negro educator, founder of Tuskegee Institute.

Stevenson, Augusta, *George Carver Boy Scientist*. Indianapolis: Bobbs, 1959. R.L. 4.3. Childhood biography of the Negro scientist.

Yates, Elizabeth, *Prudence Crandall: Woman of Courage*. New York: Dutton, 1955. R.L. 5-6. Prudence Crandall founded a school for Negro girls in 1833, but was driven from her state.

Yates, Elizabeth, *Amos Fortune: Free Man*. New York: Dutton. 1950. R.L. 5.6. True story of Amos Fortune who eventually buys his freedom and earns respect as a free man.

Young, Margaret B., *The First Book of American Negroes*. New York: Watts, 1966. R.L. 6.0. Survey of the life of the American Negro from the advent of slavery to the present.

(Jr.—Sr. H. S. Level)

Adams, Russell L., *Great Negroes Past and Present*. Chicago: Afro-American, 1964. R.L. 6-7. Short biographies of 150 outstanding Negroes.

Angell, Pauline, *To the Top of the World: The Story of Peary and Henson*. Chicago: Rand, 1964. R.L. 7-8. The story of two explorers who were dependent on each other for the accomplishment of their life work. Robert E. Peary and Mathew Henson, a Negro.

Bernard, Jacqueline, *Journey Toward Freedom: The Story of Sojourner Truth*. New York: Norton, 1967. R.L. 7-8. Biography of a civil rights leader.

Bontemps, Arna, *Chariot in the Sky: A Story of the Jubilee Singers*. New York: Holt, 1951. R.L. 6-7. Through the story of Caleb Williams, the early struggles of Fisk University and of the Jubilee singers is told.

Foster, G. A., *The Eyes and Ears of the Civil War*. New York: Criterion, 1963. R.L. 6-7. The role of Negroes as couriers and spies during the Civil War.

Graham, Shirley, *The Story of Phillis Wheatley*. New York: Messner, 1949. R.L. 6-7. The tragic life of an early Negro poetess.

Hardwick, Richard, *Charles Richard Drew: Pioneer in Blood Research*. New York: Scribner, 1967. R.L. 7-8. Charles Drew became an authority on the storage of human blood.

Harris, Joel C., *Uncle Remus: His Songs and Sayings*. New York: Grosset. R.L. 9.3. Stories about Negroes, once considered quite humorous.

Hoyt, Edwin P., *Paul Robeson, the American Othello*. Cleveland: World, 1967. R.L. 7-8. Biography of the great Negro singer.

Hughes, Langston, *Famous Negro Heroes of America*. New York: Dodd, 1958. R.L. 7-8. Seventeen biographies of Negro men and women who have achieved success in various fields.

Kelly, Josephine, *Dark Shepherd*. Paterson: St. Anthony. R.L. 7-8. Story of Bishop Healey, first Negro Catholic bishop in the United States.

Knight, Frank, *The Slaver's Apprentice*. New York: St. Martin's, 1961. R.L. 6-7. John is an apprentice on a slave ship in 1794.

Leckie, William H., *The Buffalo Soldiers: A Narrative of the Negro*

Cavalry in the West. Norman: University of Oklahoma, 1967. R.L. 8-9. Adventures of the little-known Negro cavalry.

Lee, Irwin H., *Negro Medal of Honor Men.* New York: Dodd, 1967. R.L. 6-7. Stories of the 44 valiant Negroes who received this decoration.

Lester, Julius, editor, *To Be a Slave.* New York: Noble. (Paperback.) R.L. 7-8. A documentary based on journals, diaries, etc., depicting life as a slave.

McPherson, James M., *The Negro's Civil War: How Negroes Felt and Acted During the War for the Union.* New York: Pantheon, 1965. R.L. 6-7. Documentary material on the Negro's contribution to the Northern cause.

Means, Florence, *Carver's George: A Biography of George W. Carver.* Boston: Houghton, 1952. R.L. 6-7.

Meltzer, Milton, *Thaddeus Stevens and the Fight for Negro Rights.* New York: Crowell, 1967. R.L. 7-8. Civil rights activities in the period of Thaddeus Stevens.

Meltzer, Milton, *In Their Own Words: A History of the American Negro 1619-1865.* New York: Crowell, 1964. (Paperback) R.L. 6-7. One of three volumes covering the period from the beginning of slavery in the United States to the close of the Civil War. This book reflects American Negro thought and the conditions faced by both slaves and freemen.

Meltzer, Milton, *Tongue of Flame: The Life of Lydia Maria Child.* New York: Crowell, 1965. R.L. 6-7. Biography of an early fighter for civil rights.

Meltzer, Milton and Meier, August, *Time of Trial: Time of Hope.* New York: Doubleday, 1966. R.L. 6-7. Advancement of the black since World War I.

Mirsky, Jeanette, *The Gentle Conquistadors.* New York: Random, 1969. R.L. 6-7. Four men, three Spanish captains and a negro slave wander through Mexico for ten years.

Nathan, Dorothy, *Women of Courage.* New York: Random, 1964. R.L. 6-7. Short biographies of outstanding Negro and white women.

Onstott, Kyle, *Mandingo.* Greenwich: Fawcett. (Paperback). R.L. 7-8. A brutally realistic novel of slavery in 1827-35. For mature readers.

Pauli, Hertha, *Her Name Was Sojourner Truth.* New York: Appleton, 1962. R.L. 7-8. A little-known leader of the black people.

Peare, Catherine O., *Mary McLeod Bethune.* New York: Vanguard, 1951. R.L. 6-7. Mary McLeod started a college for Negroes with not much more than her faith and her industry.

Petry, Ann, *Tituba of Salem Village.* New York: Crowell, 1964. R.L. 7-8. Tituba, a Negro slave woman, is one of the first three persons condemned in the Salem witch trials.

Richardson, Ben, *Great American Negroes.* New York: Crowell, 1956. R.L. 6-7. Short biographies of twenty-six American Negroes who achieved prominence.

Robinson, Bradley with Mathew Henson, *Dark Companion: The Story of Mathew Henson,* Greenwich: Fawcett. (Paperback). R.L. 7-8. Biography of Mathew Henson, who, with Peary, discovered the North Pole.

Starkey, Marion L., *Striving to Make It My Home*: *The Story of Americans from Africa*. New York: Norton, 1964. R.L. 6-7.

Sterling, Dorothy, *Freedom Train*: *The Story of Harriet Tubman*. New York: Doubleday, 1954. R.L. 6-7. A simple biography of Harriet Tubman, "conductor" on the Underground Railway.

Sterling, Dorothy, *Captain of the Planter*: *The Story of Robert Smalls*. New York: Doubleday, 1958. R.L. 6-7. Robert Smalls, a Civil War Negro pilot, fights and works for his people.

Sterling, Dorothy, *Lucretia Mott*: *Gentle Warrior*. New York: Doubleday, 1964. R.L. 6-7. Excellent biography of a woman crusader.

Sterling, Dorothy, *Forever Free—The Story of the Emancipation Proclamation*. New York: Doubleday, 1963. R.L. 7-8. A review of America's treatment of her black people.

Sterne, Emma G., *Blood Brothers*: *Four Men of Science*. New York: Knopf, 1959. R.L. 7-8. The text describes the research and discoveries of four great scientists, one a Negro, Charles Richard Drew, who pioneered in the field of blood plasma preservation.

Sterne, Emma G., *Mary McLeod Bethune*. New York: Knopf, 1957. R.L. 6-7. Mary overcomes dire poverty to become a teacher and educator.

Stowe, Harriet B., *Uncle Tom's Cabin*. New York: Barziller, 1966. R.L. 6-7. Adapted for younger readers.

Styron, William, *The Confessions of Nat Turner*. New York: New American, 1968. (Paperback). R.L. 7-8. First-person account of a bloody slave revolt in the South.

Tarry, Ellen, *Young Jim*: *The Early Years of James Weldon Johnson*. New York: Dodd, 1967. R.L. 6-7. Johnson eventually became one of America's greatest poets.

Washington, Booker T., *Up From Slavery*. New York: Dell. Paperback. R.L. Autobiography of the controversial Negro educator.

Weinstein, A. and Gatell, F. O., *American Negro Slavery*: *A Modern Reader*. New York: Oxford University, 1968. R.L. 7-8. A collection of documentary and other materials.

Yates, Elizabeth, *Howard Thurman*: *Portrait of a Practical Dreamer*. New York: Day, 1964. R.L. 6-7. Biography of a revered religious leader.

CHAPTER VI

The Black American Today

THE role of the present-day Black American is revealed in the story of the civil rights movement and in the lives of his leaders in politics, sports, entertainment, literature and other fields. The stories of prejudice, segregation and ghetto life fill out this picture. This list attempts to bring together the mass of literature, factual and fictional, that tells the reader what it is like to be black in the 20th century. Both blacks and whites should be familiar with this contemporary material, if they are ever to understand each other or themselves.

(Primary Level)

Beim, Jerrold, *Swimming Hole*. New York: Morrow, 1961. R.L. 3. Steve is not accepted at the swimming hole until he learns that skin color isn't important.

Beim, Lorraine and Jerrold, *Two is a Team*. New York: Harcourt, 1945. R.L. 3.5. Paul and Ted pay for their carelessness in a cooperative effort.

Brown, Jeanette P., *Ronnie's Wish*. Drawings by Jean Martinez. New York: Friendship Press, 1954. R.L. 3-4. A small Negro boy has interesting adventures in the children's zoo.

Courlander, Harold, *Terrapin's Pot of Sense*. New York: Holt, 1957. R.L. 3-4. A collection of folk tales.

Gipson, Fred, *Trail-Driving Rooster*. New York: Harper, 1955. R.L. 3-4. Dick, a scrawny rooster, fights to stay out of the frying pan. Later he becomes involved in fighting segregation.

Grifalconi, Ann, *City Rhythms*. Indianapolis: Bobbs, 1965. R.L. 2-3. Text and pictures interpret a Negro child's awareness of the city about him.

Horvath, Betty, *Hooray for Jasper*. New York: Watts, 1966. R.L. 3-4. Jasper proves his courage in an integrated suburban setting.

Jaynes, Ruth, *Friends, Friends, Friends*. Glendale: Bowmar, 1967. R.L. 1-2. A simple story of multi-ethnic friendships in a city setting.

Justus, May, *New Boy in School*. New York: Hastings, 1963. R.L. 3-4 Story of a Negro boy in a newly integrated school.

Justus, May, *A New Home for Billy*. New York: Hastings, 1966. R.L. 2-3. A little Negro boy and his family find a new home and friends.

Katzoff, Betty and Sy, *Cathy's First School*. New York: Knopf, 1964. R.L. 3-4. Cathy goes to an integrated nursery school. Largely a picture book.

Keats, Ezra J., *Whistle for Willie*. New York: Viking, 1964. R.L. 2.8. Willie, a little Negro boy, tries to learn to whistle.

Keats, Ezra J., *The Snowy Day*. New York: Viking, 1962. R.L. 3.1. Peter, a Negro boy, enjoys the excitement of snow.

Kessler, Leonard, *Here Comes the Strikeout*. New York: Harper, 1965. R.L. 1.5. Bobby simply couldn't get a hit, no matter how hard he tried. Finally, with the coaching and encouragement of his friend Willie, Bobby did get a hit that won the ball game.

Laugh With Larry. Chicago: Follett, 1962. R.L. 2.0. A primer with illustrations of a Negro family in an urban setting. Written by the Writer's Committee under the leadership of Dr. Gertrude Whipple.

Lewis, Mary, *Hallow'een Kangaroo*. New York: Washburn, 1964. R.L. 3-4. Jeffery has real troubles with the zipper on his kangaroo costume.

Lexau, Joan M. *Benjie*. New York: Dial, 1964. R.L. 3-4. Benjie tries to find his grandmother's earrings.

Lexau, Joan M. *I Should Have Stayed in Bed*. New York: Harper, 1965. R.L. 2-3. Sam was really upset when he thought that his Negro friend Albert had deserted him.

Lipkind, William and Mordinoff, Nicholas, *Four-Leaf Clover*. New York: Harcourt, 1959. R.L. 3-4. Two boys, one white and one Negro, search successfully for a four-leaf clover. But their greatest luck is in their friendship.

Martin, Patricia M., *The Little Brown Hen*. New York: Crowell, 1960. R.L. 3-4. An easy to read story about Willie and how he finds his lost hen.

Randall, Blossom E., *Fun for Chris*. Chicago: Whitman, 1956. R.L. 3.0. Chris' mother helps him understand that difference in skin color is no barrier to friendship.

Rosenbaum, Eileen, *Ronnie*. New York: Parents, 1969. R.L. 2-3. Illustrated by true-to-life photographs, the book offers a simple story of a day in a black city boy's life.

Selsam, Millicent E., *Tony's Birds*. New York: Harper, 1961. R.L. 2.6. Tony is an avid bird-watcher.

Shackleford, Jane, *Happy Days*. Washington, D.C.: Associated Publishers, 1944. R.L. 3-4. Daily life of a Negro boy in a middle class Northern home.

Sharpe, Stelle G., *Tobe*. Chapel Hill: University of North Carolina Press, 1939. R.L. 3-4. The illustrations and text describe the daily activities of a rural Negro family and a little boy named Tobe.

Weddle, Ethel M., *Joel Chandler Harris*. Indianapolis: Bobbs-Merrill, 1964. R.L. 3.5. Biography of the famous writer of Negro humor stories.

Williamson, Stan, *No Bark Dog*. Chicago: Follett, 1962. R.L. 1.5. A story about a little boy and his dog that wouldn't bark. The dog about whom everyone is so concerned does bark at an appropriate time.

Young, Margaret B., *The Picture Life of Martin Luther King, Jr*. New York: Watts, 1968. R.L. 2-3. Told in pictures and simple text.

(Intermediate Level)

Agle, Nan H., *Joe Bean*. New York: Seabury, 1967. R.L. 3-4. An eleven-year-old Negro boy spends a summer on a horse farm and learns a great deal about horses and himself.

Ball, Dorothy W., *Hurricane: The Story of a Friendship*. Indianapolis: Bobbs, 1964. R.L. 4-5. Luke, a fatherless Negro boy, must prove his innocence of a knifing.

Baum, Betty, *A New Home for Theresa*. New York: Knopf, 1968. R.L. 5-6. Theresa tries to adjust to her foster home.

Baum, Betty, *Patricia Crosses Town*. New York: Knopf. 1965. R.L. 3-4. Bussing Negro children to a white school creates feelings among parents, but not among the children.

Beattie, Jessie L., *Black Moses: The Real Uncle Tom*. Toronto: Ryerson, 1957. R.L. 5-6. Story of a slave who escaped to Canada and founded a Negro refugee colony in Ontario.

Blassingame, Wyatt, *Jake Gaither: Winning Coach*. Champaign: Garrard, 1969. R.L. 4.0. A winning football coach who is an inspiration to his boys.

Bontemps, Arna, *Sad Faced Boy*. Boston: Houghton, 1937. R.L. 4. Three small Negro boys from Alabama visit New York.

Bontemps, Arna, *Famous Negro Athletes*. New York: Dodd, 1964. R.L. 5-6. Short, biographical stories of sports figures.

Brodsky, Mimi, *House at 12 Rose Street*. New York: Abelard, 1966. R.L. 4-5. Two boys, one white and one black, bring harmony to the neighborhood.

Burchardt, Nellie, *Reggie's No-Good Bird*. New York: Watts, 1967. R.L. 4-5. Reggie's cruelty to a bird backfires upon him to lead him to a better relationship with his multi-ethnic peers.

Campanella, Roy, *It's Good to Be Alive*. Boston: Little, 1959. R.L. 5-6. Roy tells his own story from his childhood to his present convalescence.

Carlson, Natalie S., *The Empty Schoolhouse*. New York: Harper, 1965. R.L. 4.7. Going to a desegregated school raises many physical and emotional problems.

Chandler, Ruth F., *Ladder to the Sky*. New York: Abelard, 1959. R.L. 5-6. The problems of a Negro family living in a predominantly white Northern community are told simply and directly.

Clayton, Ed., *Martin Luther King: the Peaceful Warrior*. Englewood Cliffs: Prentice-Hall, 1964. R.L. 4-5. An official biography of this martyred civil rights leader.

Cobb, Alice, *The Swimming Pool*. New York: Friendship, 1957. R.L. 4-5. Preston is not allowed to use the new swimming pool, but, with the help of his friends raises money for one in his part of town.

de Angeli, Marguerite, *Bright April*. Garden City, New York: Doubleday, 1946. R.L. 4.7. April learns about prejudice from her friends.

Eaton, Jeanette, *Trumpeter's Tale: The Story of Young Louis Armstrong*. New York: Morrow, 1955. R.L. 6-7. Boyhood of the great Negro trumpeter.

Etter, Les, *Golden Gloves Challenger*. New York: Hastings, 1967. R.L. 6-7. Realistic story of a Negro amateur boxer.

Faulkner, Georgene and Becker, John, *Melindy's Medal*. New York: Messner, 1945. R.L. 3-4. Melindy lives up to the courage of her family history.

Faulkner, Georgene, *Melindy's Happy Summer*. New York: Messner, 1949.

R.L. 4-5. Melindy's summer vacation with a white family is marred by her boasting.

Finlayson, Ann, *Stars of the Modern Olympics*. Champaign: Garrard, 1967. R.L. 4.0. Biographies of athletes of recent times.

Fisher, Aileen, *A Lantern in the Window*. New York: Nelson, 1957. R.L. 5-6. Twelve-year-old Peter learns that the farm is a station on the underground railroad. A fascinating account of the perils involved in its operation.

Fox, Paula, *How Many Miles to Babylon?* New York: White, 1967. R.L. 5-6. A ten-year-old Negro boy is caught up by his life in Coney Island, Brooklyn.

Freeman, Don, *Corduroy*. New York: Viking, 1968. R.L. 4.0. This is the story of a toy bear that no one wanted. He was finally bought by a little Negro girl.

Gates, Doris, *Little Vic*. New York: Viking, 1951. R.L. 4.5. In training his horse, Tony learns that his being a Negro has no influence upon his success.

Gould, Jean, *That Dunbar Boy*. New York: Dodd, 1958. R.L. 5-6. Biography of the great Negro poet.

Graham, Lorenz, *South Town*. Chicago, Follett, 1958. R.L. 5.2. The life of a Negro family living in a small Southern community is disrupted by prejudices of some white citizens.

Graham, Lorenz, *North Town*. New York: Crowell, 1965. R.L. 6-7. Continuation of the story of the Williams family in a Northern town.

Hamilton, Virginia, *Zeely*. New York: Macmillan, 1967. R.L. 4-5. Zeely is tall, quiet and aloof like an African queen.

Hayes, Florence, *Skid*. Boston: Houghton Mifflin, 1948. R.L. 5-6. When Skid's family moves north and he is the only Negro in his school, he experiences a difficult adjustment.

Hogan, Inez, *Nappy Has a New Friend*. New York: Dutton, 1947. R.L. 4-5. A pleasant little story of interracial friendships.

Hunt, Mabel L., *Ladycake Farm*. Philadelphia: Lippincott, 1952. R.L. 4.9. A Negro family earns respect and acceptance in an all-white community.

Jackson, Jesse, *Tessie*. New York: Dell, 1969. Paperback. R.L. 5-6. A young girl's conflict between the standards of her Harlem home and the private school she attends.

Klein, Larry, *Jim Brown—The Running Back*. New York: Putnam, 1965. R.L. 6-7. Story of a great American athlete from high school days on.

Kugelmass, J.A., *Ralph J. Bunche, Fighter for Peace*. New York: Messner, 1952. R.L. 5.2. Ralph J. Bunche overcomes poverty and prejudice to become a leading statesman.

Lee, Harper, *To Kill a Mockingbird*. Philadelphia: Lippincott, 1960. R.L. 5.4. Two young children discover how brave their father really is when he defends a Negro in court.

Lenski, Lois, *Mama Hattie's Girl*. Philadelphia: Lippincott, 1953. R.L. 4-5. Lula Bell goes north with her mother, to meet the joys and prejudices of a new life.

Lewis, Richard W., *A Summer Adventure.* New York: Harper, 1962. R.L. 4-5. Ross eventually realizes that the animals in his backyard zoo would be happier if he freed them.

Liss, Howard, *The Making of a Rookie.* New York: Random, 1968. R.L. 4-5. The exciting stories of Gale Sayers and other football figures.

Miles, Miska, *Mississippi Possum.* Boston: Little Brown, 1965. R.L. 5-6. A Negro family took refuge on the top of a hill during a flood in the lower Mississippi. Among the evacuees was a shy, frightened possum who was befriended by the two children of the family.

Morse, Evangeline, *Brown Rabbit: Her Story.* Chicago: Follett, 1967. R.L. 5.5. A simple story of race relations.

Norfleet, Mary C., *Hand-Me-Down House.* Richmond: John Knox, 1962. R.L. 4-5. Jake, a young Negro boy, helps his family accept a new white neighbor.

Orsborn, Peggy A., *The Meeting.* Chicago: Afro-American. A one act play based on multi-ethnic theme. Boxed with 15 copies of play and teaching guide.

Paige, Satchel and Lipman, David, *Maybe I'll Pitch Forever.* New York: Doubleday, 1962. R.L. 6-7. Satchel grew up through the slums and major league baseball to become a well-liked person.

Palmer, Cadida, *Snow Storm before Christmas.* Philadelphia: Lippincott, 1965. R.L. 4-5. Two Negro brothers are caught in a snowstorm which nearly ruins their presents and the holiday.

Patterson, Lillie, *Martin Luther King, Jr.: Man of Peace.* Champaign: Garrard, 1969. R.L. 4.0. The life and works of the great Civil Rights leader.

Richards, Kenneth G., *People of Destiny—Louis Armstrong.* Chicago: Children's Press, 1967. R.L. 5.9. Biography of the greatest trumpeter.

Robinson, John R. and Duckett, Alfred, *Breakthrough to the Big League: The Story of Jackie Robinson.* New York: Harper, 1965. R.L. 6-7. Biography of Jackie's childhood and early manhood.

Robinson, Louie, *Arthur Ashe Tennis Champion,* New York: Doubleday, 1967. R.L. 4.6. Biography of the tennis champion.

Rowan, Carl, *Wait Until Next Year.* New York: Random, 1960. R.L. 6-7. Jackie Robinson struggles to achieve the respect his athletic skill justifies.

Russell, William F., *Go Up for Glory.* New York: Coward, 1966. R.L. 6-7. Professional basketballer's story.

Ruthland, Eva, *The Trouble with Being a Mama.* New York: Abingdon, 1964. R.L. 6-7. A mother's problems with four lively youngsters.

Rydberg, Ervie, *The Dark of the Cave.* New York: McKay, 1965. R.L. 5-6. After his cataract operation, Ronnie discovers that his best friend is a Negro.

Schoor, Gene, *Roy Campanella.* New York: Putnam, 1959. R.L. 4.9. Story of the baseball figure.

Schoor, Gene, *Willie Mays.* New York: Putnam, 1960. R.L. 5.2. Tells story of Willie Mays' career in baseball.

Shapiro, Milton J., *The Roy Campanella Story*. New York: Messner, 1958. R.L. 6-7. The story of Roy's difficulties as a Negro in bigtime baseball.

Shapiro, Milton J., *Jackie Robinson (of the Brooklyn Dodgers)*. New York: Messner, 1965. R.L. 5.7. Biography of the first major league Negro ball player.

Snyder, Zilpha K., *The Egypt Game*. New York: Atheneum, 1967. R.L. 5-6. A group of boys create a game around an old Egyptian statue.

Stevenson, Janet, *Singing to the World—Marian Anderson*. Chicago: Encyclopedia Britannica, 1963. R.L. 5-6. Biography of the great Negro singer.

Stiles, Martha B., *The Strange House at Newburyport*. New York: Dial, 1963. R.L. 4-5. Two little girls discover that their grandmother is helping Negro slaves escape to Canada.

Stolz, Mary, *A Wonderful, Terrible Time*. New York: Harper, 1967. R.L. 3-4. Two little Negro girls from the city spend a frightening summer in camp.

Sullivan, George, *The Cassius Clay Story*. New York: Fleet, 1964. R.L. 6-7. The colorful career of the famous heavyweight fighter.

Undry, Janice M., *What Mary Jo Shared*. Chicago: Whitman, 1966. R.L. 4-5. Mary Jo was shy at sharing time until she hit on the idea of sharing her father.

Vogel, Ilse-Margaret, *Hello, Henry*. New York: Parents, 1965. R.L. 4-5. Two boys find a friendship in a supermarket, despite their racial differences.

Vroman, Mary E., *Harlem Summer*. New York: Putnam, 1967. R.L. 4.5. John comes from the South to spend the summer in Harlem.

Weik, Mary H., *The Jazz Man*. New York: Atheneum, 1966. R.L. 5-6. Music and courage give hope to a crippled Negro boy who lives in poverty and deprivation.

Wier, Esther, *Easy Does It*. New York: Vanguard, 1965. R.L. 6-7. Although Chip is only eleven, he is more mature in his relations with the new Negro neighbors, than his own family or the rest of the community.

Wills, Maury and Gardner, Steve, *It Pays to Steal*. Englewood Cliffs: Prentice-Hall, 1963. R.L. 6-7. A detailed account of Will's struggle to achieve a baseball career.

Woody, Regina, *Almena's Dogs*. New York: Farrar, 1954. R.L. 4-5. Almena finds a way to show her love for dogs and other pets, despite the restrictions of the apartment house.

(Jr.-Sr. High School Levels)

Arthur, Ruth M. *Portrait of Margarita*. New York: Atheneum, 1968. R.L. 6-7. Margarita feels alone at boarding school, partly because she is orphaned; partly because she is black.

Ashe, Advantage and Gewecke, C.G., Jr., *Advantage Ashe*. New York: Coward, 1967. R.L. 6-7. Success story of a determined Negro tennis player.

Baldwin, James, *Nobody Knows My Name: More Notes of a Native Son*.

New York: Dial, 1961. Paperback. R.L. 6-7. This Negro writer again studies the relationships between races.

Baldwin, James, *Go Tell It on the Mountain.* New York: Noble & Noble. Paperback. R.L. 7-8. Novel of the life of a Harlem family. Abridged edition.

Barrett, William E., *Lilies of the Field.* New York: Doubleday, 1962. R.L. 6-7. Homer helps a group of nuns build a chapel for them, and as a gift to their faith.

Bennett, Lerone, *What Manner of Man*: A Biography of Martin Luther *King.* Chicago: Johnson, 1964. R.L. 6-7.

Blanton, Catherine, *Hold Fast to Your Dreams.* New York: Messner, 1955. R.L. 6-7. Emy Lou persists in her attempt to become a ballet dancer despite the obstacles created by prejudice against her race.

Board of Education, City of New York, *Call Them Heroes.* Morristown, N.J.: Silver, Burdett. R.L. 5-6. Series of 4 small paperbacks. Short biographies of minority figures.

Bradbury, Bianca, *Lots of Love, Lucinda.* New York: Washburn, 1966. R.L. 7-8. A Negro girl goes to live with a white family in the Northeast.

Breitman, George, *Last Year of Malcolm X: Evolution of a Revolutionary.* New York: Schocken, 1968. R.L. 7-8. Reviews the philosophy and speeches of Malcolm X during the last year of his life.

Butters, Dorothy G., *Masquerade.* New York: Macrae, 1961. R.L. 6-7. Cora inadvertently passes as a white while living in a school dormitory. When the masquerade is discovered, she is surprised at her roommate's actions.

Carmichael, Stokely and Hamilton, C. V., *Black Power.* New York: Random, 1968. (Paperback) R.L. 6-7. A call to the Negro community to take action in its own behalf.

Cavanna, Betty, *A Time for Tenderness.* New York: Morrow, 1962. R.L. 5.6. Members of a white family living in Brazil react differently to the country's attitudes toward race.

Christmas, Walter, editor, *Negroes in Public Affairs and Government.* Yonkers: Educational Heritage, 1965. R.L. 6-7. Biographical materials.

Clarke, John, *Black Soldier.* New York: Doubleday, 1968. R.L. 4. Story of George Bunty, a Negro draftee, in World War II.

Cleaver, Eldridge, *Soul on Ice.* New York: McGraw-Hill, 1968. R.L. 7-8. In autobiographical style, Cleaver reveals his change in attitude towards whites from anger and hatred to gradual acceptance.

Cohen, J. and Murphy, W.S., *Burn, Baby, Burn.* New York: Dutton, 1966. R.L. 7-8. The story of the riots in Watts, Los Angeles.

Colman, Hila, *Classmates by Request.* New York: Morrow, 1964. R.L. 6-7. Integration creates problems for some girl students of a Northern high school.

Davis, Sammy Jr., *Yes I Can.* New York: Farrar, 1965. R.L. 6-7. Autobiographical material on a great black entertainer.

DeJong, Dola, *One Summer's Secret.* New York: McKay, 1963. R.L. 6-7. Laurie encounters trouble when she tries to help a run-away Negro girl.

deLeeuw, Adele, *The Barred Road.* New York: Macmillan, 1964. R.L.

6-7. Friendship between a Negro and a white girl tests the town's prejudices.

Douglas, Marjory S., *Freedom River*. New York: Scribner, 1953. R.L. 6-7. Three boys of different races find their freedom in Florida.

Fairbairn, Ann, *Five Smooth Stones*. New York: Crown, 1966. R.L. 8-9. A young black gives his life to and for the cause of civil rights.

Fall, Thomas, *Canalboat to Freedom*. New York: Dial, 1966. R.L. 7-8. A bound servant escapes at the cost of the life of his friend, a Negro freedman.

Finis, Farr, *Black Champion: The Life of Jack Johnson*. Greenwich: Fawcett. (Paperback) R.L. 7-8. Story of the first Negro heavyweight boxing champion; his achievements and his persecution.

Freed, Leonard, *Black in White America*. New York: Viking. (Paperback) R.L. 8-9. Portrayal of the black's feelings in a white-oriented America.

Friermood, Elizabeth H., *Whispering Willows*. New York: Doubleday, 1964. R.L. 6-7. The Washington family is changed by the coming of their niece and her friendship with a Negro girl.

Gibson, Althea, *I Always Wanted to be Somebody*. New York: Harper, 1958. (Paperback) R.L. 7-8. An autobiography of a leading woman tennis player.

Gregory, Dick, *Nigger: An Autobiography*. New York: Dutton, 1964. (Paperback) R.L. 6-7. Autobiography of a contemporary black entertainer and militant civil rights worker.

Gregory, Dick, *The Shadow That Scares Me*. New York: Doubleday, 1968. R.L. 6-7. A humorous view of the hypocrisy of the middle class white and Negro.

Griffin, John H., *Black, Like Me*. Boston: Houghton, 1960. R.L. 6-7. The author darkened his skin and spent five weeks in the South playing the role of a Negro.

Haas, Ben, *The Troubled Summer*. Indianapolis: Bobbs-Merrill, 1966. R.L. 6-7. A black boy grows from hatred to cooperation.

Haley, Alex, editor, *Autobiography of Malcolm X*. New York: Grove, 1965. R.L. 6-7. The story of a striking Negro leader who lost his life in his civil rights efforts.

Hansberry. Lorraine, *A Raisin in the Sun*. New York: Random, 1959. R.L. 7-8. The world through a black's eyes.

Hennessy, M. and Sauter, E. Jr., *Soldier of Africa*. New York: Washburn, 1965. R.L. 6-7. Story of a Nigerian, a professional soldier, honored by Queen Elizabeth.

Hentoff, Nat, *Jazz Country*. New York: Harper, 1965. R.L. 7-8. An adult novel of jazz world in New York.

Huie, Wm. B., *Klansman*. New York: Dell, 1967. R.L. 6-7. When outsiders try to work for integration, the Klan strikes back with terror and violence.

Hunter, Kristin, *The Soul Brothers and Sister Lou*. New York: Scribner, 1968. R.L. 7-8. A sophisticated novel. Family life of a Negro family in a Northern city.

Jackson, Jesse, *Call Me Charley*. New York: Harper, 1945. R.L. 6-7. As the only Negro boy in the junior high school, Charley has quite a struggle to establish himself.

Jackson, Jesse, *Anchor Man*. New York: Harper, 1948. R.L. 6-7. A sequel to *Call Me Charley*. Charley's efforts to rise above racial prejudice and bring honor to his race and his school on the track. See also *Charley Starts from Scratch*.

Jackson, Mahalia, *Movin' On Up*. New York: Hawthorn, 1966. R.L. 7-8. Biography of the gospel singer.

Johnson, James W., *Autobiography of an Ex-Coloured Man*. New York: Hill and Wang. (Paperback) R.L. 7-8.

Keil, Charles, *Urban Blues*. Chicago: University of Chicago Press, 1969. R.L. 6-7. Emphasizes Negro music and musicians as evidence of the Negro culture.

Kennedy, Jay R., *Favor the Runner*. Cleveland: World, 1965. R.L. 7-8. A novel dealing with the gradual deterioration of a partnership between a white lawyer and a black singer.

Lawrence, J. D., *Barnaby's Bells*. New York: Macmillan, 1965. R.L. 6-7. A mystery story with ghosts, hidden treasure and all the rest.

Lee, Mildred, *The Rock and the Willow*. New York: Lothrop, 1963. R.L. 6-7. Enie lived in an old shack in Alabama but struggles to make her life count.

Lessing, D., *Going Home*. New York: Ballantine, 1957. R.L. 7-8. A native South African journalist returns home to further disillusionment.

Marshall, Catherine, *Julie's Heritage*. New York: McKay, 1957. R.L. 7-8. Julie wants to be accepted as a person first, and as a Negro afterwards.

Mather, Melissa, *One Summer in Between*. New York: Harper, 1967. R.L. 8-9. A Southern Negro girl spends her summer as a helper on a Vermont farm.

Means, Florence C., *Reach for a Star*. Boston: Houghton, 1957. R.L. 7-8. Middleclass Negro life at Fisk University.

Miers, Earl S., *Big Ben*. Philadelphia: Westminster, 1942. R.L. 6-7. A fictionalized story of the youth of Paul Robeson.

Moody, Anne, *Coming of Age in Mississippi*. New York: Dell, 1969 (Paperback). R.L. 8-9. Autobiography of a young woman who grew out of poverty to a place in the civil rights movement.

Newell, Hope, *A Cap for Mary Ellis*. New York: Harper, 1953. R.L. 6-7. Two Negro girls enter an all-white nursing school.

Newman, Shirlee P., *Marian Anderson: Lady from Philadelphia*. Philadelphia: Westminster, 1966. R.L. 7-8. A sympathetic biography.

Olsen, Jack, *Black Athletes in Revolt*. New York: Time-Life, 1968. R.L. 7-8. Negro athletes and their feelings about their exploitation.

Olsen, Jack, *Black is Best*. New York: Putnam, 1967. R.L. 7-8. Cassius Clay story of revolt against white power.

Panger, Daniel, *Ol' Prophet Nat*. Greenwich: Fawcett. (Paperback). R.L. 7-8. A popular novel on Nat Turner who led the famous 1831 slave rebellion.

Parks, Gordon, *A Choice of Weapons*. New York: Harper, 1966 (Paperback). R.L. 7-8. An autobiography of a Negro photographer who lifted himself to success.

Parks, Gordon, *The Learning Tree*. Greenwich: Fawcett. (Paperback). An autobiographical novel by a Life photographer about a Negro boy growing up in Kansas in the 20's.

Patterson, Floyd and Gross, Milton, *Victory over Myself*. New York: Random, 1962. R.L. 7-8. Floyd overcame childhood delinquency to become the youngest Negro heavyweight boxing champion.

Petry, Ann, *The Street*. Boston, Houghton-Mifflin, 1946. R.L. 6-7. A mother experiences difficulties in making a decent home for her son in overcrowded Harlem.

Powell, Adam C., *Keep the Faith Baby*. New York: Trident, 1967. R.L. 7-8. Collection of Pastor Powell's sermons.

Robinson, James H., *The Road Without Turning*. New York: Holt, 1950. R.L. 6-7. This famous Negro minister learns to overcome his hatred for whites when he comes to an interracial church in Harlem.

Rodman, Bella, *Lions in the Way*. Chicago: Follett, 1966. R.L. 5.8. A story about high school integration in a Tennessee town and the troubles that ensued.

Rowan, Carl, *Go South to Sorrow*. New York: Random, 1957. R.L. 7-8. A journalist goes South to view the progress in desegregation.

Sprague, Gretchen, *A Question of Harmony*. New York: Dodd, 1965. R.L. 7-8. Three young musicians of mixed races encounter racial prejudice.

Sterling, Dorothy, *Mary Jane*. New York: Doubleday, 1959. R.L. 6-7. Mary Jane, one of the two Negroes in a recently desegregated junior high school, overcomes rejection to find a friend.

Sterling, Dorothy, *Tender Warriors*. New York: Hill, 1958. R.L. 6-7. The story of the Negro children who began the integration of schools in Little Rock, Arkansas.

Sterne, Emma G., *I Have a Dream*. New York: Knopf, 1965. R.L. 7-8. Short biographical studies of nine Negro civil rights leaders.

Stolz, Mary, *Who Wants Music on Monday?* New York: Harper, 1963. R.L. 6-7. A teenage novel which touches on family and race relations quite candidly.

Stone, Chuck, *Tell It Like It Is*. New York: Trident. R.L. 8-9. A Negro columnist speaks out, straight from the shoulder.

Strachan, Margaret P., *Where Were You That Year?* New York: Washburn, 1965. R.L. 5-6. Polly, a college student, goes to Mississippi to help Negroes to register and vote, and encounters violent hostility.

Terzian, James P., *The Jimmy Brown Story*. New York: Messner, 1964. R.L. 7-8. Biography of an outstanding football player.

Thomas, Piri, *Down These Mean Streets*. New York: Knopf, 1967. R.L. 7-8. The sights and sounds of Harlem's crime-ridden streets.

Tunis, John R., *All-American*. New York: Harcourt, 1942. R.L. 6-7. An old football story, but still presenting the problem of today, integration and acceptance of a Negro player.

Tunnell, Emlen with Gleason, Wm., *Footsteps of a Giant*. New York: Doubleday, 1966. R.L. 6-7. Autobiography of the first Negro football players for the New York Giants.

Wallace, Irving, *The Man*. Greenwich: Fawcett. (Paperback) R.L. 7-8. A Negro senator succeeds to the presidency in this popular novel.

Waters, Ethel, *His Eye Is on the Sparrow*. New York: Doubleday, 1951. R.L. 7-8. A moving autobiography of the Negro actress.

Whitney, Phyllis A., *Willow Hill*. New York: McKay, 1947. R.L. 6-7. The Negro and white students at Willow Hill are helped to accept each other by Val and her friends.

Wright, Charles, *The Messenger*. Greenwich: Fawcett. (Paperback) R.L. 7-8. Story of a Harlem Negro boy who is plunged into the world of junkies and homosexuals.

Wright, Richard, *Black Boy*. New York: Harper, 1945. R.L. 6-7. Racial discrimination embitters a young Negro.

CHAPTER VII

The American Indian Background and History

The story of the relations of the American Indian and the white man is more than a recounting of the almost constant exploitation of the red man and the consequent warfare. These publications date from the earliest meeting of the two races in America through the end of the last century. They try to present a fuller picture, both real and fictional, of the life and achievements of the Indian during this long, bitter period. Perhaps most Americans ought to be familiar with this background, if they are to understand the position of the Indian today, and help him find his rightful place in the America of tomorrow.

(Primary Level)

Anderson, A. M., *Friday the Arapaho Indian.* New York: Harper. R.L. 2.5. Written especially for poor readers.

Anderson, A. M., *Portugee Phillips and the Fighting Sioux.* New York: Harper. R.L. 3.0. Adventure story written to interest the poor reader.

Anderson, A. M., *Squanto and the Pilgrims.* New York: Harper. R.L. 2.6. The story of the first interracial friendship in the New World.

Beals, Frank L., *Chief Black Hawk.* New York: Harper, 1943. R.L. 3.5. Biography of the Great chief.

Blassingame, Wyatt, *Sacagawea: Indian Guide.* Champaign: Garrard, 1965. R.L. 3.0. Biography of the Indian girl who served as a guide for part of the Lewis and Clark expedition.

Blassingame, Wyatt, *Osceola: Seminole War Chief.* Champaign: Garrard, 1967. R.L. 3.2. Biography of the great and tragic leader of the Seminole Indians of Florida.

Bulla, Clyde R., *Squanto, Friend of the White Men.* New York: Crowell, 1954. R.L. 3-4. The old story of Squanto and the early settlers.

Chandler, Edna W., *Juanito Makes a Drum.* Chicago: Benefic, 1961. R.L. 1-2. Story of a Pueblo Indian boy who makes a drum for the rain dance.

Dobrin, Norma, *Delawares.* Chicago: Melmont, 1963. R.L. 3.1. Delaware Indians—their daily life and customs.

Dolch, Edward, *Lodge Stories.* Champaign: Garrard, 1957. R.L. 2.5. Folklore of Indians of the Southeast. See also *Navaho Stories* (2.5) *Pueblo Stories* (2.5) *Tepee Stories* (2.5) and *Wigwam Stories.* (2.5) by the same author and publisher.

Estep, Irene, *Seminoles.* Chicago: Melmont, 1963. R.L. 3.4. The dwellings, games, costumes and life of the Seminole Indians of the Southeast.

Estep, Irene, *Iroquois*. Chicago: Melmont, 1961. R.L. 3.2. Descriptive and historical account of the Iroquois.

Falk, Elsa, *Tohi, Chumash Indian Boy*. Chicago: Melmont, 1965. R. L. 3.5. Simple story of a coastal Californian Indian boy.

Fenton, Carroll L. and Epstein, Alice, *Cliff Dwellers of Walnut Canyon*. New York: Day, 1960. R.L. 3.4. Life of the Indian Cliff Dwellers of the Southwest.

Graff, Stewart and Polly A., *Squanto: Indian Adventurer*. Champaign: Garrard, 1965. R.L. 3.0. Another semi-historical story of Squanto, friend of the Pilgrims.

Hood, Flora M., *Something for the Medicine Man*. Chicago: Melmont, 1962. R.L. 3.9. A simple story of Indian life.

Latham, Jean L., *Wa O'Ka*. Indianapolis: Bobbs, 1961. R.L. 2.7. An old story retold by a noted author. Life, customs, games and dances of Indian life are depicted.

Meadowcroft, Enid L., *Crazy Horse: Sioux Warrior*. Champaign: Garrard, 1965. R.L. 3.0. Biography of the great Sioux war chief.

Montgomery, Elizabeth Rider, *Chief Seattle: Great Statesman*. Champaign: Garrard, 1966. R.L. 3.0. Biography of the leader of the Northwest Indians.

Montgomery, Elizabeth R., *Chief Joseph: Guardian of His People*. Champaign: Garrard, 1969. R.L. 3.0. The Nez Perce who tried to protect the rights of his people, first by peace and later by a brilliant campaign.

Stevenson, Augusta, *Squanto*. Indianapolis: Bobbs, 1962. R.L. 3.3. Biography of a friendly Indian who helped the Pilgrims adjust to their new land.

Stoutenberg, Adrien, *The Mud Ponies*. New York: Coward, 1963. R.L. 3-4. Based on a Pawnee myth of a boy who creates ponies out of mud.

Wilkie, Katharine, *Pocahontas: Indian Princess*. Champaign: Garrard, 1969. R.L. 3.0. The famous Indian princess who helped white men.

Worthylake, Mary M., *Nika Illahee (My Homeland)*. Chicago: Melmont, 1962. R.L. 3.2. An Indian girl's home life.

Worthylake, Mary M., *Children of the Seed Gatherers*. Chicago: Melmont, 1964. R.L. 3.0. Story of the plants and seeds known to American Indians and their uses.

(Intermediate Level)

Alter, Robert E., *Time of the Tomahawk*. New York: Putnam, 1964. R.L. 5.4. An historical novel of Indian vs. Colonist.

Bailey, R. L., *Indian Fighter*. New York: Morrow, 1965. R.L. 6-7. Semi-historical story of war between the white man and the American Indian.

Baker, Betty, *Killer-of-Death*. New York: Harper, 1963. R.L. 6-7. The son of an Apache chief grows in manhood to take his place among the warriors.

Baker, Charlotte, *Sunrise Island*. Toronto: Musson, 1952. R.L. 5-6. Story of the Northwest coast Indians before the coming of the white man.

Baldwin, Gordon C., *America's Buried Past*. New York: Putnam, 1962. R.L. 5.8. Factual account of the Indians of long ago.

Baldwin, Gordon C., *How Indians Really Lived*. New York: Putnam, 1967. R.L. 5.2. Factual material on Indian life and customs.

Barbeau, Charles M., and Melvin, Grace W., *The Indian Speaks*. Toronto: Macmillan, 1955. Indian legends and folk tales.

Bleeker, Sonia, *The Mission Indians of California*. New York: Morrow, 1956. R.L. 4-5. Background material.

Buff, Mary and Conrad, *Hah-Nee of the Cliff Dwellers*. Boston: Houghton, 1965. R.L. 4-5. The tribe is forced to leave its home site during a great drought.

Buffalo Child Long Lance, *Long Lance*. Toronto: British Book Service, 1956. R.L. 6-7. Autobiography of a Blackfoot Indian.

Chafetz, Henry, *Thunderbird and Other Stories*. New York: Pantheon, 1964. R.L. 5-6. American Indian explanations of thunder and lightning, evil and the use of the peace pipe.

Clark, Electa, *Osceola, Young Seminole Indian*. Indianapolis: Bobbs, 1965. R.L. 4.6. A history of the Seminole Warrior and tribal leader.

Colver, Anne, *Bred-and-Butter Indian*. New York: Holt, 1964. R.L. 4-5. Barbara makes friends with a hungry Indian and learns the difference between friends and enemies.

Cooke, David C., *Apache Warrior*. New York: Norton, 1963. R.L. 6-7. Mangus Colorado, Apache Chief, changed from a peace-loving man to a savage warrior in his efforts for his people.

Cooke, Ronald J. V., *Algonquin Adventure*. Toronto: Ryerson, 1958. R.L. 6-7. Adventure among the Algonquin Indians in Canada.

Cooper, James F., *The Last of the Mohicans*. Chicago: Scott, Foresman, 1950. R.L. 4.5. Adapted version of the classic.

Curry, Jane L., *Down from the Lonely Mountain*. New York: Harcourt, 1965. R.L. 4-5. California Indian folktales.

Davis, Russell G. and Ashbranner, Brent K., *Chief Joseph, War Chief of the Nez Perce*. New York: McGraw-Hill, 1962. R.L. 6-7. The heartbreaking struggle to find freedom is strongly presented in this biography.

Edwards, C.A.M., *Son of the Mohawks*. Toronto: Ryerson, 1954. R.L. 6-7. Fictionalized account of Pierre Radisson's capture by the Mohawks; his adventures and escape.

Famous Indians—A Collection of Short Biographies. Washington, D.C.: Government Printing Office, R.L. 5-6. Vignettes of historical chiefs and other American Indians.

Farnsworth, Frances J., *Winged Moccasins*. New York: Messner, 1967. R.L. 4.9. Semi-historical account of the famous Indian girl guide.

Fisher, O. M., and Tyner, C. L., *Totem, Tipi and Tumpline: Stories of Canadian Indians*. Toronto: Dent, 1956. R.L. 5-6. A collection of Indian stories.

Gardner, Jeanne, *Mary Jemison, Seneca Captive*. New York: Harcourt, 1966. R.L. 4-5. Captured by the Senecas, Mary gradually changed her hatred to trust and understanding. A true account.

Garst, Shannon, *Sitting Bull—Champion of His People.* New York: Messner, 1946. R.L. 5-6. Biography of the famous Sioux leader.

Garst, Shannon, *Red Cloud.* Chicago: Follett, 1965. R.L. 4-3. Biography of the great Sioux chieftain.

Grey, Zane, *Stranger from the Tonto.* New York: Grosset, 1956. R.L. 5.5. An adult novel.

Haig-Brown, Roderick, *The Whale People.* New York: Morrow, 1963. R.L. 5-6. Whale hunting of the pre-Columbian Indians of the Northwest.

Harmon, Daniel W., *Sixteen Years in the Indian Country.* Toronto: Macmillan, 1957. R.L. 6-7. Travels in Western Canada, by a representative of the North West Company.

Harris, Christie, *Once Upon a Totem.* New York: Atheneum, 1963. R.L. 5-6. Legends of the Northwest American Indians.

Hofsinde, Robert, *The Indian and the Buffalo.* New York: Morrow, 1961. R.L. 5.1. Authentic explanation of the way in which the Indian exploited his uses of the buffalo.

Hofsinde, Robert, *The Indian and His Horse.* New York: Morrow, 1960. R.L. 5.2. Factual account of the way the Indian learned to use the horses left behind by Spanish explorers.

Hofsinde, Robert, *The Indian Medicine Man.* New York: Morrow, 1966. R.L. 5.8. The beliefs, customs and rites of the Indian medicine man.

Hofsinde, Robert, *Indian Hunting.* New York: Morrow, 1962. R.L. 4-5. Hunting techniques.

Hofsinde, Robert, *Indians at Home.* New York: Morrow, 1964. R.L. 5.0. Authentic account of types of dwellings and home life in various Indian tribes.

Hofsinde, Robert, *Indian Warriors and Their Weapons.* New York: Morrow, 1965. R.L. 5.8. The great warriors and their weapons.

Houston, James, *Eagle Mask: A West Coast Indian Tale.* New York: Harcourt, 1966. R.L. 4-5. Skemshan undergoes difficult trials to prove his manhood.

Indians of the Plains. New York: American Heritage, 1960. R.L. 5.2. Informational material on the Plains Indians.

Israel, Marion, *Ojibway.* Chicago: Melmont, 1962. R.L. 5.3. Factual material on the Ojibway Indians or the Chippewas of the Northeast woodlands.

Israel, Marion, *Cherokees.* Chicago: Melmont, 1961. R.L. 4.3. Informational material on the Cherokees of the Southeastern United States.

Jones, Weyman, *Edge of Two Worlds.* New York: Dial, 1968. R.L. 5-6. Calvin, the only survivor of a Comanche massacre, attempts to find a new life.

Knox, Olive E., *Black Falcon.* Toronto: Ryerson, 1954. R.L. 5-6. Fictionalized account of John Tanner, an Ohio boy captured by Indians and taken to Canada.

La Farge, Oliver, *The American Indian.* New York: Golden, 1960. R.L. 4.5. Informational material and many pictures of Indian life.

Lenski, Lois, *Indian Captive.* Philadelphia: Lippincott, 1941. R.L. 4-5.

True story of Mary Jemison who chose to remain with the Indians who had captured her.

Lomask, Milton, *Saint Isaac and the Indians*. Toronto: Ambassador, 1956. R.L. 6-7. Story of Father Isaac Jogues.

Luce, Willard and Celia, *Sutter's Fort: Empire on the Sacramento*. Champaign: Garrard, 1969. R.L. 4.0. Story of the fort during the 1840's.

Martin, Patricia, *Pocahontas*. New York: Putnam, 1964. R.L. 4.4. Story of an Indian princess who was courted by an Englishman.

MacMillan, Cyrus, *Glooskap's Country and Other Indian Tales*. Toronto: Oxford, 1955. R.L. 5-6. A collection of Indian tales.

McNeer, May, *War Chief of the Seminoles*. New York: Random, 1954. R.L. 4-5. One of the Landmark series, the story of Osceola and his unbeatable Seminoles.

Miller, Hanson O., *Raiders of the Mohawk*. Toronto: Macmillan. 1954. R.L. 7-8. The story of Butler's Rangers against the Mohawks.

Morris, Loverne, *The American Indian as Farmer*. Chicago: Melmont, 1963. R.L. 4.4. Non-fiction account of the American Indian as a farmer.

Myron, Robert. *Shadow of the Hawk*. New York: Putnam, 1964. R.L. 5.7. The story of the development of the Mound Builders (Ohio River Valley).

Needler, George H., *Louis Riel*. Toronto: Burns, 1957. R.L. 6-7. Story of a half-breed who led an Indian uprising against the white man in Western Canada.

Oberreich, Robert, *The Blood Red Belt*. New York: Doubleday, 1961. R.L. 4. Peter and a friendly Iroquois boy outwit dangerous spies.

Peckham, Howard, *Pontiac*. Indianapolis: Bobbs, 1963. R.L. 4.9. Childhood biography of the Ottawa war leader who led a large number of tribes against the British in 1763.

Rachlis, Eugene and Ewers, John C., *Indians of the Plains*. New York: American Heritage, 1960. R.L. 5-6. Story of the Plains Indians from prehistoric times until the Sioux uprising in 1890.

Raskin, Joseph and Edith, *Indian Tales*. New York: Random, 1969. R.L. 4-5. Retelling of legends of the Hudson Valley Indians.

Robinson, Barbara, *Trace Through the Forest*. New York: Lothrop, 1965. R.L. 6-7. Adventure story of a 14-year-old who meets the Indians that had abducted his father.

Robinson, William G., *Tales of Kitimat*. Kitimat, B.C.: S. Sough, 1956. R.L. 6-7. Collection of legends, folk stories and customs of the West Coast Indians of British Columbia.

Rounds, Glen, *Buffalo Harvest*. Toronto: Saunders, 1952. R.L. 4-5. Buffalo hunting by North American Indians.

Rushmore, Helen, *The Magnificent House of Man Alone*. Champaign: Garrard, 1968. R.L. 4.0. The mixing of the Indian and the new cultures.

Russell, Don, *Sioux Buffalo Hunters*. Chicago: Encyclopedia Britannica, 1962. R.L. 5.5. A semi-fictional account of the Sioux buffalo hunters.

Scheele, William E., *The Mound Builders*. Cleveland: World, 1960. R.L. 6.6. Semi-historical account of the Mound Builders of the Ohio Valley.

Schoor, Gene, *The Jim Thorpe Story*. New York: Messner, 1965. R.L. 5.3. Biography of Thorpe, one of America's greatest athletes.

Scott, Paul and Beryl, *Eliza and the Indian War Pony*. New York: Lothrop, 1961. R.L. 4-5. Based on memoirs of a woman who worked as a missionary among the Nez Perce in Oregon.

Seymour, Flora W., *Pocahontas, Brave Girl*. Indianapolis: Bobbs, 1961. R.L. 4.2. Biography of the legendary Indian princess.

Shannon, Terry, *Wakapoo and the Flying Arrows*. Chicago: Whitman, 1963. R.L. 5.0. Fictional account attempting to give some background information about Indian life.

Snow, Dorothea J., *Sequoyah, Young Cherokee Guide*. Indianapolis: Bobbs, 1960. R.L. 4-5. Biography of the noted Indian educator, creator of the Cherokee written language.

Stevenson, Augusta, *Sitting Bull. Dakota Boy*. Indianapolis: Bobbs, 1960. R.L. 4.5. Biography of the great Sioux chieftain.

Stevenson, Augusta, *Tecumseh*. Indianapolis: Bobbs, 1962. R.L. 4.2. Childhood biography of Chief Tecumseh, leader of the Shawnee against the encroachment of the white man.

Terrell, John U., *Black Robe*. New York: Doubleday, 1964. R.L. 6-7. The life of Father Pierre-Jean De Smet whose influence upon the Indians was most significant.

Van Riper, Guernsey, Jr., *Jim Thorpe*. Indianapolis: Bobbs, 1961. R.L. 5.0. Biography of the greatest athlete America has probably ever produced.

Voight, Virginia F. *Sacajawea*. New York: Putnam, 1967. R.L. 4.2. Biography of the Indian guide for the Lewis and Clark expedition.

Voight, Virginia F. *The Adventures of Hiawatha*. Champaign: Garrard, 1969. R.L. 4.0. A famous Indian legend.

Vrooman, John J., *Council Fire and Cannon*. Chicago: Follett, 1962. R.L. 4.9. Indian-white relations in the Northeast in the early years of American history.

Witten, Herbert, *Desperate Journey*. Chicago: Follett, 1960. R.L. 5.3. Dangers of frontier life, a fictional account.

Witten, Herbert, *The Warriors' Path*. Chicago: Follett, 1962. R.L. 5.1. Fictional account of Indian-white relationships in the early days of America.

Wood, Kerry, *The Great Chief*. Toronto: Macmillan, 1957. R.L. 6-7. Biography of the warrior of the Crees, Maskepetoon.

Wyatt, Edgar, *Geronimo: The Last Apache War Chief*. New York: McGraw-Hill, 1952. R.L. 5-6. A biography of the great chief, with many line drawings by his great-grandson.

(Jr.-Sr. H. S. Level)

Day, A. Grove, *Coronado and the Discovery of the Southwest*. Des Moines: Meredith, 1967. R.L. 6-7. Based on the explorer's journals. Includes descriptions of Indian life as Coronado saw it.

Doughty, Wayne D., *Crimson Moccasins*. New York: Harper, 1966. R.L.

7-8. Quick Eagle discovers he is not an Indian but really an adopted white boy and experiences real difficulty in trying to find a sense of identity.

Drucker, Philip, *Indians of the Northwest Coast.* Toronto: McGraw-Hill, 1955. R.L. 6-7. Informational material.

Frazier, Neta L., *Sacajawea: The Girl Nobody Knows.* New York: McKay, 1967. R.L. 7-8. Biography based on the Lewis and Clark journals.

Garcia, Andrew, *Tough Trip through Paradise.* Boston: Houghton, 1967. R.L. 9-10. A novel laid in the Northwest during the Nez Perce war.

Hall-Quest, Olga, *Flames Over New England.* New York: Dutton, 1967. R.L. 9-10. The story of King Philip's War in 1675-76.

Henry, Will, *Custer's Last Stand.* Philadelphia: Chilton, 1966. R.L. 7-8. Both sides of the battle of the Little Big Horn.

Lauritzen, Jonreed, *The Legend of Billy Bluesage.* Boston: Little, 1961. R.L. 6-7. Raised by the Utes, Billy breaks away to spend his life guiding travelers and protecting them from the Indians. Based on fact.

Mulcahy, Lucille, *Natoto.* Camden: Nelson, 1960. R.L. 6-7. Natoto, a pre-Columbian Indian girl, finds romance and marriage despite the wars with other tribes.

Myron, Robert, *Mounds, Towns and Totems: Indians of North America.* Cleveland: World, 1966. R.L. 6-7. Three North American Indian cultures.

Orrmont, Arthur, *Diplomat in Warpaint: Chief Alexander McGillvray of the Creeks.* New York: Abelard, 1967. R.L. 7-8. An unknown Creek chieftain during the Revolutionary War.

Richter, Conrad, *The Light in the Forest.* New York: Knopf, 1966. R.L. 6-7. An old but classic story of the conflict in the life of a white boy adopted by Indians.

Roland, Albert, *Great Indian Chiefs.* New York: Crowell-Collier, 1966. R.L. 7-8. The struggle for survival as related through the efforts of nine great chiefs.

Sandoz, Mari, *Cheyenne Autumn.* New York: Hastings, 1961. R.L. 7-8. The heartbreaking flight of the Nez Perce toward Canada and their eventual capture.

Tunis, Edwin, *Indians.* Cleveland: World, 1959. R.L. 6-7. Informational material.

Waltrip, Lela and Rufus, *Indian Women.* New York: McKay, 1964. R.L. 6-7. Fourteen short biographies of important Indian women.

Wyatt, Edgar, *Cochise: Apache Warrior and Statesman.* New York: McGraw-Hill, 1953. R.L. 6-7. An attractive biography.

CHAPTER VIII

The American Indian Today

T HE place of the American Indian in contemporary America is still ambiguous. Is he to continue to be segregated in reservations? Or shall he be urged to leave the reservation to be assimilated into the slums of urban life? Should we continue to subsidize his semi-tribal life and private schools, or force him to make his way wherever and however he can? These are some of the questions this collection touches upon in presenting literature which is concerned with the American Indian, as he is, and as the white man views him today.

(Primary Level)

Baker, Betty, *Little Runner of the Longhouse*. New York: Harper, 1962. R.L. 2.0. Little Runner cannot take part in the tribal games and ceremonies.

Benchley, N., *Red Fox and His Canoe*. New York: Harper. R.L. 1.5. Red Fox's canoe is large enough for him but not for the bears, otters, raccoons and moose that join him.

Brenner, Anita, *A Hero by Mistake*. New York: Scott, 1953. R.L. 3.5. A frightened Indian boy overcomes his fears.

Bulla, Clyde, *Indian Hill*. New York: Crowell, 1963. R.L. 2.8. A Navajo boy moves from the reservation to an apartment in Los Angeles.

Clark, Ann N., *Desert People*. New York: Viking, 1962. R.L. 3-4. Indians of the desert areas; their present-day life.

Clark, Ann N., *Little Indian Basket Maker*. Chicago: Melmont, 1957. R.L. 2-3. See also her little *Indian Pottery Maker* by the same publisher for stories on Navaho Indians.

Clark, Ann N., *Little Navajo Bluebird*. New York: Viking, 1943. R.L. 4.3. Navajo community and family life.

Deming, Therese O., *Indians in Winter Camp*. Chicago: Whitman, 1957. R.L. 2-3. Indian sports in winter.

Farquhar, Margaret C., *Indian Children of America*. New York: Holt, 1964. R.L. 2.9. Family life in various North American Indian tribes.

Friskey, Margaret, *Indian Two Feet and His Eagle Feather*. Chicago: Childrens Press. 1967. R.L. 3.1. See also *Indian Two Feet and His Horse* by same author.

Harvey, Lois, *Toyanuki's Rabbit*. Chicago: Melmont, 1964. R.L. 2.9. Simple story of a North American Indian boy.

Holling, Holling C. and Lucille, *Paddle to the Sea*. Boston: Houghton, 1941.

R.L. 3-4. Travels of a toy Indian canoe through the Great Lakes and the St. Lawrence.

Wolcott, H. F., *A Kwakiutl Village and School*. New York: Holt, 1967. R.L. 4-5. Story of the Northwest Indians and their daily life.

(Intermediate Level)

Allen, T.D., *Tall as Great Standing Rock*. Philadelphia: Westminster Press, 1963. R.L. 5-6. Conflict between the Navajo and the white man is eventually resolved for the central boy character.

Armer, Laura A., *In Navajo Land*. New York: McKay, 1962. R.L. 5-6. Photography and text offer a different side of Navajo life.

Armer, Laura A., *Waterless Mountain*. New York: McKay, 1966. R.L. 5-6-. Stories of Navaho Indians.

Baker, Betty, *The Shaman's Last Raid*. New York: Harper, 1963. A pair of Indian twins help their grandfather forsake his belief in the old ways.

Bannon, Laura M., *Hat for a Hero: A Tarascan Boy of Mexico*. Chicago: Whitman, 1954. R.L. 4-5. A young Indian boy proves his courage.

Bleeker, Sonia, *The Navajo*. New York: Morrow, 1964. R.L. 5.2.

Bleeker, Sonia, *The Sioux Indians*. New York: Morrow, 1967. R.L. 4.5.

Bothwell, Jean, *The Silver Mango Tree*. New York: Harcourt, 1960. R.L. 6-7. Indian family life.

Buff, Mary and Conrad, *Magic Maize*. Boston: Houghton Mifflin, 1953. R.L. 4-5. A young Guatemalan Indian boy helps his father overcome distrust of the gringos.

Carroll, Ruth and Latrobe, *Tough Enough's Indians*. New York: Walck, 1960. R.L. 4.6. The Tatum boys learn about present-day Indians when they meet a Cherokee family.

Clark, Ann N., *In My Mother's House*. New York: Viking, 1941. R.L. 4.6. Life in a pueblo.

Elting, Mary and Folsom, Michael, *The Secret Story of Pueblo Bonito*. New York: Harvey, 1963. R.L. 4.3. Indian pueblo life in New Mexico.

Faulkner, Cliff, *The White Peril*. Boston; Little, 1966. R.L. 6-7. The peril of the white man as seen through the eyes of a Blackfoot boy.

Hoffine, Lyla, *The Eagle Feather Prize*. New York: McKay, 1962. R.L. 5-6. Billy Youngbear tries to make the choices which will determine his future life.

Hoffine, Lyla, *Jennie's Mandan Bowl*. New York: McKay, 1960. R.L. 4-5. Jennie is ashamed of her Indian ancestry until she appreciates the values of her people. See also *Running Elk* and *Carol Blue Wing* by this author.

Hooker, Forestine C. *Star: The Story of an Indian Pony*. New York: Doubleday, 1964. R.L. 6.4. Indian life as viewed by a pony.

Kirk, Ruth, *David: Young Chief of the Quitentes*. New York: Harcourt, 1967. R.L. 5-6. An eleven-year-old bridges the gap between old and new ways.

Kroeber, Theodora, *Ishi, Last of His Tribe*. Berkeley: Parnassus, 1964. R.L. 5-6. Narrative of Ishi, last of the Yahi tribe in California.

Lampman, Evelyn S., *Navaho Sister*. New York: Doubleday, 1956. R.L. 5-6. Sad Girl, an orphan, not only finds friends but even a blood relative at the government school.

Mason, Miriam, *Pony Called Lightning*. New York: Macmillan, 1948. R.L. 5-6. An Indian pony that loved to run.

Mulcahy, Lucille, *Fire on Big Lonesome*. Los Angeles: Elk Grove, 1967. R.L. 4-5. Phillip, a Zuni Indian boy, helps fight a forest fire.

Nixon, Joan L., *Mystery of the Haunted Woods*. New York: Criterion, 1967. R.L. 5.4. A superstitious Indian housekeeper contributes to the fears of the visiting youngsters.

Norbeck, O.E., *Indian Crafts for Campers*. New York: Association, 1967. (Paperback). R.L. 6-7. How campers can use Indian tricks and ways.

Quimby, Myrtle, *The Cougar*. New York: Criterion, 1968. R.L. 5-6. A half-breed youngster learns to live with his heritage and the prejudice it engenders.

Rambeau, John and Nancy, *Chumash Boy*. San Francisco: Field, 1967. R.L. 4-5. Story of American Indian boy written to portray the contribution of his race to America.

Robinson, Barbara, *Across from Indian Shore*. New York: Lothrop, 1962. R.L. 4-5. Luke neglects his duties and nearly misses the opportunity of meeting an Indian Princess.

Russell, Paulson, *Navaho Land—Yesterday and Today*. Chicago: Melmont, 1961. R.L. 4.4.

Sandoz, Mari, *The Story Catcher*. Philadelphia: Westminster, 1963. R.L. 6-7. Lance attempts to record the story of his people, the Plains Indians.

Sandoz, Mari, *The Buffalo Hunters*. Toronto: Saunders, 1954. R.L. 6-7. The extermination of the buffalo herds of the U.S. by the greedy white man.

Shirreffs, Gordon D., *The Rebel Trumpet*. Philadelphia: Westminster. R.L. 4.3. Stories of the Southwest.

Smucker, Barbara, *Wigwam in the City*. New York: Dutton, 1966. R.L. 4-5. Problems of an Indian girl who moves to Chicago.

Stinetorf, Louise A., *The Treasure of Tolmec*. New York: John Day, 1967. R.L. 4.6. Action and mystery among the Tarascan Indians in Mexico.

Sutton, F., *The How and Why Wonder Book of North American Indians*. New York: Grosset, 1967. R.L. 6-7. Pictures, drawings and text give broad background on the American Indian.

Thompson, Eileen, *The Apache Gold Mystery*. New York: Abelard, 1965. R.L. 4.6. Indians, adventure and mystery.

Thompson, Hildegard, *Getting to Know American Indians Today*. Chicago: Follett, R.L. 5.8. Informational material on present-day Indians.

Waltrip, Lela and Rufus, *Quiet Boy*. New York: McKay, 1961. R.L. 5-6. Conflict between the Indian and white cultures as seen through the eyes of a twelve-year-old Navajo boy.

Warren, Mary P., *Walk in My Moccasins*. Philadelphia: Westminster, 1966. R.L. 5-6. A young Sioux girl, adopted by whites, finds understanding and friendships.

Williams, Barbara, *Let's Go to an Indian Cliff Dwelling*. New York: Putnam 1965. R.L. 4.8.

Wilson, Holly, *Snowbound in Hidden Valley*. New York: Messner, 1957. R.L. 5-6. An Indian family comes to live in a white community.

(Jr.-Sr. H. S. Level)

Ball, Zachary, *Swamp Chief*. New York: Holiday, 1952. R.L. 6-7. Joe Panther tries to help the older Indians give up tribal ways and cooperate with the white man.

Barnouw, Victor, *Dream of the Blue Heron*. New York: Delacorte, 1966. R.L. 6-7. A Chippewa boy growing up amid the conflict of his and the white world.

Bell, Margaret, *The Totem Casts a Shadow*. New York: Morrow, 1949. R.L. 7-8. A father disowns his son when the boy marries an Indian girl.

Carlson, Natalie S.. *The Tomahawk Family*. New York: Harper, 1960. R.L. 6-7. The problems of Indians who seek to become Americanized.

Clark, Ann N., *Medicine Man's Daughter*. New York: Farrar, 1963. R.L. 7-8. Tall-Girl is disturbed by the conflict between Indian and White man's medicine.

Davis, Russell G. and Ashabranner, Brent, *The Choctaw Code*. New York: McGraw, 1961. R.L. 7-8. Despite his Indian friends, Tom finds it hard to understand the Choctaw law which condemns his Indian friend, Jim, to death.

Gates, Doris., *North Fork*. New York: Viking, 1945. R.L. 5.0. Drew antagonizes the Indians who work at the sawmill.

O'Dell, Scott, *Island of the Blue Dolphins*. Boston: Houghton Mifflin, 1960. R.L. 5.0. An Indian girl is deserted by her tribe and faces eighteen years of solitude.

Silverberg, Robert, *The Old Ones: Indians of the American Southwest*. New York: N.Y. Graphic, 1965. R.L. 7-8. Pueblo Indian life past and present.

Sommerfelt, Aimee, *The White Bungalow*. New York: Criterion, 1964. R.L. 4-5. Lalu must choose between a doctor's career and replacing his sick father on the farm.

Steele, William O., *Wayah of the Real People*. New York: Holt, 1964. R.L. 6-7. A year at school, away from his tribe, makes Wayah feel ill at ease with his own people.

Voss, Carroll, *White Cap for Rechinda*. New York: Washburn, 1966. R.L. 6-7. An American Indian girl attempts to choose among the values of Indian and white society.

CHAPTER IX

Eskimo and Alaska

(All Levels)

Andrist, Ralph K., *Heroes of Polar Exploration*. New York: American Heritage, 1962. R.L. 6.6. Biographies of Arctic explorers.

Annixter, Jane and Paul, *The Great White*. New York: Holiday, 1966. R.L. 6-7. Conflict between an Eskimo boy and a great polar bear.

Beim, L. L., *Little Igloo*. New York: Harcourt, 1941. R.L. 3-4. A simple Arctic story.

Bell, Margaret, *Watch for a Tall White Sail*. New York: Dunlap, 1948. R.L. 4.5. A sixteen-year-old struggles against the terrors of Alaskan life in the 1880's.

Bell, Margaret E., *Flight from Love*. New York: Morrow, 1968. R.L. 7-8. A sixteen-year-old falls in love with a bush pilot.

Berry, Erick, *A World Explorer: Fridtjof Nansen*. Champaign: Garrard, 1969. R.L. 4.0. An explorer of the 1800's who nearly reached the North Pole.

Berry, Erick, *Men, Moss and Reindeer: The Challenge of Lapland*. New York: Coward, 1959. R.L. 5-6. Story of the far North.

Berry, Erick, *Robert E. Peary: North Pole Conqueror*. Champaign: Garrard, 1963. R.L. 2.5. Biography of the great explorer.

Bleeker, Sonia, *The Eskimo: Arctic Hunters and Trappers*. New York: Morrow, 1967. R.L. 5.9. Stories of Indian and Eskimo hunters and trappers.

Bonsall, Crosby, *What Spot?* New York: Harper, 1963. R.L. 2-3. An Arctic story. An easy to read story for the beginner.

Brewster, Benjamin, *First Book of Eskimos*. New York: Watts, 1952. R.L. 5.0. Informational material on Eskimos.

Builard, Robert, *My Eskimos*. Toronto: Ambassador, 1956. R.L. 4-5. Story of a priest in the Arctic.

Calder, Ritchie, *Men Against the Frozen North*. Toronto: Nelson, 1957. R.L. 6-7. Adventure in the far North.

Castle, Douglas, *Arctic Assignment*. Toronto: Ryerson, 1952. R.L. 7-8. Spy story set in the Canadian North.

Copeland, Donald M., *True Book of Little Eskimos*. Chicago: Childrens, 1953. R.L. 2.9. Informational material on Eskimo life.

Creekmore, Raymond, *Lokoshi Learns to Hunt Seals*. New York: Macmillan, 1946. R.L. 2-3. An Eskimo boy begins to grow up.

Crisp, William, *Ook-Pik*. Toronto: Dent, 1952. R.L. 4-5. Simple story of an Eskimo boy.

Darbois, Dominique, *Achouna—Boy of the Arctic*. Chicago: Follett, 1962. R.L. 4.6. About an Eskimo family, their customs, animals, life, homes, and play.

deLeeuw, Adele, *Richard E. Byrd: Adventurer to the Poles*. Champaign: Garrard, 1963. R.L. 2.5. The first man to explore both poles.

deLeeuw, Cateau, *A World Explorer: Roald Amundsen*. Champaign: Garrard, 1965. R.L. 4.0. Amundsen, the North Pole explorer, was a friend to the Eskimos.

Dolch, Edward, *Stories from Alaska*. Champaign: Garrard, 1961. R.L. 4.3 Folklore and animal stories drawn from the lore of the Arctic regions.

Epstein, Samuel and Williams, Beryl, *The Real Book About Alaska*. New York: Watts, 1952. R.L. 6-7. A simple historical account of Alaska.

Foster, Eliza and Williams, Slim, *The Friend of the Singing One*. New York: Atheneum, 1967. R.L. 4-5. Eskimo folkways.

Frankel, Haskel, *Adventure in Alaska*. New York: Doubleday, 1963. R.L. 4.3. An adventure story laid in Alaska.

Freedman, Benedict and Nancy, *Mrs. Mike*. New York: Coward-McCann, 1947. (Paperback) R.L. 7-8. Kathie learns to adjust to her marriage and new life in the far North.

Gidal, Sonia and Tim, *Follow the Reindeer*. New York: Pantheon, 1959. R.L. 4-5. Informational material on Eskimo life.

Guillot, Rene, *A Boy and Five Huskies*. Toronto: Ryerson, 1957. R.L. 4-5. Life with a dog team in Northern Canada.

Harrington, Lyn, *Ootook, Young Eskimo Girl*. New York: Abelard, 1956. R.L. 4-5. Real life pictures portray daily life in an Eskimo village.

Harris, Christie, *Forbidden Frontier*. New York: Atheneum, 1968. R.L. 5-6. Two girls of different backgrounds clash with their own cultures, 100 years ago.

Herrmanns, Ralph, *Children of the North Pole*. New York: Harcourt, 1964. R.L. 5-6. A boy and a girl try to take the place of their injured father, and to secure food for their family.

Holsaert, Eunice, *Life in the Arctic*. New York: Harvey, 1957. R.L. 5.3. Factual account of the animals and people of the area.

Hopkins, Marjorie, *The Three Visitors*. New York: Parents, 1967. R.L. 4.7. An Eskimo girl adds three animal visitors to her igloo.

Houston, James A. *White Archer: An Eskimo Legend*. New York: Harcourt, 1967. R.L. 4-5. Vowing to avenge the killing of his parents, a young Eskimo finds a better answer than counter-violence.

Iglauer, Edith, *The New People: The Eskimo's Journey into Our Time*. New York: Doubleday, 1966. R.L. 8-9. A first-hand account of the Eskimo's efforts to participate in the modern world.

Janes, Edward, *When Men Panned Gold in the Yukon*. Champaign: Garrard, 1968. R.L. 4.0. The gold rush in the Yukon territory.

Jenness, Aylette, *Gussuk Boy*. Chicago: Follett, 1967. R.L. 4.7. Boy story of adventure in Alaska.

Jenness, Diamond, *Dawn in Arctic Alaska*. Toronto: Allen, 1957. R.L. 6-7. The author's experiences among the Eskimos of Arctic Alaska, while he was a member of the Stefansson Expedition of 1913.

Kjelgaard. Jim, *Kalak of the Ice*. New York: Holiday, 1949. R.L. 5-6. Man against the polar bear.

Lestina, Dorothy, *Alaska*. New York: Holt, 1962. R.L. 3.2. A simple history of Alaska.

Lindquist, Willis, *Alaska: The Forty-Ninth State*. New York: Whittlesey, 1959. R.L. 7-8. A history of the State of Alaska beginning with earliest settlement.

Lipkind, William, *Boy with a Harpoon*. New York: Harcourt, 1952. R.L. 4-5. Adventures of an Eskimo boy.

Liversidge, Douglas, *The First Book of the Arctic*. New York: Watts, 1967. R.L. 4-5. Survey of geography, wildlife, and the family life of the Eskimos and Indians.

Lutgen, Kurt, *Two Against the Arctic*. Toronto: McClelland, 1957. R.L. 6-7. Two humans brave the elements in Greenland and Alaska.

Machetanz, Frederick, *Panuck, Eskimo Sled Dog*. New York: Scribner, 1939. R.L. 4.5. Story of Eskimo boy and his dog.

Machetanz, Sara. *Puppy Named Gih*. New York: Scribner, 1957. R.L. 4-5. Children and puppies are much the same anywhere in the world.

Marsh, Roy, S. *Tundra*. New York: Macrae, 1968. R.L. 6-7. Two trading post owners separate when one leaves to hunt for gold, but he then disappears.

Maxwell, Moreau S., *Eskimo Family*. Chicago: Encyclopaedia Britannica, 1962. R.L. 5.6. Story of Eskimo family life accompanied by many photographs.

Mayberry, Genevieve, *Eskimo of Little Diomede*. Chicago: Follett, 1961. R.L. 4.6. A simple story of young Alaskans.

McNeer, May, *Alaska Gold Rush*. New York: Random, 1960. R.L. 5-6. Story of the madness of men in search of gold.

Milotte, Alfred and Elma, *The Story of an Alaskan Grizzly Bear*. New York: Knopf, 1969. R.L. 4-5. Animal life in the frozen North.

Morey, Walt, *Home is the North*. New York: Dutton, 1967. R.L. 5-6. A year in Alaska is an experience in growing up.

Mowat, Farley, *Canada North*. Boston: Little, 1968. R.L. 7-8. Deals with the Indians and Eskimos of Northern Canada. See other books by this prolific Canadian author.

Mowatt, Farley, *Lost in the Barrens*. Boston: Little, 1956. R.L. 7. Two boys must spend a winter on the Barren Grounds, land of the Eskimo.

Mowat, Farley, *People of the Deer*. Toronto: McClelland. 1952. R.L. 6-7. An account of a two-year visit with a little-known Eskimo tribe.

Neelands, Barbara S., *The Coming of the Reindeer*. New York: Lantern, 1966. R.L. 5-6. Tatuk finally wins his father's consent to go to school.

O'Neill, Hester, *Picture Story of Alaska*. New York: McKay, 1951. R.L. 4-5. Simple history and geography aided by many pictures.

Palazzo, Tony, *Jan and the Reindeer.* Champaign: Garrard, 1963. R.L. 2.5. Family life of the Laplanders.

Peck, Helen E., *Iceland and Greenland.* Nashville: Abelard, 1967. R.L. 5-6. Informational material with photographic illustrations.

Pedersen, Elsa, *Cook Inlet Decision.* New York: Atheneum, 1963. R.L. 5-6. Vivid story of the salmon fishing in Alaskan waters.

Pedersen, Elsa, *Dangerous Flight.* Nashville: Abingdon, 1960. R.L. 6-7. Stefan and his uncle are rescued from the Russians by Indian friends.

Pedersen, Elsa, *Fisherman's Choice.* New York: Atheneum, 1964. R.L. 6-7. Dave tries to follow his father's occupation but cannot.

Pine, Tillie S. and Levine, Joseph, *The Eskimos Knew.* New York: McGraw-Hill, 1962. R.L. 4.8. Science as the Eskimos know it.

Sarnoff, Paul, *Ice Pilot—Bob Bartlett,* New York: Messner, 1966. R.L. 5.6. Story of a bush pilot who lived with danger.

Shannon, Terry, *A Dog Team for Ongluk.* Chicago: Melmont, 1962. R.L. 2.8. Ongluk finally gets a dog team of his own.

Smith, Frances C., *The World of the Arctic.* Philadelphia: Lippincott, 1960. R.L. 5-6. Brief history of exploration and life of the Eskimo and Lapp.

Sperry, Armstrong, *All About the Arctic and Antarctic.* New York: Random, 1957. R.L. 6-7. The life of the Eskimos of the far North and the far South.

Spring, Norma, *Alaska, Pioneer State.* Camden, N.J.: Nelson, 1966. R.L. 6-7. A survey of Alaska, people and resources, by the wife of a photographer.

Staib, Bjorn O., *On Skis Toward the North Pole.* New York: Doubleday, 1965. R.L. 6-7. Ordeal of a Norwegian expedition attempting to cross the polar ice cap.

Steffansson. Evelyn, *Here is Alaska.* New York: Scribner, 1959. R.L. 6-7. The wife of the famous Arctic explorer contrasts the old and the new Alaska.

Strong, Charles S., *The Lost Convoy.* Philadelphia: Chilton, 1960. R.L. 6.3. Adventure with the Norwegian underground in the far North during World War II.

Tina, Dorothy L., *A Book to Begin on Alaska.* New York: Holt, 1962. R.L. 3-4. A simple introduction to the history of Alaska, and its flora and fauna. Good illustrations.

Tolboom, Wanda, *People of the Snow.* New York: Coward, 1956. R.L. 5-6. Story of the Canadian Eskimos.

Tolboom, Wanda, *Little Eskimo Hunter.* New York: Longmans, 1956. R.L. 3-4. Simple story of Eskimo life.

Tolboom, Wanda, *Tosie of the Far North: An Eskimo Story.* New York: Aladdin, 1954. R.L. 4-5. Daily life of an Eskimo child.

True, Barbara and Henry, Marguerite, *Their First Igloo on Baffin Island.* Chicago: Whitman, 1943. R.L. 5.2. Semi-fictional material on the daily life of the Eskimo family.

Viereck, Phillip, *Eskimo Island.* New York: John Day, 1962. R.L. 5.0. Story of the Bering Sea hunters.

Wilkinson, Douglas, *Land of the Long Day*. Toronto: Clarke Irwin, 1956. R.L. 6-7. Account of the author's year-long visit with an Eskimo family on Baffin Island.

Wyatt, Colin, *North of Sixty*. Toronto: Hodder, 1958. Life among the Eskimos of the Canadian Arctic.

CHAPTER X

Inner City Life

(Primary Level)

Appell, Clara and Morey, *Glenn Learns to Read*. Des Moines: Duell, 1964. R.L. 2-3. A reassuring story for young people struggling to learn to read.

Barr, Jene, *Miss Terry at the Library*. Chicago: Whitman, 1962. R.L. 3.1. Semi-fictional account of the work of the librarian.

Beim, Jerrold, *The Boy on Lincoln's Lap*. New York: Morrow, 1955. R.L. 2-3. Three city boys learn something about citizenship by cleaning up a statue.

Beim, Jerrold, *Shoeshine Boy*. New York: Morrow, 1954. R.L. 3-4. Simple story of a city boy.

Beim, Jerrold, *The Smallest Boy in the Class*. New York: Morrow, 1949. R.L. 3.5. Jim was the smallest, but the noisiest and busiest.

Beim, Jerrold, *Thin Ice*. New York: Morrow, 1956. R.L. 3. O.P. When his ability to read a warning sign helps prevent an accident, reading finally makes sense to Lee.

Bell, Norman, *Linda's Air Mail Letter*. Chicago: Follett, 1964. R.L. 2.8. More about community workers. Simple, factual material.

Belmont, Evelyn, *Playground Fun*. Chicago: Melmont, 1955. R.L. 1.9. Playground fun at an easy to read level.

Berg, Jean H., *The O'Learys and Friends*. Chicago: Follett, 1961. R.L. 2.0. Friends and neighbors, and their pets in the city.

Bonsall, Crosby, *The Case of the Cat's Meow*. New York: Harper, 1965. R.L. 1.5 A humorous story of the activities of city youngsters.

Brown, Virginia. et al., *Who Cares?* New York: McGraw-Hill, 1965. R.L. 3-4. Stories about underprivileged urban children.

Burchardt, Nellie, *Project Cat*. New York: Watts, 1966. R.L. 3-4. Betsy finally convinces the officials of the housing project that she should be allowed to keep a cat.

Chapin, Cynthia, *Squad Car 55*. Chicago: Whitman, 1966. R.L. 2.4. Police work in a large city.

Child Study Association, *Round About the City*. New York: Crowell, 1966. R.L. 3-4. A collection of short stories on city life.

Dawson, Rosemary and Richard, *A Walk in the City*. New York: Viking, 1950. R.L. 2-3. Sights of the city.

Elkin, Benjamin, *The True Book of Schools*. Chicago: Children. R.L. 2.8. All about schools, in a simple style.

Francoise, *What Do You Want to Be?*, New York: Scribner. R.L. 3.9. Role-playing games for primary children.

Frasconi, Antonio, *See Again, Say Again*. New York: Harcourt, 1964. R.L. 2-3. City scenes in four languages.

Gregor, Arthur S., *How the World's First Cities Began*. New York: Dutton, 1967. R.L. 3-4. The gradual development of urban life.

Hader, Berta and Elmer, *Big City*. New York: Macmillan, 1948. R.L. 3-4. Two city children take their cousin on a tour of a big city.

Hamond, Penny, *My Skyscraper City: A Child's View of New York*. New York: Doubleday, 1963. R.L. 3-4. Large photographs and rollicking verse present an exciting view of New York.

Harwood, Pearl A., *Mrs. Moon and the Dark Stairs*. New York: Lerner, 1967. R.L. 3.0. Children visit neighbor who lived in a large apartment house.

Harwood, Pearl A., *Mrs. Moon's Story Hour*. New York: Lerner, 1967. R.L. 2.9. Mrs. Moon goes with little boy to the library. She shows him how to travel in the subway and find his way.

Hawkinson, John and Lucy, *Little Boy Who Lives Up High*. Chicago: Whitman, 1967. R.L. 3.5. Neighbors in a city high-rise apartment.

Heilbroner, Joan, *This is the House Where Jack Lives*. New York: Harper, 1962. R.L. 2-3. Jack lives in an apartment house.

Hitte, Kathryn, *Boy, Was I Mad*. New York: Parents, 1969. R.L. 2-3. The story of a little boy and the day he ran away and finished in front of his own home.

Holland, Marion, *Billy's Clubhouse*. New York: Knopf, 1955. R.L. 4-5. Billy and his friends solve all the problems in building and using a clubhouse.

Lattin, Anne, *Peter's Policeman*. Chicago: Follett, 1958. R.L. 3.1. The police fight against crime in a great city. A semi-factual account.

Lenski, Lois, *Papa Small*. New York: Oxford, 1951. R.L. 2-3. Daddy's daily activities in and about the home.

Lenski, Lois, *Policeman Small*. New York: Walck, 1962. R.L. 2.3. The work of the city policeman.

Lenski, Lois, *We Live in the City*. Philadelphia: Lippincott, 1954. R.L. 3-4. A city newsboy's outlook on life and people.

Levenson, Dorothy, *The Day Joe Went to the Supermarket*. New York: Grosset, 1963. R.L. 2.2. Life in the big city.

Lexau, Joan, *I Should Have Stayed in Bed*. New York: Harper, 1965. R.L. 1-2. A small boy's misadventures in a school day.

Liang, Yen, *The Skyscraper*. Philadelphia: Lippincott, 1958. R.L. 2-3. How a crowded neighborhood is changed to a new apartment area.

Lyman, Susan and Szasz, Susanne, *Young Folks' New York*. New York: Lothrop, 1960. R.L. 3-4. Pictures and text present those parts of New York City of interest to young children.

Martin, Patricia M., *Show and Tell*. New York: Putnam, 1962. R.L. 2.5. Life in school, in a very simple style.

McIntire, Alta and Hill, Wilhelmina, *Billy's Neighbors*. Chicago: Follett,

1965. R.L. 2.2. Billy's friends and neighbors include the community workers.

Mike—The Mailman and Other Rebus Stories. Chicago: Parents, 1962. R.L. 2.1. Semi-picture book.

Miles, Betty, *A House for Everyone.* New York: Knopf, 1958. R.L. 2-3. All different kinds of houses.

Palmer, Candida, *A Ride on High.* Philadelphia: Lippincott, 1966. R.L. 3-4. Two Negro boys find adventure on the city elevated train.

Perl, Susan, *Surprise in the Tree.* New York: Wonder, 1962. R.L. 2.1. The story of those brave community workers, the firemen.

Scott, Ann H., *Sam.* New York: McGraw-Hill, 1967. R.L. 3-4. Sam thinks his family is too busy to care about him.

Shapp, Martha, *Let's Find Out What the Signs Say.* New York: Watts, 1959. R.L. 2-3. Simple reading of city signs.

Stanek, Muriel and Johnson, Barbara, *How People Live in the Big City.* Chicago: Benefic, 1964. R.L. 2-3. A simple introduction to the features of a big city.

Tensen, Ruth M., *Come to the City.* Chicago: Reilly, 1961. R.L. 2.8. Two children visit the city.

Tresselt, Alvin, *Wake Up, City.* New York: Lothrop, 1957. R.L. 2-3. Sights and sounds of the city in the morning.

Udry, Janice M., *Let's Be Enemies.* New York: Harper, 1967. R.L. 2-3. A childhood quarrel between friends ends on a friendly note.

Walters, George, *The Steam Shovel That Wouldn't Eat Dirt.* New York: Dutton, 1948. R.L. 3.3. Picture-story of a misbehaving steam shovel.

Wise, William, *The Story of Mulberry Bend.* New York: Dutton, 1963. R.L. 2-3. Albert and his slum playmates had never seen a flower until their friend, a newspaperman, brought some from his house.

Wright, Betty R., *I Want to Read!* Chicago: Whitman, 1965. R.L. 3.0. Semi-picture book for the beginning reader.

(Intermediate Level)

BacMeister, Rhoda W., *The People Downstairs.* New York: Coward, 1964. R.L. 5.3. Stories about city children.

Bloch, Marie H., *The House on Third High.* New York: Coward, 1962. R.L. 4-5. O. P. Jenny experiences what it is like to be considered "foreign" and "an outsider."

Brown, Pamela, *The Other Side of the Street.* Chicago: Follett, 1965. R.L. 5.3. Fictional account of city life.

Chandler, Edna W., *The Boy Who Made Faces.* Chicago: Whitman, 1964. R.L. 5.4. A slight story about peer relationship among city children.

Cleary, Beverly, *Mitch and Amy.* New York: Morrow, 1967. R.L. 4-5. Mitch has troubles with a neighborhood bully and with reading. Amy, his twin sister, tries to help.

Coles, Robert, *Dead End School.* Boston: Little, 1968. R.L. 4-5. Life in a ghetto school.

Corbett, Scott, *Cop's Kid*. Boston: Little, 1968. R.L. 4.6. Story of a policeman's boy who was in the grocery store at the time of a robbery. He decides to follow up the clues himself and ends up face to face with the robber.

Dolch, Edward, *Stories from Italy*. Champaign: Garrard, 1962. R.L. 4.4. Folktales from Italy.

Ets, Marie H., *Bad Boy: Good Boy*. New York: Crowell, 1967. R.L. 3-4. Problems of an immigrant family.

Fast, Howard, *Tony and the Wonderful Door*. New York: Knopf, 1968. R.L. 4-5. The fantastic adventures of Tony, a poor New York City boy, who finds a magic door that leads to long ago.

Fox, Paula, *How Many Miles to Babylon?* New York: White, 1968. R.L. 5-6. A small city boy gets involved in the delinquency of the older boys.

Friedman, Frieda, *The Janitor's Girl*. New York: Morrow, 1956. R.L. 4.5. Sue is snubbed because she is the "janitor's daughter."

Hays, Wilma P., *The Pup Who Became a Police Dog*. Boston: Little, 1963. R.L. 4.6. Story of the training of a police dog.

Hunt, Mabel L., *Singing Among Strangers*. Philadelphia: Lippincott, 1954. R.L. 5.1. Relationships among immigrant groups in a big city. A fictional account.

Inyart, Gene, *Susan and Martin*. New York: Watts, 1965. R.L. 3-4. Fourth-grade Susie leads her friend Martin into all sorts of scrapes.

Lenski, Lois, *High-Rise Secret*. Philadelphia: Lippincott, 1966. R.L. 4-5. Problems of children in a low-income housing project.

Malone, Mary, *Here's Howie*. New York: Dodd, 1962. R.L. 4-5. Howie means well but is always in trouble at school or at home.

McCarthy, Agnes, *Let's Go to Vote*. New York: Putnam, 1962. R.L. 4-5. All about voting.

McNeill, Janet, *The Battle of St. George Without*. Boston: Little, 1968. R.L. 4-5. City children have to fight to save their favorite play area.

Merrill, Jean, *The Pushcart War*. New York: Scott, 1964. R.L. 4-5. A witty fictional, story of the fight between the truckers and the pushcarts in the crowded streets of New York.

Neville, Emily C., *The Seventeenth-Street Gang*. New York: Harper, 1966. R.L. 4-5. Activities of big city children.

Rambeau, John and Nancy, *Stranger at Cherry Hill*. San Francisco: Harr Wagner. R.L. 4.5. Domenic finds difficulty in adjusting to a new school.

Rose, Karen, *There is a Season*. Chicago: Follett, 1967. R.L. 4-8. Katie and Jamie resolve their problem of different religions.

Schick, Eleanor, *5A and 7B*. New York: Macmillan, 1967. R.L. 3-4. Living in an apartment building, two girls eventually meet and become friends.

Scott, Ann H., *Big Cowboy Western*. New York: Lathrop, 1965. R.L. 3-4. Family life in an urban housing development.

Scott, Ann H., *Let's Catch a Monster*. New York: Lothrop. R.L. 4-5. Trick-or-treat time for inner-city youngsters.

Stolz, Mary, *The Bully of Barkham Street*. New York: Harper, 1963. R.L.

4-5. Story of a boy who overeats and bullies in retaliation for his parents' lack of interest in him.

Stolz, Mary, *The Noonday Friends*. New York: Harper, 1965. R.L. 5-6. Family life in crowded Greenwich Village in New York City.

Tarry, Ellen, and Ets, Marie, *My Dog Rinty*. New York: Viking, 1964. R.L. 4-5. David and his mischievous dog Rinty live in Harlem in New York City. The story and photographs create a warm picture of life in Harlem.

Taylor, Sydney, *All-of-a-Kind Family*. Chicago: Follett, 1951. R.L. 4.7. Life of an East Side Hebrew family.

Watts, Mabel, *Weeks and Weeks—Walking Week, Smile Week, Posture Week, Safety Week*. New York: Abelard, 1962. R.L. 4.0. Humorous stories about city life, a semi-picture book.

Wilson, Penelope C., *Fancy and the Cement Patch*. Chicago: Reilly, 1964. R.L. 4-5. A pony in a city backyard causes some problems.

(Jr.-Sr. H.S. Level)

Alcock, Gudrum, *Run, Westy, Run*. New York: Lothrop, 1966. R.L. 6-7 Westy gets in trouble with the law.

Beim, Jerrold, *Trouble After School*. New York: Harcourt, 1957. R.L. 6-7 Lee faces a choice when his gang decides to wreck a high school recreation center.

Bonham, Frank, *Durango Street*. New York: Dutton, 1965. R.L. 5-6 Rufus, a parolee, finds he must join a gang to survive.

Bowen, Robert S. *Hot Rod Rodeo*. New York: Criterion, 1964. R.L. 5-6 Larry, a hot rod enthusiast, becomes involved in a hold-up. See also *Hot Rod Angels, Hot Rod Patrol,* and *Hot Rod Showdown* by same author.

Braithwaite, E. R., *To Sir, With Love*. Englewood Cliffs: Prentice-Hall, 1959. R.L. 6-7 A Negro teacher in the slums of London finds the heart of his pupils.

Bushman, John C. *Scope*. New York: Harper, 1965. R.L. 5-? Four volumes of stories for reluctant readers of secondary urban school, probably about 5-8th grade.

Butwin, Frances, *The Jews in America*. Cincinnati: McCormick-Mathers, 1968. R.L. 7-8 A history of the major migrations of Jews to America, their integration and contributions.

Carson, John F. *The 23rd Street Crusaders*. New York: Holt, 1958. R.L. 7 A gang of hoodlums wind up in a church, seeking a place to play basketball.

Clarke, John, *High School Drop Out*. New York: Doubleday, 1964. R.L. 4.9. Teen-age fiction.

Cohen, Florence C., *Portrait of Deborah*. Chicago: Messner, 1961. R.L. 7-8. Deborah has problems in securing a musical career, and in loving a Gentile.

Eyerly, Jeannette, *Drop-Out*. Philadelphia: Lippincott, 1963. R.L. 4.9. School life and teen-age peer relationships.

Eyerly, Jeannette, *A Girl Like Me*. Philadelphia: Lippincott, 1966. R.L. 4.7.

Friedman, Frieda, *Ellen and the Gang*. New York: Morrow, 1963. R.L. 5.4. A teen age girl in a housing project makes questionable friendships.

Hinton, S. E., *The Outsiders*. New York: Noble & Noble. (Paperback). R.L. 6-7. The inner conflicts of a teenage gang.

Jackson, Jesse, *Tessie*. New York: Harper, 1968. R.L. 5-6. Tessie has problems in a multi-racial neighborhood.

Johnson, Annabel and Edgar, *Pickpocket Run*. New York: Harper, 1961. R.L. 6-7. A teen-ager cannot accept his father's cheating of the tourists.

Krumgold, Joseph, *Henry*. New York: Atheneum, 1967. R.L. 7-8. Life of a teen-age boy in the complex setting of a big city suburb.

Laklan, Carli, *Two Girls in New York*. New York: Doubleday, 1964. R.L. 4.5. Fictional account of the adventures and misadventures of two young girls in a big city.

Lariar, Lawrence, *The Teen Scene*. New York: Dodd, 1966. R.L. 6-7. A hilarious cartoon book on the world of the present-day teen-ager.

Neville, Emily C., *Berries Goodman*. New York: Harper, 1965. R.L. 6-7. Berries meets anti-Semitism when it affects his friend, Sydney.

Nickerson, Jan, *New Boy in Town*. New York: Funk, 1960. R.L. 4.6. Teen-age romance fiction.

Rizk, Salom, *Syrian Yankee*. New York: Doubleday, 1943. R.L. 6-7. What America did for a Syrian boy.

Singer, Isaac B., *Zlateh the Goat and Other Stories*. New York: Harper, 1966. R.L. 6-7. Old World Jewish folk tales.

Spiegler, Charles G., *Courage Under Fire. Against the Odds*. Columbus: Merrill, 1967. R.L. 4-7. A pair of paperback anthologies of stories for inner city adolescents.

CHAPTER XI

Mexican-American and Migrant Workers

(Primary Level)

Amescus, Carol Connor, adapted by, *The Story of Pablo Mexican Boy.* Chicago: Encyclopedia Britannica, 1962. R.L. 3.7. Mexican family life.

Baker, Charlotte, *Necessary Nellie.* New York: Coward, 1938. R.L. 3-4. A dog is the most precious possession of a group of Spanish-speaking youngsters.

Bell-Zano, Gina, *Presents for Johnny Jerome.* Boston, Ginn, 1966. R.L. 3-4. Pedro brings his father's guitar to the birthday party.

Bemelmans, Ludwig, *Quito Express.* New York: Viking, 1965. R.L. 2-3. Pedro who can say only one word, "Dadadada" takes a trip on the Quito Express.

Bulla, Clyde R., *Benito.* New York: Crowell, 1961. R.L. 3-4. Benito stands up against his uncle to demand his right to go to school.

Clark, Ann N., *Tia Maria's Garden.* New York: Viking, 1963. R.L. 3-4. A little boy and his aunt discover beauty in a desert.

Dralle, Elizabeth, *Angel in the Tower.* New York: Farrar, 1962. R.L. 3-4. Angel and his parents are bell-ringers for their village.

Ets, Marie H., *Gilberto and the Wind.* New York: Viking, 1963. R.L. 2-3. Adventures of a small Mexican boy.

Graham, Helen H., *Little Don Pedro.* New York: Abelard, 1959. R.L. 2-3. Pedro proves he is no sissy when he saves his baby sister from a fierce bull.

Graham, Helen H., *Taco, the Snoring Burro.* New York: Abelard, 1957. R.L. 2-3. Humorous, Mexican story.

Hood, Flora, *One Luminaria for Antonio.* New York: Putnam, 1966. R.L. 3.6. Mexican family life and religious beliefs.

Kirn, Ann, *Two Pesos for Catalina.* Chicago: Rand, 1962. R.L. 3.0. Catalina finally buys shoes for her two pesos—the first shoes she has ever worn.

Martin, Patricia M., *Trina's Boxcar.* Nashville: Abingdon, 1967. R.L. 3-4. Trina tries to learn to speak English.

Ormsby, Virginia H., *What's Wrong with Julio?* Philadelphia: Lippincott, 1956. R.L. 2-3. Julio wouldn't talk in either English or Spanish.

Ormsby, Virginia H., *Twenty-one Children.* Philadelphia: Lippincott, 1957. R.L. 5-6. Emalina can't speak English, but the class finds it fun to teach her, while she teaches them Spanish.

Politi, Leo, *Piccolo's Prank.* New York: Scribner, 1965. R.L. 2-3. Another story of the Mexican-American section of Los Angeles.

Politi, Leo, *Lito and the Clown*. New York: Scribner, 1964. R.L. 2.4. A carnival provides background for the story of Lito and his search for his lost kitten.

Politi, Leo, *Rosa*. New York: Scribner, 1963. R.L. 3.2. Rosa finally achieves her long-desired doll.

Prieto, Mariana B., *A Kite for Carlos*. New York: John Day, 1966. R.L. 3-4. Story is told in both English and Spanish.

Rowland, Florence W., *The Singing Leaf*. New York: Putnam, 1965. R.L. 2.4. A fictional account of Mexican family life.

Schloat, G. Warren Jr., *Conchita and Juan*. New York: Knopf. 1964. R.L. 3-4. Informational material on a typical day in Central Mexico.

Shannon, Terry, *A Playmate for Puna*. Chicago: Melmont, 1963. R.L. 2.5. Puna, a Mexican Indian child, seeks a playmate.

Storm, Dan, *Picture Tales from Mexico*. Philadelphia: Lippincott, 1941. R.L. 3-4. Short stories about "Senor Coyote" and other animals.

We Say Happy Birthday. New York: Funk, 1967. Parallel Spanish and English simple texts.

When We Go to School. New York: Funk, 1967. Parallel Spanish and English texts introduce the young student to another language.

(Intermediate Level)

Behn, Harry, *The Two Uncles of Pablo*. New York: Harcourt, 1959. R.L. 4.8. Pablo tries to adjust to the very different uncles.

Bolton, Ivy, *Father Junipero Serra*. New York: Messner, 1952. R.L. 5.9. Biography of the founder of the California Missions.

Bulosan, Carlos, *America Is in the Heart*. New York: Harcourt, 1946. R.L. 5-6. Filipino emigrants experience discrimination on the west coast.

Camille, Josephine and Albert, *Carlos and the Brave Owl*. New York: Random House, 1968. R.L. 4-5. Carlos finds a courageous, useful pet in time for the blessing of the animals at the fiesta.

Clark, Ann, *Paco's Miracle*. New York: Farrar, 1962. R.L. 4-5. Paco tries to learn the ways of a Spanish family with whom he lives in New Mexico.

Coatsworth, Elizabeth, *The Place*. New York: Holt, 1966. R.L. 5-6. Friendship between an American and a Mexican girl.

Cooper, Page, *Amigo, Circus Horse*. New York: Grosset, 1955. R.L. 4.8. Story of a circus horse.

Crosby, Alexander, *The Rio Grande: Life for the Desert*. Champaign: Garrard, 1966. R.L. 5.0. The history of this great river.

Dazey, Frank and Johnston, Agnes, *Pepe, the Bad One*. Philadelphia: Westminster, 1966. R.L. 4-5. Pepe's hunger forces him to steal.

Dolch, Edward, *Stories from Mexico*. Champaign: Garrard, 1960. R.L. 4.2. Folk stories that help children understand Mexican people and their ways.

Dusoe, R.C., *Sea Boots*. New York: McKay, 1949. R.L. 5-6. A Mexican-American boy learns the dangerous life of a commercial fisherman.

Earle, Vanya, *Wish Around the World*. Eau Claire: Hale, 1954. R.L. 4-5.

Danny learns about the customs of the Chinese, Italians and Mexicans in his home town.

Epstein, S. and Williams, B., *The First Book of Mexico*. New York: Watts, 1967. R.L. 5-6. Informational material.

Ets, Marie H., *Gilberto y el Viento*. New York: Viking, 1967. A long-time favorite folktale, translated into simple Spanish.

Ets, Marie H., and Labastida, Aurora, *Nine Days to Christmas*. New York: Viking, 1959. R.L. 4.5. Ceci enjoys each of the nine days of the posadas parties before Christmas and wins the special pinata she hopes for.

Fall, Thomas, *Wild Boy*. New York: Dial, 1965. R.L. 5-6. Roberto comes to terms with his mixed heritage eventually.

Forsee, Aylesa, *Too Much Dog*. Philadelphia: Lippincott, 1957. R.L. 4-5. A migrant boy goes with his grandfather to pick fruit in the Colorado orchards.

Frasconi, Antonio, *The Snow and the Sun*. New York: Harcourt, 1961. A dual language book offering a folk rhyme in English and Spanish.

Garthwaite, Marion, *Mario, A Mexican Boy's Adventure*. New York: Doubleday, 1960. R.L. 5-6. Left alone by his mother's illness, Mario is smuggled into California and into trouble, as a wetback.

Gates, Doris, *Blue Willow*. New York: Viking, 1946. R.L. 5-6. A family of migratory workers treasures a blue willow plate as a symbol of their hopes for a better future.

Grant, C. L. and Werner, J., *Mexico, Land of the Plumed Serpent*. Champaign: Garrard, 1968. R.L. 4.5. Factual information on customs, culture, and political events.

Hader, B. T. and Elmer, *Story of Pancho and the Bull with the Crooked Tail*. New York: Macmillan, 1942. R.L. 4-5. Fantasy story laid in Mexico.

Heck, Bessie H., *Millie*. Cleveland; World, 1961. R.L. 5-6. Millie changes school each year, as her transient father moves from one crop to the next.

Hoff, Carol, *Chris*. Chicago: Follett, 1969. R.L. 4.8. Because Chris's father, an oil driller moves frequently, Chris attends many schools: how Chris eventually solves his problem.

Jackson, Helen H., *Ramona*. New York: Grosset, R.L. 5.4. Adult romantic fiction.

Joslin, Sesyle, *La Fiesta*. New York: Harcourt, 1967. A series of amusing incidents are presented in simple Spanish.

Joslin, Sesyle, *Senor Baby Elephant, the Pirate*. New York: Harcourt, 1962. R.L. 4-5. A baby elephant learns some Spanish words as he plays at being a pirate.

Juline, Ruth B., *A Place for Johnny Bill*. Philadelphia: Westminster, 1961. O.P. R.L. 4-5. Johnny longs for a home and a school to attend where he could make friends. But his family moves constantly from place to place to follow the crops.

Knight, Ruth A., and Gardner, Claud, *Word of Honor*. New York: Farrar, 1964. R.L. 6-7. A Mexican boy helps put a horse farm back on its feet.

Krumgold, Joseph, *And Now Miguel*. New York: Crowell, 1953. R.L. 4.6. Miguel tries to take his place with the sheep herders.

Lauritzen, Jonreed, *Colonel Anza's Impossible Journey*. New York: Putnam, 1966. R.L. 5.0. History in early California.

Lenski, Lois, *Papa Pequeno. Papa Small*. New York: Walck, 1961. Spanish and English versions appear on the same page.

Lenski, Lois, *Cotton in My Sack*. Philadelphia: Lippincott, 1949. (Paperback) R.L. 5-6. Joanda's family become tenant farmers but find it very difficult to solve their money problem.

Lenski, Lois, *Judy's Journey*. Philadelpha: Lippincott, 1947. (Paperback) R.L. 4-5. Judy longs for a permanent home and school, as her migrant family follows the harvests from one place to another.

Lomas, Steve, *Fishing Fleet Boy*. New York: Doubleday, 1962. R.L. 4. Don Sebastian tries to discover the cause of the disappearance of the fish from the waters of his native village.

Parish, Helen R., *At the Palace Gates*. New York: Viking, 1949. R.L. 4-5. Paco goes to the city to earn his living as a shoe-shine boy.

Phillips, Eula M., *Chuco—The Boy With the Good Name*. Chicago: Follett, 1957. R.L. 4.5. Home life and customs of the Mexican family.

Politi, Leo, *A Boat for Peppe*. New York: Scribner, 1950. R.L. 4.4. Peppe's greatest wish was for a sailboat of his own.

Politi, Leo, *Juanita*. New York: Scribner, 1948. R.L. 4.9. The blessing of the animals at Easter among the Mexican-Americans in Los Angeles.

Politi, Leo, *Little Leo*. New York: Scribner, 1951. R.L. 4.3. A simple, fanciful tale of a Mexican boy.

Politi, Leo, *Pedro, the Angel of Olvera Street*. New York: Scribner, 1946. R.L. 4-5. Mexican style Christmas celebrated in Los Angeles by Mexican family.

Politi, Leo, *Song of the Swallows*. New York: Scribner, 1949. R.L. 4.5. A Spanish boy learns to love the swallows that return yearly to the mission.

Prieto, Mariana B., *Tomato Boy*. New York: John Day, 1967. R.L. 4.2. Friendship among the children of migrant workers.

Prieto, Mariana B., *The Wise Rooster: El Gallo Sabio*. New York: John Day, 1962. An Old World Christmas legend in English and Spanish, side by side.

Rambeau, John and Nancy, *The Magic Door*. San Francisco: Harr Wagner. R.L. 4.5. Depicts the problems of growing up for an only girl in a ranchero family.

Ritchie, Barbara, *Ramon Makes a Trade: Los Cambios de Ramon*. Berkeley: Parnassus, 1959. R.L. 4-5. A bilingual story about a young trader.

Robinson, Benelle H., *Citizen Pablo*. New York: John Day, 1967. R.L. 5-6. The efforts of a poor Mexican family to find a better way of life.

Rydberg, Ernie, *Bright Summer*. New York: McKay, 1953. R.L. 5-6. A Mexican-American family spends the summer near a small California town.

Sawyer, Ruth, *The Year of the Christmas Dragon*. New York: Viking, 1960. R.L. 4-5. Fantasy story of Pepe and the dragon who save the Christmas fiesta.

Schweitzer, Byrd B., *Amigo*. New York: Macmillan, 1963. R.L. 4.2. Story of a Mexican boy who wanted a dog. Amigo, a Prairie dog, and the boy know and understand each other's ways.

Shotwell, Louisa R., *Roosevelt Grady*. Cleveland: World, 1963. (Paperback) R.L. 4-5. A migrant worker family's hard life.

Simon, Charlie M., *Robin on the Mountain*. New York: Dutton, 1953. R.L. 4-5. Life for a family of migrant workers.

Snyder, Zilpha K., *The Velvet Room*. New York: Atheneum, 1965. R.L. 4-5. Robin's migrant family has a hard life in the depression of the 30's.

Sommerfelt, Aimee, *My Name is Pablo*. New York: Criterion, 1965. R.L. 5-6. Pablo escapes from the dope pushers of Mexico City with the help of an Anglo friend.

Stinetorf, Louise A., *A Charm for Paco's Mother*. New York: John Day, 1965. R.L. 5.3. Paco prays for a charm which will give his mother her sight.

Stinetorf, Louise A., *Manuel and the Pearl*. New York: John Day, 1966. R.L. 5.1. Manuel's father finds a great pearl but he is accused of stealing it. Manuel pitches in to clear his father's name.

Tarshis, Elizabeth K., *Village That Learned to Read*. Boston: Houghton, 1941. R.L. 4-5. Once it got started, the entire community wanted to learn to read.

Waltrip, Lela and Rufus, *White Harvest*. New York: McKay, 1960. R.L. 4-5. Susan, daughter of a migrant worker, longs to stay in one school long enough to make friends.

(Jr.-Sr. H. S. Level)

Allen, Steve, *The Ground is Our Table*. New York: Doubleday, 1966. R.L. 7-8. This noted entertainer exposes the plight of migrant workers.

Bannon, J. F., *Spanish Conquistadors: Men or Devils*. New York: Holt, 1960. R.L. 7-8. Factual material.

de Trevino, Elizabeth B., *I, Juan de Pareja*. New York: Farrar, 1965. R.L. 8-9. Story of Velasquez, the Spanish painter and his Negro slave who was also an accomplished artist.

Lawrence, Mildred, *Good Morning, My Heart*. New York. Harcourt, 1957. R.L. 6-7. Jan is roused to action by discrimination against a Mexican girl.

Lewis, Oscar, *The Children of Sanchez*. New York: Random, 1961. R.L. 7-8. Each member of the family recounts his life and the effects of poverty upon him.

Means, Florence C., *Knock at the Door, Emmy*. Boston: Houghton, 1956. R.L. 6-7. Migrant life through the eyes of Emmy, a 15-year-old.

Roberts, Suzanne, *Gracie*. New York: Doubleday, 1965. R.L. 4. Teenage daughter of a migrant crop picker is forced to fight for her people's rights.

Steinbeck, John, *The Grapes of Wrath*. New York: Viking, 1939. (Paperback) R.L. 6-7. A family of migratory workers struggles to find itself in California.

Tebbel, John, *Men of the Revolution.* New York: Doubleday, 1969. R.L. 7-8. The lives of five great Mexican leaders.

Vavra, Robert, *Felipe, the Bullfighter.* New York: Harcourt, 1967. R.L. 5-6. True story of a Spanish boy who prepares to fight his first bull.

Wier, Ester, *The Loner.* New York: McKay, 1963. R.L. 6-7. A nameless, orphaned migrant child is taken in by a woman sheepherder and finds a sense of identity.

Wojciechowska, Maia, *Shadow of a Bull.* New York: Atheneum, 1964. R.L. 6-7. Manolo is being trained to be a bullfighter, as his father was, but against his own wishes.

Young, Bob and Jan, *Good-Bye Amigos.* New York: Messner, 1963. R.L. 6-7. Sympathy for striking migrant workers brings conflict for an adolescent.

Young, Bob and Jan, *Across the Tracks.* New York: Messner, 1958. R.L. 6.7. A high school girl of Mexican descent struggles against racial barriers in her school.

CHAPTER XII

Orientals

(Primary Level)

Baruch, Dorothy W. *Kobo and the Wishing Pictures*: *A Story from Japan.* Rutland: Tuttle, 1964. R.L. 3-4. Kobo doesn't know what to wish for when he joins the spring pilgrimage to the shrine.

Bishop, Claire H., *The Five Chinese Brothers.* New York: Coward, 1938. R.L. 2.2. A well-loved Chinese folktale.

Brown, J. P., *Surprise for Robin.* New York: Friendship, 1956. R.L. 3-4. A Japanese story.

Buell, Hal, *Festivals of Japan.* New York: Dodd, 1965. R.L. 4-5. Beautifully illustrated, with simple text.

Clarke, Mollie, *Momotaro.* Chicago: Follett, 1963. R.L. 3.5. The home life of a Japanese woodcutter family.

Cloutier, Helen, *The Many Names of Lee Lu.* Chicago: Whitman, 1960. R.L. 3.4. A simple story of Lee and his names and nicknames.

D'Amelio, Dan, *Taller than Bandai Mountain*: *The Story of Hideyo Noguchi.* New York: Viking, 1968. R.L. 3-4. A Japanese boy conquers poverty, physical deformity and class barriers to become a great scientist. A true account.

Dobrin, Arnold, *Taro and the Sea Turtles*: *A Tale of Japan.* New York: Coward, 1966. R.L. 3-4. Taro is moved to action by the mistreatment of turtles.

Dolch, Edward, *Stories from Japan.* Champaign: Garrard, 1960. R.L. 3.1. Simple Japanese folktales.

Dolch, Edward, *Stories from Old China.* Champaign: Garrard, 1964. R.L. 3.5. Simple Chinese folktales.

Flack, Marjorie and Wiese, Kurt, *The Story About Ping.* New York: Viking 1966. R.L. 3.8. Story of a Chinese duck who fishes for his master.

Forester, C.S., *Poo-Poo and the Dragons.* Boston: Little, 1968. R.L. 3-4. A humorous tale.

Headland, I. T., *Chinese Nursery Rhymes.* Old Tappan: Revell, 1967.

Keating, Norman, *Mr. Chu.* New York: Macmillan, 1965. R.L. 2-3. Simple story of a small boy and his elderly friend in New York's Chinatown.

Liang, Yen, *Tommy and Dee-Dee.* New York: Walck, 1953. R.L. 2-3. A simple story of two boys.

Lifton, Betty J., *Joji and the Dragon.* New York: Morrow, 1957. R.L. 3-4. A simple Japanese story of a crow and his best friends—the scarecrows.

Matsutani, Miyoko, *The Witch's Magic Cloth*. New York: Parents', 1969. R.L. 2-3. A folktale about a brave grandmother and a witch.

Nakagawa, Rieko, *A Blue Seed*. New York: Hastings, 1967. R.L. 2-3. A boy plants a blue seed and harvests a surprise.

Pine, T. S. and Levine, J., *The Chinese Knew*. New York: McGraw-Hill, 1958. R.L. 3-4. Science as the Chinese knew it.

Politi, Leo, *Moy Moy*. New York: Scribner, 1960. R.L. 2-3. Moy Moy enjoys the Chinese New Year celebration in Los Angeles.

Wyndham, R., *Chinese Mother Goose Rhymes*. Cleveland: World, 1968.

Yoda, Junichi, *The Rolling Rice Ball*. New York: Parents', 1969. R.L. 2-3. A charming Japanese folktale.

Yolen, Jane, *The Emperor and the Kite*. Cleveland: World, 1967. R.L. 3-4. An heroic little Chinese girl rescues her father from evil men.

(Intermediate Levels)

Anderson, Joy, *The Pai-Pai Pig*. New York: Harcourt. 1967. R.L. 4-5. Festival time on Taiwan.

Appel, Benjamin, *Why the Chinese Are the Way They Are*. Boston: Little, 1968. R.L. 6-7. A social and political history of China.

Bonham, Frank, *Mystery in Little Tokyo*. New York: Dutton, 1966. R.L. 4-5. Two Japanese-American children visit their grandparents and become involved in mysterious happenings.

Boston, L. M., *A Stranger at Green Knowe*. New York: Harcourt, 1961. R.L. 5.4. Fanciful tale of a young Chinese.

Buck, Pearl S., *The Big Wave*. New York: Day, 1948. R.L. 4-5. Adventure in Japan.

Buck, Pearl S., *Chinese Children Next Door*. New York: Day, 1942. R.L. 4-5. Chinese neighbors raise some community reactions.

Buck, Pearl S., *Fairy Tales of the Orient*. New York: Simon and Schuster, 1965. R.L. 6.1.

Buck, Pearl S., *The Good Earth*. New York: Grosset, 1931. R.L. 6.5. Adult fiction laid in China.

Buck, Pearl S., *The Man Who Changed China*. New York: Random, 1953. R.L. 5.4. Biography of Sun-Yat-Sen: China's greatest leader.

Buehr, Walter, *The World of Marco Polo*. New York: Putnam, 1961. R.L. 6.1. Biography of the Italian adventurer who visited China.

Burleigh, David R., *Messenger from K'itai*. Chicago: Follett, 1964. R.L. 5.1. Semi-historical material on China.

Caldwell, John C. and Elsie, *Our Neighbors in Japan*. New York: John Day, 1960. R.L. 4.1. An introduction to the Japanese way of life.

Cavanna, Betty, *Jenny Kimura*. New York: Morrow, 1964. R.L. 6-7. Jenny visits her grandmother in America.

Chrisman, Arthur B., *Shen of the Sea*. New York: Dutton, 1966. R.L. 6.0 Newbery Award book. An excellent story.

Darbois, Dominique, *Kai Ming, Boy of Hong Kong*. Chicago: Follett, 1960. R.L. 4.7. The life of people in Hong Kong who live on the junks.

Darbois, Dominique, *Noriko Girl of Japan*. Chicago: Follett, 1964. R.L. 5.2. Tale of a young Japanese girl and her family.

Dolch, Edward, *Far East Stories*. Champaign: Garrard, 1953. R.L. 4.2. Folk tales from five of the Far Eastern countries.

Dupuy, Trevor N., Col. U.S. Army, Ret., *Asiatic Land Battles: Allied Victories in China and Burma*. New York: Watts, 1963. R.L. 6.1. An official account of the Allied campaigns in China and Burma.

Eldridge, Ethel J., *Yen-Foh—A Chinese Boy*. Chicago: Whitman, 1935. R.L. 4.5. A Chinese folk tale.

Flory, Jane, *One Hundred and Eight Bells*. Boston: Houghton, 1963. R.L. 4-5. Living in modern Tokyo presents typical big city problems for Setsuko.

Geis, Darlene, *Let's Travel in Japan*. New York: Travel Press, 1960. R.L. 6.4. Travel book offering simple history and geography matter on Japan.

Glasgow, Aline, *Old Wind and Liu Li-San*. New York: Harvey, 1962. R.L. 5.0. Liu is left alone in the house, but admits an old stranger. Later she is rewarded for her kindness. Based on a Chinese folktale.

Godden, Rumer, *Miss Happiness and Miss Flower*. New York: Viking, 1960. R.L. 4.7. Japanese doll story.

Graves, Charles P., *Marco Polo*. Champaign: Garrard, 1963. R.L. 4.2. Biography of the Italian adventurer.

Gray, Elizabeth J., *The Cheerful Heart*. New York: Viking, 1959. R.L. 4.8. Japanese family life in Modern Japan.

Hall, Elvajean, *Hong Kong*. Chicago: Rand, 1967. R.L. 4-5. Well illustrated and simply written informational matter.

Hamada, Hirosuke, *The Tears of the Dragon*. New York: Parents, 1967. R.L. 4.8. Story of a dragon who terrorized the people. Through the love and understanding of a little boy he became a happy dragon boat for the pleasure of the villagers.

Handforth, Thomas, *Mei Li*. New York: Doubleday, 1938. R.L. 4.5. A favorite Chinese folk tale.

Hawkes, Hester, *Tami's New House*. New York: Coward, 1955. R.L. 4-5. Japanese daily life.

Hawkinson, Lucy, *Dance, Dance, Amy-Chan*. Chicago: Whitman, 1964. R.L. 4.4. Amy and Susie visit their grandparents and learn more about the customs of their homeland.

Hayes, Florence, *The Boy in the 49th Seat*. New York: Random, 1963. R.L. 4.1. The people and customs of Japan woven into a fictional account.

Herrmanns, Ralph, *Lee Lan Flies the Dragon Kite*. New York: Harcourt, 1962. R.L. 4.5. Fishing with a kite, Chinese style, by children who live on a junk.

Ishie, Momoko, *The Dolls' Day for Yoshiko*. Chicago: Follett, 1966. R.L. 4.8. Story of Japanese custom of the dolls' festival.

Jakeman, Alan, *Getting to Know Japan*. New York: Coward, 1960. R.L. 5.0. Factual material on Japan.

Joy, Charles R., *Getting to Know the Two Chinas*. New York: Coward,

1960. R.L. 5.0. It tells about the people, land, economy, and life in China today.

Judson, Clara I., *The Green Ginger Jar*. Boston: Houghton Mifflin, 1949. R.L. 5.4. A favorite Chinese mystery story.

Kim, Yong-ik, *Blue in the Seed*. Boston: Little, 1964. R.L. 4-5. Rebellious Chun Bok, the only blue-eyed boy in his Korean class solves the problem of being different.

Lamb, Harold, *Genghis Khan and the Mongol Horde*. New York: Random, 1954. R.L. 5.2. Semi-historical account of the great conqueror.

Larson, Joan P., *Visit with Us in Japan*. Englewood Cliffs: Prentice-Hall, 1964. R.L. 5-6. Japanese family life and customs as viewed by American tourists.

Lattimore, Eleanor F., *Chinese Daughter*. New York: Morrow, 1960. R.L. 5-6. Chinese family life.

Lewis, Elizabeth F., *Young Fu of the Upper Yangtze*. New York: Holt, 1960. R.L. 5.6. An adventure story laid in China.

Liao, H. Y. and Bryan, D., *Let's Visit China*. Toronto: Burke, 1966. R.L. 5-6. A travel book introducing the reader to the sights of China.

Liu, Beatrice, *Little Wu and the Watermelons*. Chicago: Follett, 1954. R.L. 5.6. A Chinese folktale.

Lum, Peter, *Great Day in China*. New York: Abelard, 1963. R.L. 4-5. A little boy welcomes kite-flying, fireworks and the new Kitchen God.

Mandel, Oscar, *Chi Po and the Sorcerer*. Rutland: Tuttle, 1964. R.L. 5-6. Account of China's great painter Chi Po-Shih, with excellent pictures.

Masters, Robert V., *Japan—in Pictures*. New York: Sterling, 1966. R.L. 6.4. A pictorial geography of Japan.

Matsuno, Masako, *Chie and the Sports Day*. Cleveland: World, 1965. R.L. 4-5. A Japanese girl proves that sisters can be very nice.

Matsuno, Masako, *Taro and the Tofu*. Cleveland: World, 1962. R.L. 4-5. Taro takes a frightening night journey to return the money belonging to the storekeeper.

Mears, Helen, *First Book of Japan*. New York: Watts, 1953. R.L. 4.9. Factual material on Japan's history and geography.

Ness, Evaline, *A Double Discovery*. New York: Scribner, 1965. R.L. 4-5. Adventures of a Japanese boy, a wild pony and a monkey.

Oakes, Vanya, *Willy Wong American*. New York: Messner, 1951. R.L. 5-6. Willy learns to live within the cultures of his school and that of his grandfather.

Petersham, Maud and Miska, *Let's Learn About Silk*. New York: Harvey, 1967. R.L. 5.5. Factual material on the silk industry.

Piggott, Juliet, *Great Day in Japan: The Bigger Fish*. New York: Abelard, 1962. R.L. 5.1. Informational matter on Japan.

Piggott, Juliet, *Japanese Fairy Tales*. Chicago; Follett, 1967. R.L. 5.2. Favorite fairy tales from Japan.

Price, Olive, *The Story of Marco Polo*. New York: Grosset, 1953. R.L. 4.6. A simple biography of the Italian adventurer.

Rambeau, John and Nancy, *China Boy*. San Francisco: Field. R.L. 4-5. Story of a Chinese boy, written to portray the contributions of his group to America.

Rugoff, Milton, *Marco Polo's Adventures in China*. New York: American Heritage, 1964. R.L. 5.9. An authentic, illustrated book on Marco Polo's activities in China.

Sheldon, Walter J., *The Key to Tokyo*. Philadelphia: Lippincott, 1962. R.L. 4-5. Tokyo, the old and the new; the oriental and the western aspects of the city.

Sherer, Mary H., *Ho Fills the Rice Barrel*. Chicago: Follett, 1957. R.L. 5.2. A fictional story of family life in China.

Slobodkin, Louis, *Yasu and the Strangers*. New York: Macmillan, 1965. R.L. 5-6. Two American and a Japanese boy get lost together during Cherry Blossom time in Japan.

Spencer, Cornelia, *The Land of the Chinese People*. Philadelphia: Lippincott, 1964. R.L. 5.4. A simple history and geography book on China.

Spencer, Cornelia, *China's Leaders: In Ideas and Action*. New York: Macrae, 1966. R.L. 5-6. Lives of 12 great Chinese leaders.

Spencer, Cornelia, *The Yangtze; China's River Highway*. Champaign: Garrard, 1963. R.L. 5.0. This river is the life line of China.

Stuart, B., *Come Along to China*. Minneapolis: Denison, 1967. R.L. 5-6. Factual material on the great land of China.

Toland, John, *The Flying Tigers*. New York: Random, 1963. R.L. 5.3. Biography of General Chennault and his immortal Flying Tigers of World War II.

Treffinger, Carolyn, *Li Lun, Lad of Courage*. New York: Abingdon, 1947. R.L. 4-5. Story of an heroic Chinese boy.

Uchida, Yoshiko, *In-Between Miya*. New York: Scribner, 1967. R.L. 5-6. A Japanese girl grows in integrity.

Uchida, Yoshiko, *Mik and the Prowler*. New York: Harcourt, 1960. R.L. 5-6. Japanese family life in the U.S.

Uchida, Yoshiko, *Sumi's Special Happening*. New York: Scribner, 1966. R.L. 4-5. A little girl helps the village's oldest man celebrate his birthday.

Walsh, Richard J., *Adventures and Discoveries of Marco Polo*. New York: Random, 1953. R.L. 5.0. An historical account of the travels of Marco Polo.

Watson, Jane, *Japan: Islands of the Rising Sun*. Champaign: Garrard, 1968. R.L. 4.0. Simple stories of Japanese life.

Whitney, Phyllis A., *Secret of the Samurai Sword*. Philadelphia: Westminster. R.L. 5.2. A fantasy story with elements of mystery.

Yashima, Taro, *Crow Boy*. New York: Viking, 1955. R.L. 4.5. Story of a shy young Japanese boy who was ignored by his classmates until they found out he had much to share with them.

Yashima, Taro, *Umbrella*. New York: Viking, 1958. R.L. 4.3. A runner-up for the Caldecott Award, a picture-story of Japan.

Yashima, Taro, *The Village Tree*. Viking: New York, 1953. R.L. 4.4. Picture-story of the play of Japanese children.

(Jr.-Sr. H.S. Levels)

Bonham, Frank, *Burma Rifles: A Story of Merrill's Marauders*. New York: Crowell, 1960. R.L. 7-8. Jerry Harada is released from an American relocation center to serve as an interpreter in the war in Burma.

Breckenfeld, Vivian G., *The Two Worlds of Noriko*. New York: Doubleday, 1966. R.L. 7-8. Noriko receives a gift of a trip to see her grandparents upon graduation from college. A good comparison of Japanese and American ways.

Goldston, Robert, *The Rise of Red China*. Indianapolis: Bobbs, 1967. R.L. 7.1. Semi-historical account of the growth of Communism in China.

Harrington, Lyn, *China and the Chinese*. New York: Nelson, 1966. R.L. 6-7. Present-day China.

Haugaard, Kay, *Myeko's Gift*. New York: Abelard, 1966. R.L. 6-7. Myeko, newly arrived from Japan, finds that being different is not necessarily a handicap.

Kinmond, William, *The First Book of Communist China*: New York: Watts, 1962. R.L. 6.3. Informational material on Communist China.

Leathers, Noel L., *The Japanese in America*. Cincinnati: McCormick-Mathers, 1967. R.L. 7-8. Story of the attitudes toward the Japanese. and their contributions to American culture.

Lee, C.Y., *Land of the Golden Mountain*. Des Moines: Meredith, 1967. R.L. 7-8. A young chinese girl stows away on a ship to reach California during the Gold Rush days.

Lin, Yutang, *Chinese Way of Life*. Cleveland: World, 1959. R.L. 6-7. An interpretation of Chinese ways by a noted author.

Lin, Yutang, *Lady Wu*. New York: Putnam, 1965. R.L. 7-8. Semi-fictional Chinese story.

Martin, R. G., *A Boy from Nebraska*. New York: Harper, 1946. R.L. 5-6. A Nisei boy is rejected by his fellow-soldiers despite his heroism.

Means, Florence C., *The Moved Outers*. Boston: Houghton, 1945. R.L. 4-5. Story of a Japanese family in a relocation center.

Nach, James, *Hong Kong in Pictures*. (*Visual Geography Series*). New York: Sterling, 1963. R.L. 7.1. A pictorial geography of Hong Kong.

Newman, Robert, *The Japanese: People of the Three Treasures*. New York Atheneum, 1964. R.L. 8-9. Japanese culture, political and social history is covered briefly but interestingly.

Osada, Arata, *Children of the A-Bomb*. New York: Putnam, 1963. R.L. 6-7. In their own words, victims of the Hiroshima bombing tell it like it was. A shocking account.

Scott, J., *China—The Hungry Dragon*. New York: Parents, 167. R.L. 6-7. Background on history and culture.

Strachan, Margaret P., *Patience and a Mulberry Leaf*. New York: Washburn, 162. R.L. 6-7. Oriental and Caucasian high school youngsters learn to live together.

Tregaskis, R., *China Bomb*. New York: Doubleday, 1967. (Paperback) R.L. 7-8. The story of China's development of an atomic bomb.

CHAPTER XIII

Puerto-Ricans

Archibald, Joe, *Big League Busher*. New York: Macrae, 1963. R.L. 7-8. Ernie learns from Alguno the values of a struggle for a professional baseball career.

Baker, Nina B., *Juan Ponce de Leon*. New York: Knopf, 1957. R.L. 5-6. Biography of the great explorer.

Belpré, Pura, *Perez Y Martina*. New York: Warne, 1966. A popular Puerto-Rican folktale about a cockroach and her love for a mouse, translated into Spanish.

Belpré, Pura, *The Tiger and the Rabbit*. Philadelphia: Lippincott, 1965. R. 4-5. Eighteen Puerto-Rican folk tales.

Bishop, Curtis, *Little League Amigo*. Philadelphia: Lippincott, 1964. R.L. 6-7. Carlos, a refugee from Cuba, must conquer his pride before becoming a good little leaguer.

Brenner, Barbara, *Barto Takes the Subway*. New York: Knopf, 1961. R.L. 5-6. A Puerto Rican boy and his sister experience their first subway ride.

Christopher, Matthew F., *Baseball Flyhawk*. Boston: Little, 1963. R.L. 3-4. Chico feels that he must overcompensate for being a Puerto Rican, if he is to succeed in baseball.

Colman, Hilda, *The Girl from Puerto Rico*. New York: Morrow, 1961. (Paperback) R.L. 6-7. Problems and disappointments of a Puerto Rican family that moves to New York.

Colorado, Antonio J., *First Book of Puerto Rico*. New York: Watts, 1965. Photographs and maps enliven this social studies resource book.

Edell, Celeste, *A Present from Rosita*. New York: Messner, 1952. (Paperback) R.L. 7. Rosita finds life in New York quite different than that in her Puerto Rican village.

Felt, Sue, *Rosa-Too-Little*. New York: Doubleday, 1950. R.L. 4-5. A little Puerto Rican girl tries to join the public library.

Fleischman, H. Samuel, *Gang Girl*. New York: Doubleday, 1967. R.L. 4. Maria Gomez, from Spanish Harlem, tries to find a better way of life than being a gang member.

Heuman, William, *City High Five*. New York: Dodd, 1964. R.L. 6-7. Mike and his Puerto Rican friend Pedro experience the effects of prejudice that spoil their basketball fun.

Jackson, Jesse, *Room for Randy*. New York: Friendship, 1959. R.L. 5-6. Puerto Rican and Negro children are transferred to another school under difficult conditions.

Keats, Ezra J. and Cherr, Pat, *My Dog is Lost*. New York: Crowell, 1960. R.L. 4-5. Children of Harlem join in a search for Pepito.

Lewiton. Mina, *Candita's Choice*. New York: Harper, 1959. R.L. 5-6. Candita, a Puerto Rican girl, learns to speak English when the situation demands.

Lewiton, Mina, *That Bad Carlos*. New York: Harper, 1964. R.L. 4-5. Carlos finds his new home in New York demands many changes in his behavior.

Lexau, Joan M., *Jose's Christmas Secret*. New York: Dial, 1963. R.L. 3-4. Jose and his family learn to like New York City.

Lexau, Joan, *Maria*. New York: Dial, 1964. R.L. 2-3. The family sacrifices a treasure to secure a doll for Maria.

Mann, Peggy, *The Street of the Flower Boxes*. New York: Coward, 1966. R.L. 5.1. Carlos tends to the flowers of the neighborhood and eventually finds his place in the multi-racial setting.

Manning. Jack, *Young Puerto Rico*. New York: Dodd, 1962. R.L. 3-4. An introduction to the schools, housing and industry of Puerto Rico.

McGuire, Edna, *Puerto Rico*. New York: Macmillan, 1963. R.L. 7-8. The history, people and their progress in present-day Puerto Rico.

Norris, Marianna, *Father and Son for Freedom*. New York: Dodd, 1968. R. 7-8. Story of Munoz Marin, Puerto Rico's greatest leader.

Schloat, G. W., *Maria and Ramon: A Girl and Boy of Puerto Rico*. New York: Knopf, 1966. R.L. 4-5. Typical day in a Puerto Rican town.

Speevack, Yetta, *The Spider Plant*. New York: Atheneum, 1965. R.L. 4-5. Carmen gradually wins acceptance in a big city school.

Sterling. Philip, *The Quiet Rebels*. New York: Doubleday, 1968. R.L. 7-8. The biographies of four of Puerto Rico's leading figures.

Stolz, Mary S. *The Noonday Friends*. New York: Harper, 1965. R.L. 5-6. Franny learns to live with poverty with the aid of her Puerto Rican family.

Talbot, Charlene J., *Tomas Takes Charge*. New York: Lothrop, 1966. R.L. 5-6. Two motherless Puerto Rican children try to establish a life of their own.

Tor, Regina, *Getting to Know Puerto Rico*. New York: Coward, 1955. R.L. 4-5. Simple, informational material.

CHAPTER XIV

Social Science and Science

(Primary Level)

Barr, Jene, *What Can Money Do?* Chicago: Whitman, 1967. R.L. 2.8. Simple informational material on the uses of money in commerce and industry.

Edwards, Mary M., *World Friends: The City's Children.* New York: Friendship, 1963. Picture album of 15 photographs with descriptive text.

Goldin, Augusta, *Straight Hair, Curly Hair.* New York: Crowell, 1966. R.L. 3-4. A scientific, informational book.

Grossbart, Francine B., *A Big City.* New York: Harper, 1966. R.L. 2-3. An alphabet book based on the objects of the city.

Hoffman, Elaine and Hefflefinger, Jane, *About Friendly Helpers Around Town.* Chicago: Melmont, 1967. R.L. 2.6. Community workers and helpers—factual accounts.

Holtan, Gene, *At the Bank.* Chicago: Melmont, 1959. R.L. 3.1. Workings of a city bank, in simple language.

Leavitt, Jerome E., *America and Its Indians.* Chicago: Childrens Press, 1962. R.L. 3-4. A child's history of American Indians.

Map Skills for Today. Columbus: American Education. R.L. 2-6. A series of workbooks for successive elementary grades. A two book series for junior high is also offered.

Miner, O. I. S., *The True Book of Our Post Office and Its Helpers.* Chicago: Childrens Press, 1955. R.L. 3.6. Work of the Post Office and its helpers; city life and transportation.

Neurath, Marie, *They Lived Like This in Ancient Africa.* New York: Watts, 1967. R.L. 3-4. Everyday life of the ancient Africans.

Newman, S. and Sherman, D., *About People Who Run Your City.* Chicago: Melmont, R.L. 3.8. A simple explanation of city government.

Parish, Peggy, *Let's Be Indians.* New York: Harper, 1962. R.L. 3-4. Indian games, dress-up activities, etc.

Phillips, Eleanor, *About the Driver of a Bus.* Chicago: Melmont, 1963. R.L. 2.9. The work of the city bus driver.

Roy, Bert, *We Live in the City.* New York: Childrens Press, 1963. R.L. 3-4. A child's view of Chicago and its places of interest.

Sasek, M., *This Is New York.* New York: Macmillan, 1960. R.L. 3-4. A humorous presentation of various aspects of New York City.

Schneider, Herman and Nina, *Let's Look Under the City.* New York: Scott, 1954. R.L. 3-4. The underground works of the city.

Showers, Paul, *Look at Your Eyes*. New York: Crowell, 1962. R.L. 2-3. A simple science story in which the only character is a curious Negro boy.

Smith, Eunice Y., *Denny's Story*. Chicago: Whitman, 1952. R.L. 2.6. Simple stories of the work of community helpers.

Stanek, Muriel and Johnson, Barbara, *How People Live in the Big City*. Chicago: Benefic, 1964. R.L. 2-3. Portrait of city life in simple style.

Udry, Janice M., *End of the Line*. Chicago: Whitman, 1962. R.L. 3.2. Semi-factual account of a city street car system.

Urell, Catherine, *Big City Homes*. Chicago: Follett, 1954. R.L. 3.0. Homes and other buildings in the city. Factual material.

Urell, Catherine, *The Big City and How It Grew*. Chicago: Follett, 1958. R.L. 3.5. How a big city starts and how it grows.

Urell, Catherine, *Big City Fun*. Chicago: Follett, 1953. R.L. 3.4. Play and fun activities in a big city.

Urell, Catherine, et al., *Big City Water Supply*. Chicago: Follett, 1953. R.L. 3.2. How the big city gets its water.

Urell, Catherine and Goldman, Lillian, *Big City Neighbors*. Chicago: Follett 1955. R.L. 2.8. Family life in a large city.

Williams, Barbara, *I Know a Mayor*. New York: Putnam, 1967. R.L. 3.3. How the city is governed.

Year's Pictorial History of the American Negro. Maplewood, N.J.: C. S. Hammond, 1965.

(Intermediate Level)

Adler, Irving and Ruth, *Communication*. New York: John Day, 1967. R.L. 5.5. Factual material on the communication systems within a city.

Alpenfels, Ethel J., *Sense and Nonsense about Race*. New York: Friendship, 1959. R.L. 5-6. In answer to children's questions.

An American Album. Chicago: Science Research. Offers kit of 300 reading selections in American history graded from 3rd to 9th grade.

Bernheim, Marc and Evelyne, *From Bush to City: A Look at the New Africa*. New York: Harcourt, 1966. R.L. 6-7. Text and many photographs give excellent overview of the life of modern Africa.

Bleeker, Sonia, *The Masai Herders of East Africa*. New York: Morrow, 1966. R.L. 5.8. The life of the Masai herders of East Africa.

Bleeker, Sonia. *The Ashanti of Ghana*. New York: Morrow, 1966. R.L. 4.9. Peoples of Ghana, their life and ways.

Bowen, J. D., *The Island of Puerto Rico*. Philadelphia: Lippincott, 1968. R.L. 6-7. Factual, background information.

Brown, Jack and Vashti, *Proudly We Hail*. Boston: Houghton, 1968. R.L. 5-6. Negro history book for elementary schools.

Caldwell, John C. and Elsie F., *Our Neighbors in Africa*. New York: John Day, 1961. R.L. 4.5.

Century, *Negro-American Heritage*. Chicago: Century Consultants. R.L. 5-6. Profusely illustrated, biographical material on Negro-Americans.

Chu, Daniel and Skinner, Elliott, P., *A Glorious Age in Africa: The Story*

of Three Great African Empires. New York: Doubleday, 1965. R.L. 5-6.
Simple, informative material on the Sudanese empires.

Cochrane, Joanna, *Let's Go to the United Nations Headquarters.* New
York: Putnam, 1958. R.L. 4.9. An informative visit to the headquarters
of the United Nations.

Colby, C. B., *Night People.* New York: Coward, 1961. R.L. 6.0. Factual
account of the workers at night in a great city.

Dorian Edith, *Hockahey! American Indians Now and Then.* New York:
McGraw-Hill, 1957. R.L. 5-6. Attempts to cover the customs and leaders
of the seven Indian groups of our country.

Drisko, Carol and Topping, Edgar A., *Unfinished March.* New York: Doubleday, 1967. R.L. 6. The progress of the American black from Recon-
struction period to World War II.

Epstein, Edna, *The First Book of the United Nations.* New York: Watts,
1966. R.L. 6.0. A simple presentation of the work, and purposes of the
United Nations.

Faulkner, H. V. and Rosenthal, H., *A Visual History of the United States.*
New York: McGraw-Hill, 1961. R.L. 5-6. Uses charts, graphs, diagrams
and pictures to make history readable.

Feigenbaum, Lawrence H., *This Is a Newspaper.* Chicago: Follett, 1965.
R.L. 4.0. The insides of a city newspaper.

Fisher, Lois, *You and the United Nations.* Chicago: Children, 1947. R.L.
4.9. The work of the international organization is presented in simple
terms.

Garelick, May, *Manhattan Island.* New York: Crowell, 1957. R.L. 5-5.
Factual material on New York City.

Goldman, Peter, *Civil Rights: The Challenge of the Fourteenth Amendment.* New York: Coward, 1965. R.L. 6-7. Factual, background material.

Gunther, John, *Meet South Africa.* New York: Harper, 1955. R.L. 6.4.
Travel author writes about South Africa.

Hoffman, Elaine and Hefflefinger, *About Helpers Who Work at Night.*
Chicago: Melmont, 1963. R.L. 4.4. Night workers in a large city.

Hughes, Langston, *The First Book of Africa.* New York: Watts, 1964.
R.L. 5. History, government and problems of the new nations of Africa.

Hughes, Langston, *The First Book of the West Indies.* New York: Watts,
1956. R.L. 5-6. Each group of islands is discussed in terms of its history,
people and ways of living.

Hughes, Langston and Meltzer, Milton, *A Pictorial History of the Negro
in America.* New York: Crown, 1968. R.L. 4-5.

Kaye, Geraldine, *Great Day in Ghana—Kwasi Goes to Town.* New York:
Abelard, 1962. R.L. 4.7. Life in Ghana today.

Landes, Ruth, *Latin Americans of the Southwest.* St. Louis: Webster,
1965. (Paperback). Biographical material.

Lavine, David, *Under the City.* New York: Doubleday, 1967. R.L. 4-5.
A look at the maze of activities that go on under the city.

Lerner, Marguerite R., *Red Man, White Man, African Chief.* New York:
Lerner, 1961. R.L. 4-5. A simple explanation of skin coloring.

McCarthy, Agnes, *Let's Go to Vote*. New York: Putnam, 1962. R.L. 4.9. How our government works.

McIntire, Alta and Hill, Wilhelmina, *Working Together*. Chicago: Follett, 1962. R.L. 4.3. Workers of the community.

McNeer, May, *The American Indian Story*. New York: Farrar, 1963. R.L. 4-5. The history of the North American Indian.

Peet, Creighton, *The First Book of Skyscrapers*. New York: Watts, 1964. R.L. 6.3. All about skyscrapers.

Pine, Tillie S. and Levine, Joseph, *The Africans Knew*. New York: McGraw Hill, 1967. R.L. 4.7. Science as the Africans knew it.

Platt, Kin, *Big Max*. New York: Harper, 1965. R.L. 4.1. The work of the police department of a large city.

Quinn, Vernon, *Picture Map Geography of Africa*. Philadelphia: Lippincott, 1964. Reference material to thirty independent countries of Africa.

Radlauer, Ruth S., *About Men at Work*. Chicago: Melmont, 1967. R.L. 4.0. Brief descriptions of the activities of various workers of the community.

Romano, Louis G., and Georgiady, Nicholas P., *This Is a Department Store*. Chicago: Follett, 1962. R.L. 4.8. The workings of a large department store in a big city.

Schwartz. Alvin, *The City and Its People*. New York: Dutton, 1967. R.L. 4-5. The story of one city's government.

Shackelford, Jane D., *First Book of Negro History*. Washington: Associated, 1968. R.L. 4-5. A child's story of Negro history.

Slobodkin, Louis, *Read About the Busman*. New York: Watts, 1967. R.L. 4-5. A simple history of transportation and the work of the bus driver. See also the author's similar books on the policeman, the postman and the fireman.

Speiser, Jean, *Unicef and the World*. New York: John Day, 1965. R.L. 4.6. The activities of UNICEF in the areas of health and education.

Spencer, Cornelia, *Made in China: The Story of China's Expression*. New York: Knopf, 1943. R.L. 6-7. China's art and culture.

Sterne, Emma G., *I Have a Dream*. New York: Knopf, 1965. R.L. 8-9. A high moment in the life of each of ten leaders in the Civil Rights movement.

Table and Graph Skills. Columbus: American Education. R.L. 3-6. A series of four workbooks for successive grades.

Watson, Jane W., *Nigeria—Republic of a Hundred Kings*. Champaign: Garrard, 1967. R.L. 4.0. History of Nigeria.

Wattenberg, Ben, and Smith, Ralph L., *New Nations of Africa*. New York: Hart, 1963. R.L. 6.4. Brief stories of the new African nations.

Wolfe, Louis, *Let's Go to a City Hall*. New York: Putnam, 1958. R.L. 4.8. Let's find out how our city is governed.

Woodson, Carter C., and Wesley, Charles H., *Second Book of Negro History*. Washington: Associated, 1968. R.L. 5-6. A simple history for intermediate grades of Negro makers of history.

(Jr.-Sr. H. S. Level)

Abramowitz, Jack, *American History Study Lessons*. Chicago: Follett, 1963. Nine separately collated units—each emphasizing fundamental ideas and events in American history. Adapted for poor readers.

Abramowitz, Jack, *Study Lessons on Documents of Freedom*: *The Declaration of Independence, the Constitution, the Bill of Rights*. Chicago: Follett, 1964. Social studies materials for educationally-deprived students. Written at a low reading level.

Abramowitz, Jack, *World History Study Lessons*. Chicago: Follett, 1963. Nine separately collated units. Adapted for poor readers.

Baxter, Zenobia L. and Marion, Ester A., *Your Life in a Big City*. St. Louis: Webster, 1967. R.L. 6-7. Picture textbook on urban life.

Bennett, Lerone, *Before the Mayflower*: *History of the Negro in America 1619-1966*. Chicago: Johnson, 1967. (Paperback) R.L. 7-8.

Buell, H., *The World of Red China*. New York: Dodd, 1967. R.L. 9-10. Traces the historical events leading to the revolution of Mao Tse-Tung.

Chambers, Bradford, compiler, *Chronicles of Negro Protest*. New York: Parents Magazine, 1968. R.L. 7. Selected historical documents and other materials dealing with racial struggle in the U.S.

Chu, Daniel and Samuel, *Passage to the Golden Gate*. New York: Doubleday, 1967. R.L. 7-8. History of the Chinese in America to 1910.

Clemons, Lulamae: Hollitz, Erwin and Gardner, Gordon, *The American Negro*. St. Louis: Webster, 1965. (Paperback). R.L. 6-7. Biographical materials.

Cuban, Larry, *The Negro in America*. Chicago: Scott, Foresman, 1964. R.L. 6-7. For use as resource material in social studies.

Davidson, Basil, *Black Mother*: *The Years of the African Slave Trade*. Boston: Little, 1961. R.L. 8-9. A carefully researched and very readable account of the slave era.

Davidson, Basil, *A Guide to African History*. New York: Doubleday, 1965. R.L. 6-7. From bondage to independence.

Dobler, L. and Brown, W. A., *Great Rulers of the African Past*. New York: Doubleday. R.L. 6.0. Biographies of five great African rulers in the 14-17th centuries.

Du Bois, W. E. B., *The Souls of Black Folk*. Greenwich: Fawcett. (Paperback). R.L. 7-8. A story of the bitter struggle for human rights by an early Negro scholar and historian.

Dunbar, Ernest, *Black Expatriates*. New York: Dutton, 1968. R.L. 8-9. Story of 15 American blacks who went into exile from America.

Elkins, Stanley M., *Slavery*. Chicago: University of Chicago, 1969. R.L. 7-8. Study of the impact of slavery upon Negro personality and life.

Embree, E. R., *Indians of the Americas*. Boston: Houghton-Mifflin, 1939. R.L. 8-9. Sympathetic description of all major Indian groups in the Western Hemisphere.

Fletcher, Sydney E., *The American Indians*. New York: Grosset, 1954. Background information and illustrations.

Fulks, Bryan, *Black Struggle*: *A History of the Negro in America*. New York: Dell, 1969. (Paperback). R.L. 7-8. Traces history of the Negro in America from the slavery period to the present.

Giddings, J. L., *Ancient Men of the Arctic*. New York: Knopf, 1967. R.L. 9-10. A careful historical account of Eskimo history, based on the expeditions of the author and others.

Grant, Joanne, *Black Protest*. Greenwich, Fawcett. R.L. 8-9. Documentary materials covering three and one-half centuries of black protest.

Griffin, Ella, *Africa Today*: *Continent in a Hurry*. New York: Coward, 1962. R.L. 7-8. A 19-year-old college student reports on the new countries of Africa, as he saw them.

Hennessy, M., and Sauter, E., Jr., *Sword of the Hausas*. New York: Washburn, 1964. R.L. 6-7. Story of the Hausas, a Nigerian regiment in World War II.

Hoff, Rhoda, *America's Immigrants*: *Adventures in Eyewitness History*. New York: Walck, 1967. R.L. 7-8. Firsthand accounts by new Americans.

Hughes, John, *The New Face of Africa*: *South of the Sahara*. New York: McKay, 1961. R.L. 7-8. Background material from an American journalist on the developing African nations.

Kaula, Edna, *The Land and People of Rhodesia*. Philadelphia: Lippincott, 1967. R.L. 7-8. The land, the people, the problems of this country.

Leinward, Gerald, editor, *Problems of American Society*. New York: Washington Square. R.L. 7-8. A series of paperbacks on urban problems such as: The Negro; Civil Rights; Crime; Poverty; Drugs; Schools; Pollution.

Lowenthal, Leo and Guterman, Norbert, *Prophets of Deceit*. New York: Harper, 1949. (Paperback) R.L. 7-8. Analyzes professional agitators—their speeches, writings and techniques.

McCarthy, Agnes and Reddick, Lawrence, *Worth Fighting For*. New York: Doubleday, 1965. R.L. 6.0. Minority groups and their contributions to the development of America.

McCormick-Mathers, *In America Series*. Cincinnati: McCormick-Mathers. R.L. 7-8. A twenty-volume series on immigrant groups, their contributions to America, and their search for human rights.

Mooney, Chase C., *Civil Rights and Liberties*. Boston: Holt, 1964. (Paperback). R.L. 7-8. Resource materials for social studies classes.

Patrick, John J., *The Progress of the Afro-American*. Westchester, Illinois: Benefic Press, 1968. R.L. 6-7. Documentary materials, charts, speeches, letters and diaries illustrate the race questions of today.

Pei, Mario A., *Our National Heritage*. Boston: Houghton, 1965. R.L. 7-8. Contributions of the many groups that compose America.

Ritter, Ed and Helen, and Spector, Stanley, *Our Oriental Americans*. St. Louis: Webster, 1965. R.L. 6-7. Biographical and historical material.

Salk, E. A., editor, *A Layman's Guide to Negro History*. New York: McGraw-Hill, 1967. R.L. 7-8. An overview of Negro history.

Savage, Katherine, *The Story of Africa South of the Sahara*. New York: Walck, 1961. R.L. 7-8. Struggles of the young African nations.

Schecter, Betty, *The Peaceable Revolution*. Boston: Houghton, 1963. R.L.

7-8. The story of nonviolent resistance from Thoreau, to Gandhi to present-day America.

Scholastic Book Services, *Curriculum Unit—Prejudice*. Englewood Cliffs: Scholastic. A kit of 61 paperbacks ranging in difficulty from 4-6; for use in middle grades in social studies.

Sterling, Dorothy, *Tear Down the Walls: A History of the American Civil Rights Movement*. New York: Doubleday, 1968.

Teitz, Ronald, *The Black American Past and Present*. Wilkinsburg, Pa.: Hayes School Publishing. A study unit on the heritage, history, culture and achievements of Black Americans. Spirit masters and transparencies available.

Thompson, Eliza B., *Africa: Past and Present*. Boston: Houghton, 1966. R.L. 6-7. A very readable history of Africa.

Turnbull, Colin M., *Tradition and Change in African Tribal Life*. Cleveland: World, 1966. R.L. 7-8. Changes in tribal cultures.

Turner, Mary, *We, Too Belong: An Anthology about the Minorities in America*. New York: Dell, 1969. (Paperback). R.L. 7-8. A collection of essays and other writings.

Vlahos, Olivia, *African Beginnings*. New York: Viking, 1967. R.L. 7-8. Africa's past comes alive in an up-to-date account.

Wade, Richard C., editor, *The Negro in American Life: Selected Readings*. Boston: Houghton, 1965. (Paperback). Intended as resource material for social studies.

Waskow, A. I., *From Race Riot to Sit-In, 1919 and the 1960's*. New York: Doubleday, 1967. R.L. 8-9. A review of the Civil Rights movement.

Williams, John A., *This Is My Country Too*. Cleveland: World. (Paperback) R.L. 7-8. A Negro's demand for recognition as an American first-class citizen.

Woodson, Carter G., *Education of the Negro Prior to 1861*. Washington: Associated Publishers. (Paperback). Historical review of Negro education prior to the Civil War.

Woodson, Carter G. and Wesley, Charles H., *Third Book of Negro History*. Washington: Associated, 1968. A history for senior high school students. See also *Fourth Book of Negro History,* which is offered for the college level student.

Wright, Betty A., *Urban Education Studies*. New York: Day, 1965. Series of albums, each about a theme of city life; chartsize photographs of urban scenes and activities.

CHAPTER XV

Reading Improvement

(Primary Level)

Bank Street College of Education, *The Bank Street Readers*. New York: Macmillan. A basic reading series from preprimer to third grade for urban children.

Baugh, Dolores M., and Marjorie P. Pulsifer, *Chandler Language-Experience Readers*. San Francisco: Chandler, 1964-66 (Paperback). Readers for urban children based on the language experience approach.

Black, Millard H., etal., *Visual Experiences for Creative Growth*. Columbus: Merrill, 1967. Ten large pictures of children in physical activities. Lesson plan includes activities in coordination, language, rhyming, art, etc., to stimulate the language abilities of children lacking in experimental background.

Brown, Frank E., *Adventuring in the City*. New York: Globe, 1968. R.L. 4. Short stories with reading exercises.

Brown, Virginia, etal., *Skyline Series*. St. Louis: Webster, 1965. Primary stories of real interest to urban children. A realistic series.

Colonius, Lillian and Schroeder, Glenn W., *At the Library*. Chicago: Melmont, 1967. R.L. 3.3. Simple, semi-fictional account of the workings of a library.

Funk, Tom, *I Read Signs*. New York: Holiday, 1962. R. L. 2.1. Functional reading for the retarded or beginning reader.

Glendinning, Sally, *Jimmy and Joe Catch an Elephant*. and *Jimmy and Joe Find a Ghost*. Champaign: Garrard, 1969. R.L. 1.5. A pair of boys, one black and one white have simple adventures together.

Goldberg, Herman R., etal., *New Rochester Occupational Reading Series*. Chicago: Science Research. Primary reading level materials on vocational guidance.

Know Your World. Columbus: American Education. R.L. 2-3. A weekly newspaper offering such features as short stories, skill development exercises and reading tests.

Lancaster, Louise, *Introducing English*: *An Oral Pre-Reading Program for Spanish-Speaking Primary Pupils*. Boston: Houghton, Mifflin, 1966. Intended to lay a language foundation for bilingual children.

Lexau, Joan, *Olaf Reads*. New York: Dial, 1961. R.L. 2.1. Humorous story of a boy who doesn't read very well.

The Name of the Game. Jericho, N.Y.: New Dimensions in Education. A multi-media reading program for inner-city adolescents.

New York, New York. New York: Random House. A school newspaper reflecting the urban life of New York. Printed in five editions from kindergarten to junior high school.

News for You. Syracuse: Laubach Literacy. Parallel editions of weekly newspapers at grades 3-4 and 5-6.

Schueler, Nancy; Feldstein, Mark and Becker, Stanley, *The City Is My Home.* New York: John Day. Readers for urban children based on language experience approach.

Shafter, Fanny and George, *Words and Action: Role-Playing.* New York: Holt, 1967. Twenty large, dramatic pictures to stimulate verbal expression and role-playing, among young children.

Woolman, Myron, *Reading in High Gear.* Chicago: Science Research, 1964. A programmed developmental reading series.

Writer's Committee of the Great Cities School Improvement Program of the Detroit Public Schools, *City Schools Reading Program.* Chicago: Follett, (Paperback). A basic reading series from preprimer through second grade for urban children.

(Intermediate Level)

Orsborn, Peggy A., *The Meeting.* Chicago: Afro-American. A one act play based on a multi-ethnic theme. Boxed with 15 copies of the play and a teacher's guide.

Reading Success Series. Columbus: American Education. R.L. 4-6. Six basic reading skill workbooks for remedial pupils, ages 10-16. Emphasize word analysis and word meaning training.

(Jr.-Sr. H.S. Level)

Gershenfeld, Howard and Edwards, Burton Ardis, *Stories for Teen-Agers.* New York: Glove Book, 1965. Books one and two are offered on the 5-6th grade reading level; Book A on 3rd-4th grade level. Each is a collection of short stories adapted from current periodicals.

Lerner, Lillian and Moller, Margaret, *Vocational Reading Series.* Chicago: Follett, 1965. A series on vocations.

Neufeld, Rose Goldman, *Reading Fundamentals for Teen-Agers: A Workbook of Basic Skill Building.* New York: John Day, (Paperback) 1963.

Negro History Bulletin. Washington: Association for Study of Negro Life and History. A monthly offering features such as editorials, current events, biographies, book reviews, historical materials and many pictures.

Scholastic Book Services, *Reluctant Reader Libraries.* Englewood Cliffs: Scholastic. Collections of paperbacks.

Scope. Englewood Cliffs: Scholastic Magazines. A weekly intended for urban disadvantaged teenagers. Written at about 4-6 grade level.

Smith, Edwin H., *Reading Development.* Menlo Park: Addison-Wesley. Kit A, one of the 3 offered, is intended for adolescent poor readers. Kit includes diagnostic tests, reading selections graded in difficulty, exercises in skill development.

Spiegler, Charles G., editor, *Mainstream Books*. Columbus: Chas. E. Merrill. R.L. 4-7. Five paperback anthologies for inner-city youth.

Turner, Richard H., *The Turner-Livingston Communication Series*. Chicago: Follett, 1965-66. For the teenaged slow reader, a four book series.

Turner, Richard H., *The Turner-Livingston Reading Series*. Chicago: Follett, 1962. Six workbooks designed to improve reading skills by meeting the interests and activities of teen-age readers. Reading level, grades 5-6.

Zenith Books. New York: Doubleday. R.L. 6. A series of books about minority groups paralleling social science and English courses in the secondary school. Written especially for reluctant readers. For separate titles, see lists above.

CHAPTER XVI

Materials for Instructional Units in Art, Music, Literature and Human Relations Among Minority Groups

(Primary Level)

Brooks, Gwendolyn, *Bronzeville Boys and Girls*. New York: Harper, 1956. R.L. 3-4. A collection of poems about city children by the well-known Negro poet and Pulitzer Prize Winner.

Burden, Shirley, *I Wonder Why*. New York: Doubleday, 1963. Touches on the rejection of people because of race. Excellent photographs.

Cavanah, Frances, *Our Country's Freedom*. Chicago: Rand, 1966. R.L. 3-4. The struggles of minority groups to attain recognition and true freedom.

Hofmann, Charles, *American Indians Sing*. New York: John Day, 1967. R.L. 5.9. Music and songs of the American Indian.

Hofsinde, Robert, *Indian Costumes*. New York: Morrow, 1968.

Hofsinde, R., *Indian Sign Language*. New York: Morrow, 1956.

Hofsinde, Robert, *Indian Music Makers*. New York: Morrow, 1967. R.L. 5.7. Indian music, dances and songs as described by a recognized authority.

Indian and Eskimo Children. Washington: Bureau of Indian Affairs, 1967. R.L. 4.5. An inexpensive pamphlet.

Lewiton, Mina, *Faces Looking Up*. New York: Harper, 1960. R.L. 3-4. Stories and pictures of children in school in twelve different countries.

U.S. Committee for UNICEF, *Hi Neighbor*. New York: Hastings, 1961. R.L. 3-4. Children of other lands are introduced by pictures, songs, stories and maps.

Wherry, J., *Indian Masks and Myths of the American West*. New York: Funk and Wagnalls, 1968.

Whiting, Helen A., *Negro Folk-Tales*. Washington: Associated Publishers. R.L. 3-4. Folktales of Africa.

Wiese, Kurt, *You Can Write Chinese*. New York: Viking, 1945. R.L. 3-4. A simple introduction to Chinese writing.

(Intermediate Level)

Bealer, Alex W., *Picture-Skin Story*. New York: Holiday, 1957. R.L. 5-6. Indian writing.

Boatright, M. C., editor, *Mexican Border Ballads and Other Lore*. Dallas: Southern Methodist University Press, 1946.

Bontemps, Arna, *American Negro Poetry*. New York: Hill and Wang, 1964.

Bontemps, Arna, *Golden Slippers*. New York: Harper, 1941. An anthology of poetry written by American blacks.

Brewer, J. M., *American Negro Folklore*. Chicago: Quadrangle, 1968.

Brinton, Margaret C. et al., *Candles in the Dark*. Philadelphia: Philadelphia Yearly Meeting of Friends, 1964. R.L. 6-7. Anthology of 50 stories about people who put their beliefs about brotherhood into action.

Century Consultants, *Negro American Heritage*. Chicago: Century Consultants, 1968. R.L. 6-7. Background material on race relations.

Cohen, Robert, *The Color of Man*. New York: Random, 1968. R.L. 5-6. A book intended to promote better self-concept and pride in one's own race.

Colby, C.B., *First Bow and Arrow*. New York: Coward, 1955. R.L. 4-5. How to hunt and fish safely with bow and arrow.

Cullen, Countee, *On These I Stand*. New York: Harper, 1947. R.L. 6-7. What the poet considered to be the finest of his works.

Culver, Eloise, *Great American Negroes in Verse, 1723-1965*. Washington: Associated, 1966. R.L. 4-5. Short poems on Negro history from the time of slavery to the present.

De Angulo, J., *Indian Tales*. New York: Hill and Wang.

De Onis, H., *Spanish Stories and Tales*. New York: Washington, 1968.

Dietz, B. W. and Olatunji, M. B., *Musical Instruments of Africa*. New York: John Day, 1965. R.L. 5-6. Fascinating study of African music, accompanied by a record.

Doob, Leonard W., *A Crocodile Has Me by the Leg*. New York: Walker, 1967. Traditional poetry of Africa.

Dover, Cedric, *American Negro Art*. New York, N.Y. Graphic Society, 1965.

Dunbar, Paul L., *Little Brown Baby*. New York: Dodd, 1940. R.L. 5-6. A selection of the author's poems for children and young people.

Eoff, S.H. and King, P.C., *Spanish American Short Stories*. New York: Macmillan. R.L. 7-8.

Feiffer, Jules, *Feiffer on Civil Rights*. New York: B'nai B'rith, 1966. Sharp cartoons on the white man's thinking about Civil rights.

Fenner, Phyllis R., *The Dark and Bloody Ground*. New York: Morrow, 1963. R.L. 6-7. The contributions of various ethnic and racial groups to America's growth.

Fisher, Aileen and Rabe, Olive, *Human Rights Day*. New York: Crowell. 1966. R.L. 4-5. Man's quest for freedom is exemplified in this holiday.

Glubok, Shirley, *The Art of Africa*. New York: Harper, 1965. R.L. 5-6. Beautifully illustrated and simply written.

Glubok, Shirley, *The Art of the Eskimo*. New York: Harper, 1964. R.L. 6-7. Excellent illustrations and simple text.

Glubok, Shirley, *The Art of the North American Indian*. New York: Harper 1964. R.L. 4-5. Illustrated with many photographs.

Golden, Harry, *Mr. Kennedy and the Negroes*. Cleveland: World, 1964. (Paperback) R.L. 6-7. President Kennedy's civil-rights goals.

Goldman, Peter, *Civil Rights: The Challenge of the Fourteenth Amendment*. New York: Coward, 1965. R.L. 6-7. A semi-historical account of the Negro in the United States.

Grossman, Ronald P., *The Italians in America*. New York: Lerner, 1966. R.L. 5.8. A history of Italian immigrants.

Hague, E., *Spanish-American Folk Songs*. Austin: University of Texas Press, 1917.

Hannum, Sara and Read, Gwendolyn E., compilers, *Lean Out of the Window*. New York: Atheneum, 1966. R.L. 4.7. Looking over the city—a poetry collection.

Heady, Eleanor, *When the Stones Were Soft*. New York: Funk and Wagnalls, 1968. R.L. 6-7. East African fireside tales.

Hughes, Langston, *Famous Negro Music Makers*. New York: Dodd, 1955. R.L. 5-6. A collection of brief biographies of sixteen Negro musicians, jazz musicians and Jubilee Singers.

Jacobs, J., *Indian Folk and Fairy Tales*. New York: Putnam.

Johnson, Emily P., *Flint and Feather*. Toronto: Musson, 1946. A collection of poems dealing with Canada, its white and Indian people.

Johnson, James W., *The Book of American Negro Spirituals*. New York: Viking, 1940. Volumes one and two of American Negro Spirituals are combined in one volume. The book is highly recommended for its preface, which includes authoritative information on the history and development of Negro Spirituals.

Kelen, Emery, *Peace is an Adventure*. Des Moines: Meredith, 1967. R.L. 5-6. Work of the men and women of U.N. around the world.

Kenworthy, Leonard, *Three Billion Neighbors*. Boston: Ginn, 1965. A photographic approach to the commonalities among peoples.

Leuzinger, Elsy, *Africa: The Art of the Negro Peoples*. New York: Crown, 1960. Survey of African sculpture, painting and other art forms.

Lewis, Richard, *The Moment of Wonder*. New York: Dial, 1964. Collection of Chinese and Japanese poetry.

Lewis, Richard, *In a Spring Garden*. New York: Dial, 1965. R.L. 4-5. Dramatic pictures illustrate the Japanese haiku.

Lomax, Louis E., *The Reluctant African*. New York: Harper, 1960. R.L. 6-7. Lomax, an American black journalist, examines the concept of black racism very frankly.

Mieri, Lorraine A., *Dear American Friends*. New York: Vanguard, 1960. R.L. 5-6. Letters from school children of 32 countries, telling of their hopes and plans.

Moon, Bucklin, *The High Cost of Prejudice*. New York: Messner, 1947. R.L. 6-7. O.P. A forceful, factual presentation of the costs of prejudice against Negroes.

New Indian Series. Bureau of Indian Affairs. Washington: Government Printing Office. A 13-booklet series on Indians in various geographical areas of our country.

Powers, William K., *Indian Dancing and Costumes*. New York: Putnam, 1956. R.L. 5.5. How to do Indian dances and make Indian costumes.

Richardson, Willis, *Plays and Pageants from the Life of the Negro.* Washington: Associated Publishers, 1930.

Rollins, Charlemae, *Famous American Negro Poets.* New York: Dodd, 1965. R.L. 7-8. Mrs. Rollins introduces twelve Negro poets, some of whom aren't well known. A useful resource for elementary school teachers and the more capable sixth grade reader.

Rollins, Charlemae, *Famous Negro Entertainers of Stage, Screen and T.V.* New York: Dodd, 1967. R.L. 6-7. Brief biographical sketches.

Segal, Edith, *Come with Me.* New York: Citadel, 1963. R.L. 4-5. Poems about children of different races.

Shapiro, Irwin, *Heroes in American Folklore.* New York: Messner, 1962. R.L. 5-6. Folk figures of many races in America.

Squires, John L. and McLean, Robert E., *American Indian Dances.* New York: Ronald, 1963. R.L. 4-5. Twenty-three dances are described step by step, with drum-beat notations.

Whiting, Helen A., *Negro Art, Music and Rhyme.* Washington: Associated, 1938. R.L. 6-7. Works of the African Negroes.

(Jr.-Sr. H. S. Level)

Adoff, Arnold, *I Am the Darker Brother.* New York: Macmillan, 1968. R.L. 7-8. Anthology of modern poems by black Americans.

Baldwin, James. *The Fire Next Time.* New York: Dell, 1963. (Paperback) R.L. 7-8. A well-known Negro writer speaks out forcefully.

Baldwin, James, *Blues for Mister Charlie.* New York: Dell. (Paperback) R.L. 7-8. The play reconstructs the murder of a young Negro, and the inevitability of his fate.

Barbour, Floyd B., *The Black Power Revolt.* Boston: Extending, 1968. R.L. 7-8. Story of the struggle for civil rights.

Baruch, Dorothy W. *Glass House of Prejudice.* New York: Morrow, 1946. R.L. 7-8. A frank, readable discussion of the causes and effects of prejudice.

Bowen, Joshua D., *The Struggle Within: Race Relations in the United States.* New York: Norton, 1965. R.L. 7-8. Many facets of race relations in America.

Bowles, Chester, *Africa's Challenge to America.* Berkeley: University of California Press, 1957. R.L. 8-9. Bowles examines critically our policies and actions toward emerging African nations.

Braden, Charles S., *These Also Believe.* New York: Macmillan, 1949. R.L. 7-8. The religious ideas of many cults and minority groups.

Brink, William and Harris, Louis, *Black and White: A Study of Racial Attitudes in America Today.* New York: Simon, 1967. R.L. 8-9. Nationwide survey of feelings and opinions.

Brooks, Charlotte, *The Outnumbered.* New York: Dell. (Paperback) A collection of stories, essays and poems about minority groups.

Brotherston, G., *Spanish American Modernista Poets.* New York: Harcourt, 1968 (Paperback)

Cain, Alfred E., editor, *The Winding Road to Freedom*: *A Documentary Survey of Negro Experiences in America*. Yonkers: Educational Heritage, 1966.

Chapman, Abraham, *Black Voices*. New York: New American. An anthology of black literature.

Chapman, Abraham, *The Negro in American Literature*. Oshkosh: Wisconsin Council of Teachers of English. Extensive material on Negro writers. Outlines a unit of study in this area for high or college students.

Clarke, J.H., *American Negro Short Stories*. New York: Hill and Wang.

Clemons, L. etal., *The American Negro*. New York: McGraw-Hill, 1965. R.L. 7-8. Informational book on Negro culture, contributions and present status.

Coles, R., *Children of Crisis*. Boston: Little, 1967. (Paperback) R.L. 8-9. Interviews by a psychiatrist with the children involved in desegregation, both Negro and white.

Damerell, Reginald G., *Triumph in a White Suburb*. New York: Morrow, 1968. Story of Teaneck, N.J., first town to vote for integrated schools.

Dorson, Richard M., *American Negro Folktales*. Greenwich: Fawcett. (Paperback) R.L. 7-8. A collection of tales and tall stories.

Dunbar, Paul L., *Complete Poems*. New York: Dodd, 1940. The complete poems of the celebrated Negro poet of the late 19-20th centuries.

Durham, Philip and Jones, Everett L., *The Negro Cowboy*. New York: Dodd, 1965. Superbly written, carefully researched factual account of the Negroes' participation in the settling of the West.

Ellison, Ralph, *Shadow and Act*. New York: Random, 1964. A collection of essays on literature and folklore, music and intercultural relations between the Negro and the white.

Emanuel, James and Gross, Theodore, *Dark Symphony*. New York: Free Press. A collection of the work of black writers.

Evans, Eva K., *All About Us*. New York: Capitol, 1957. Frank discussions of skin color, race and prejudice.

Forbes, J.D., *Indian in America's Past*. Englewood Cliffs: Prentice Hall.

Franklin, John H. and Starr, Isidore, *Negro in Twentieth Century America*. New York: Random, 1967.

Friedman, Leon, editor, *Civil Rights Reader*. New York: Walker, 1967. Collected materials.

Goldston, Robert, *The Negro Revolution*. New York: Macmillan, 1968. The story began in the slave trade and continues today in a recurring cycle of suppression and rebellion.

Grant, Campbell, *Rock Art of the American Indian*. New York: Crowell, 1967. R.L. 8-9. Color and black-white photos lend realism to the text.

Gross, Seymour L. and Hardy, John E., editors, *Images of the Negro in American Literature*. Toronto: University of Toronto Press, 1966. The changing image of the Negro in American fiction and poetry from Colonial times to the present.

Harris, Christie, *Raven's Cry*. New York: Atheneum, 1966. R.L. 7-8.

Through a study of one tribe, the author shows the cultural conflict between Indian and white man.

Harris, Janet, *The Long Freedom Road: The Civil Rights Story*. New York: McGraw-Hill, 1967. R.L. 7-8. Case histories and anecdotes lighten the account.

Heaps, Willard A., *Riots U.S.A.* New York: Seabury, 1966. The story of 13 riots and their contributing causes.

Hentoff, Nat, *Our Children Are Dying*. New York: Viking, 1966. One school in Harlem attempts to meet the real needs of its pupils.

Hill, Herbert, *Soon One Morning*. New York: Knopf, 1963. A collection of American Negro writing over the previous two decades.

Hughes, Langston, *The Best Short Stories by Negro Writers*. Boston: Little, 1967. Examples of the best stories by Negro writers from 1899 to the present.

Hughes, Langston and Bontemps, Arna, *Book of Negro Folklore*. New York: Dodd, 1958. An anthology of Negro folk material—songs, rhymes, games, spirituals, sermons, prayers, tales, street cries and prose selections. The book is valuable for its inclusiveness and for the background information contained in the introduction.

Jackson, Helen H., *Century of Dishonor: The Early Crusade for Indian Reform*. New York: Harper, (Paperback)

Johnston, Johanna, *Together in America: The Story of Two Races and One Nation*. New York: Dodd, 1965. R.L. 7-8. An informal history of a number of Negro men and women.

Katz, Wm. L., *Eyewitness: The Negro in American History*. New York: Pitman, 1967.

Kaula, Edna M., *Leaders of the New Africa*. Cleveland, World, 1966. R.L. 7. Brief sketches of African leaders of the new nations.

King, Martin L., *A Martin Luther King Treasury*. Yonkers: Educational Heritage, 1966. R.L. 7-8. A collection of articles, speeches and essays.

King, Martin L., *Stride Toward Freedom*. New York: Harper, 1958. The hopes and accomplishments of the civil rights movement.

King, Martin L., *Where Do We Go From Here: Chaos or Community?* New York: Harper, 1967. Dr. King charts a course of action leading to collaboration between blacks and whites.

King, Martin L., *Why We Can't Wait*. New York: Harper, 1964. (Paperback). Dr. King outlines the urgency of social changes.

Landeck, Beatrice, *Echoes of Africa in Folk Songs of the Americas*. New York: McKay, 1961. R.L. Shows the continuity of African traditions in American music.

Lee, Alfred M. and Humphrey, Norman D., *Race Riot*. New York: Dryden, 1943. (Paperback) R.L. 7-8. A detailed analysis of the Detroit riot of 1943, with suggestions for prevention of such incidents.

Lin Yutang, editor, *Famous Chinese Short Stories*. New York: Washington. (Paperback)

Lowe, David, *Ku Klux Klan: The Invisible Empire*. New York: Norton, 1967. R.L. 9-10. Based on the CBS documentary program.

MacEoin. Gary, *All of Which I Saw: Part of Which I Was: Autobiography of George K. Hunton*. New York: Doubleday, 1967. Founder of the Catholic Interracial Council, Hunton tells of his struggle against racial injustice.

McNeer, May and Ward, Lynd, *Give Me Freedom*. Nashville, Abingdon, 1964. R.L. 7-8. Short stories of figures who have contributed to the cause of human freedom.

Mayerson, Charlotte L., editor, *Two Blocks Apart*. New York: Holt, 1965. R.L. 7-8. Two seventeen-year-old boys living in New York City, Puerto Rican Juan Gonzales and Irish Peter Quinn, talked to Miss Mayerson very freely about such concerns as civil rights and segregation.

Myrus, Donald, *Ballads, Blues and the Big Beat*. New York: Macmillan, 1966. R.L. 7-8. Folk songs, their composers and performers.

Rutherford, Peggy, editor, *African Voices: An Anthology of Native African Writing*. New York: Vanguard, 1960. R.L. 8-9. A collection of poems, folk tales, essays and other African literature.

Schulberg, Budd, editor, *From the Ashes: Voices of Watts*. New York: New American, 1967. Writings on ghetto living from a workshop founded on the ashes of Watts.

Schwartz, Alvin, *What Do You Think?* New York: Dutton, 1966. R.L. 7-8. How opinions and prejudices are formed.

Swift, Hildegarde, *North Star Shining*. New York: Morrow, 1947. R.L. 6-7. A brief history of the American Negro written in free verse and movingly illustrated with lithographs.

Terkel, Studs, *Division Street: America*. New York: Pantheon, 1967. Interviews with the people of Chicago.

Warner, W. Lloyd etal., *Democracy in Jonesville*. New York: Harper, 1949. Study of the social strata of a typical American town, and the consequent effect upon behavior.

CHAPTER XVII

Audio-Visual Resources

African Heritage. New York: Pitman. Offers sets of posters, eight color filmstrips and four LP stereo records on Afro-American people and events.

Allison, Mary L., editor, *New Educational Materials.* New York: Scholastic, 1968. Annual compilation of evaluation of materials for nursery to grade 12 levels. All types of instructional materials are included.

American Council for Nationalities Service, 20 West 40th Street, New York, New York 10018. Offers a brochure on foreign festival customs.

American Federation of Arts, 41 East 65th Street, New York, New York 10021. Write for loan of exhibit materials.

American Society of African Culture, 15 East 40th Street, New York, New York 10016. Write for loan of exhibit materials.

American Traveler's Guide to Negro History. 910 South Michigan Ave., Chicago, Illinois 60680: American Oil Co. An illustrated 60-page brochure on famous American Negroes.

Art for World Friendship Committee, Friendly Acres, Media, Pennsylvania 19063. Conducts an exchange of children's pictures with all countries of the world.

Asia Society, 112 East 64th Street, New York, New York 10021. Packet of reprints of articles on Asia, other cultures. Packet is $2.00.

Aubrey, Ruth H., *Selected Free Materials for Classroom Teachers.* Palo Alto: Fearon, 1965.

Bibliographic Survey: The Negro in Print. Washington: Negro Bibliographic. Published bimonthly.

Buckingham Enterprises, Inc. 160-08 Jamaica Ave., Jamaica, New York, 11432. Write for information about teaching kits of records, filmstrips, workbooks on Afro-American leaders.

Bureau of Indian Affairs, Department of the Interior, Washington, D.C. 20025. Write for various bulletins or information on materials, newspapers and magazines dealing with Indians.

Carroll, Hazel Horn, *Play-Like Series.* Dallas: Taylor Publishing, 1969. Three collections of playlets (role-paying) plus sound filmstrip and story sequence cards.

Cooper, Dolores, "The Black Man's Contribution to Social Change," *The Instructor.* 78 (March 1969) 95-105, 152. Suggestions for the classroom teacher on how to approach such questions as: civil rights, black power, sit-ins, freedom riders, etc. Offers a sizeable bibliography of books and teaching aids.

Cooperative Recreation Service, Inc. Radnor Road, Delaware, Ohio 43015. Publishes songbooks of collections from different countries.

Critical Moments in Teaching Series. New York: Holt. Offers a half-dozen 10-12 minute color films dealing with such facets as: working with a handicapped child; teaching low socio-economic adolescents; interpreting a child's ability to his parents; teaching reading to low socio-economic children; and building self confidence in an elementary school child.

Department of State, Washington, D.C. 20025. Write for materials on specific African nations.

Dever, Esther, *Sources of Free and Inexpensive Educational Materials.* Newburg, West Virginia: Fellowsville School, 1959. A comprehensive list of all types of free and inexpensive materials.

Directory of Free Teaching Aids. Los Angeles: Publications Co. 1220 Maple Avenue, 90015. Free educational aids of all types are listed, and classified by subject-matter areas.

Doubleday and Co. See catalog for many Super 8 mm sound films on various aspects of Indian life, the problems of the Cities, life in Japan and China, Africa, the Arctic, etc.

Ebony. 1820 East Michigan Avenue, Chicago, Illinois 60616. A monthly magazine in the style of "Life." Pictures and articles on Negroes are frank and informative. See also "Tan" and "Negro Digest" published by same company.

Education and Urban Society. Sage Publications, 275 South Beverly Drive, Beverly Hills, California 90212. A quarterly dealing with the problems of urban education.

Education Exchange, 2203 Miller Street, Seattle, Washington 98102. Offers Indian realia-tipis, headdresses, sign writing, etc. at small cost.

Enriching the Curriculum with Materials By and About Negroes, by Leon County Teachers, Tallahassee, Florida, 1966. Extensive lists of materials related to each content area of teaching in the elementary grades.

Film and Filmstrips on Afro-Americans and other minority groups— Write for catalogs from the following:

    Afro-American Heritage House, 24 Whittier Drive, Englishtown, New Jersey 07726

    Association Production Materials, 600 Madison Ave., New York, New York 10022

    Atlantic Productions Inc., 894 Sheffield Street, Thousand Oaks, California 91360

    Bailey Films, Inc., 6509 DeLongpre Ave., Hollywood, California 90028

    Churchill Films, 662 N. Robertson Blvd., Los Angeles, California 90069

    Contemporary Films Inc., 267 W. 25th Street, New York, New York 10001

    Robert Disraeli Films, P.O. Box 343 Cooper Station, New York, New York 10003

    Educational Projections Corp., 527 S. Commerce Street, Jackson, Mississippi 39201

Enrichment Teaching Materials Inc., 246 Fifth Avenue, New York, New York 10001

Film Associates of America, 11559 Santa Monica Blvd., Los Angeles, California 90025

Filmstrip House, 432 Park Ave. S., New York, New York 10016

Hudson Photographic Industries, Irvington-on-Hudson, New York 10533

International Communication Films, 1371 Reynolds Ave., Santa Ana, California 92705

Journal Films, 909 W. Diversey Pkwy., Chicago, Illinois 60614

National Instruction Films, 58 E. Route 59, Nanuet, New York 10954

Popular Science Publishing Co., 355 Lexington Ave., New York, New York 10017

New York Times, 229 West 43rd Street, New York, New York 10036.

Alan Sands Productions, 565 Fifth Avenue, New York, New York 10017

Warren Schloat Productions Inc., Palmer Lane West, Pleasantville, New York 10570

Scholastic Social Studies Filmstrips, 802 Sylvan Ave., Englewood Cliffs, New Jersey 07632

Universal Education and Visual Arts, 221 Park Ave. S., New York, New York 10003

Wolfe Worldwide Films, 1657 Sawtelle Blvd., Los Angeles, California 90025

International Communications Foundation, 9033 Wilshire Blvd., Beverly Hills, California 90210

Anti-Defamation League of B'nai B'rith, 29 East 10th Street, New York, New York 10022.

See also catalogs of standard filmstrip supply houses such as Encyclopaedia Britannica, Eye Gate House, McGraw-Hill, Society for Visual Education, etc. See article by Cooper above for further details.

Free and Inexpensive Learning Materials. Nashville, George Peabody College for Teachers, 1964. Lists more than 2000 items.

Freedomways. 799 Broadway, New York, New York 10003. A quarterly review of literature dealing with the civil rights movement.

Great Negroes, Past and Present. Chicago: Afro-American. The kit contains a book of short biographies and filmstrips, transparencies, display pictures, and other materials.

Harmon Foundation, Inc., 140 Nassau Street, New York, New York 10038. Write for loan of exhibit materials.

Illustricrafts, P.O. Box 381, Alameda, California 94501. Indian craft kits and materials.

Inter-Tribal Indian Ceremonial Assn. Dept. ETG, P.O. Box 1029, Gallup, New Mexico, 87301. Write for a list of the free and inexpensive teaching aids prepared by this organization.

Jefferson, Louise E., *Twentieth Century Americans of Negro Lineage*, New York: Friendship, 1965. Picto-map with resource pamphlet. Portrait portfolio also available.

Kreutzig, L. T., editor, *The Story of the Afro-American Correlated to the Growth and Development of the United States.* Milwaukee: The News Pictorial. An illustrated time-line chart.

Letters Unlimited, P.O. Box 35143, Houston, Texas 70035. Arranges pen pals for American children and youth.

McGraw-Hill, *Instructional Materials for Antipoverty and Manpower Training Programs.* New York: McGraw-Hill, 1965. Brief lists of instructional materials for basic education, clerical and sales service, and trades and production occupations. Includes audio-visual aids as well as books and programmed materials.

Miller, Bruce, *Sources of Free and Inexpensive Teaching Aids.* Box 369, Riverside, California 92500. The Author. A brief list.

Negro Bibliographic and Research Center, Inc., 117 R Street N.W., Washington, D.C. 20002. Supplies a variety of services in research and a bimonthly bibliography of printed materials bearing on Negroes.

Negro Heritage. P.O. Box 8153, Chicago, Illinois 60680. A monthly four-page periodical offering articles, biographical material and information on Negro life.

Negro Heritage. Paramus: Educational Visual Aids. A group of transparencies on the American Black, and another on the Indians of America.

Negro Heritage Calendar. New York: Educational Heritage, 1965. A calendar of Negro contributions to society.

Negro History Program Package. Chicago: Afro-American. Offers a package of a textbook, pictures, filmstrips, tapes and transparencies.

Osborn, Merton B. and Miller, Bruce, *Sources of Free Pictures.* Box 369, Riverside, California 92500. The Author, 1964. Lists pictures under more than 250 categories which may be found in back issues of magazines and other sources.

Pennsylvania State University, Audio-Visual Services, University Park, Pennsylvania 16802. Documentary on Africa Series—A group of 15-27 minute color films on various countries of Africa.

Of Black America Series—Ten or more films of 25-60 minutes. Some narrated by prominent Negroes, others documentary.

Posters, pictures and other display materials on Afro-Americans and other groups—
Write for catalogs from:
AEVAC, Dept 109, 500 Fifth Ave., New York, New York 10036
Jackson Publications, Box 337, Santee, California 92071
Hayes School Publishing Co., Wilkinsburg, Pennsylvania 15221
DCA Educational Products Inc., 4829 Stenton Ave., Philadelphia, Pennsylvania 19144
Rand McNally & Co., Box 7600, Chicago, Illinois 60680
Friendship Press, 475 Riverside Drive, New York, New York 10027

Government Information Office, Union of South Africa, 655 Madison Ave., New York, New York 10021

British Information Services, 30 Rockefeller Plaza, New York, New York 10020

Imperial Ethiopian Embassy, 2134 Kalorma Road, N.W. Washington, D.C. 20008

Commonwealth of Puerto Rico, Dept of Labor, 88 Columbus Ave., New York, New York 10023

Office of the Commonwealth of Puerto Rico, 2210 R Street, N.W. Washington, D.C. 20008

Fairbanks Land Office, P.O. Box 110, Fairbanks, Alaska 99701

Alaska Resources Development Board, P.O. Box 50, Juneau, Alaska 99801

Information Office, Alaska Dept. of Agriculture, P.O. Box 1828, Palmer, Alaska 99645

Chinese News Service, 30 Rockefeller Plaza, New York, New York, 10010

China Society of America, 125 East 65th Street, New York, New York 10021

Japan Travel Information Service, 10 Rockefeller Plaza, New York, New York 10020

Embassy of Japan, Information Section, 2514 Massachusetts Ave., N.W., Washington, D.C. 20008

Indian Rights Assn., 1505 Race Street, Philadelphia, Pennsylvania 19102

Field Enterprises Educational Corp., Merchandise Mart Plaza, Chicago, Illinois 60654

Marguerite Brown Study Prints, 700 West Raymond St., Compton, California 90220

Informative Classroom Picture Publishers, 31 Ottawa Ave., N.W. Grand Rapids, Michigan 49500

School Service Division, National Geographic Society, 16th and M Streets, Washington, D.C. 20006

Alaska Steamship Co., Pier 2, Seattle, Washington 98100

Institute of Pacific Relations, 1 East 54th St., New York, New York 10022

Department of the Interior, U.S. Indian Service, Washington, D.C. 20025 (also Division of Territories and Possessions)

Foreign Policy Assn., 22 East 38th Street, New York, New York 10016

Pan American Union, Washington, D.C. 20006

National Railways of Mexico, Traffic Dept., 610 South Broadway, Los Angeles, California 90014

The Grolier Society, 2 West 45th Street, New York, New York 10019

Letcher Visual Aids, 1436 H St., N.W. Washington, D.C. 20002

Tourist Division, Dept. of Development, State Capitol, Sante Fe, New Mexico 87501

United Nations, UNESCO Publications Center, 801 Third Avenue, New York, New York 10022

Curriculum Materials Center, 5128 Venice Blvd., Los Angeles, California 90019

Pupil to Pupil Program Inc., 261 Constitution Ave., N.W. Washington, D.C. 20001. Sponsors communication between American children and those of other lands.

The Queen's Printer, Ottawa, Canada. Write for "Canadian Eskimo Art" a 40-page booklet. Not free.

Round the World by Mail, 505 Fifth Avenue, New York, New York 10017. A subscription yields a small package from a different country each month. Includes native products, crafts, newspapers and magazines, etc.

Salisbury, Gordon and Sheridan, Robert, *Catalog of Free Teaching Aids*. Box 942, Riverside, California 94501.: The Authors. Materials from over 1000 organizations.

Smithsonian Institute, Traveling Exhibition Service, Washington, D.C. 20025. Write for loan of exhibit materials.

Tapes and Records on Afro-American and other minority groups—Write the following for catalogs:

Classroom World Productions, 516 W. 34th Street, New York, New York 10001

Doubleday & Co., Garden City, New York 11530

Folkways/Scholastic Records, 906 Sylvan Ave., Englewood Cliffs, New Jersey 07632

Imperial International Learning, 247 W. Court Street, Kankakee, Illinois 60901

National Instruction Films, 58 East, Route 59, Nanuet, New York 10954

Tapes Unlimited, 13113 Puritan Avenue, Detroit, Michigan 48227

H.W. Wilson Corp., 555 W. Taft Drive, South Holland, Illinois 60473

Children's Music Center, 5373 W. Pico Blvd., Los Angeles, California 90019

Pennsylvania State University, Audio-Visual Aids Library, University Park, Pennsylvania 16802

Enrichment Teaching Materials, 246 Fifth Ave., New York, New York 10001

The Urban Review. New York: Center for Urban Education. A monthly review of inner city events.

Wagner, Guy and Mork, Dorlan, *Free Learning Materials for Classroom Use*. Extension Service, U. of Northern Iowa, Cedar Falls, Iowa, 1967.

Wright, Betty Atwell, *Urban Education Studies*. New York: Day, 1965. Series of albums, each about a theme of city life; chartsize photographs of urban scenes and activities.

CHAPTER XVIII

Professional Resources

Abbott, Mary K., *The Culturally Handicapped Student and the Reading Process.* San Francisco Unified School District, School-Community Improvement Program.

Africa: An Annotated List of Printed Materials Suitable for Children. New York: U.S. Committee for UNICEF, 1968. A list of more than 300 items published in nine countries.

Allen, Harold B., *Tenes—A Survey of the Teaching of English to Non-English Speakers in the United States.* Champaign: National Council of Teachers of English, 1966. Deals largely with theories, approaches and methodology of second language learning, not with the problems of dealing with bilingual children.

Allport, Gordon W., *The Resolution of Intergroup Tensions.* New York: National Conference of Christians and Jews, 1952.

American Council on Education, *Reading Ladders for Human Relations.* Washington: American Council on Education, 1963. Classified and annotated list of books for children.

Anderson, Margaret, *The Children of the South.* New York: Dell. Paperback. A guidance counselor describes the social and emotional effects of school desegregation upon her students.

Baker, Augusta, *Books about Negro Life for Children.* New York: The Public Library, 1963. Titles suitable for elementary and high school ages, arranged by subject and grade level.

Barnes, Robert F. and Hendrickson, Andrew, *Graded Materials for Teaching Adult Illiterates.* Columbus: Center for Adult Education, Ohio State University, 1965. Comprehensive, annotated list.

Baughman, E. Earl and Dahlstrom, W. Grant, *Negro and White Children: A Psychological Study in the Rural South.* New York: Academic Press, 1968. R.L. 8-9. Ability differences, intellectual changes, personal attributes and perspectives.

Berdrow, John R., *Reading Programs and Evaluation of Materials for Basic and Continuing Adult Education.* Springfield, Illinois: State Department of Public Instruction, 1965. Adult Education, Curricular Series Bulletin A-167.

Blueprint for American Community Programs on Africa. New York: African-American Institute. Suggestions for programs, and units of study on Africa.

Bookazine, 303 West 10th Street, New York, New York 10014. Offers a series of inexpensive paperbacks from Africa intended for children.

Books for Friendship. American Friends Service Committee and Anti-Defamation League of B'nai B'rith, Philadelphia, 1968. Books recommended for children. An excellent list.

Boston Public Library, *Negro Life and History*. Boston: The Library, 1968. A brief list of current books for children.

Boston Public Library, *The Negro in America*. Boston: The Library, 1968. A brief list of recent books for adults.

Bosworth, Allen R., *America's Concentration Camps*. New York: Norton, 1967. America's racial hysteria against the Japanese-Americans during World War II.

Brau, Maria, *Island in the Crossroads*. New York: Doubleday, 1968. A history of Puerto Rico.

Brown, Spencer, *They See for Themselves: A Documentary Approach to Inter-Cultural Education*. New York: Harper, 1945. Intercultural research projects for high school students, through the medium of documentary plays.

Chase, Judith W., *Books to Build World Friendship*. Dobbs Ferry, New York: Oceana. Books ranging from elementary to secondary levels are briefly annotated.

Chesler, Mark and Fox, Robert, *Role-Playing Methods in the Classroom*. Chicago: Science Research, 1966. A teacher's guide to role-playing.

Cheyney, Arnold B., *Teaching Culturally Disadvantaged in the Elementary School*. Columbus: Merrill, 1967. Despite the snobbish title, there are some good fragments, particularly in Chapter 6.

Coles, Robert, *Children of Crisis*. New York: Dell. (Paperback). A psychiatrist examines the meaning of race and racial struggle in the lives of individuals.

Conant, James B., *Slums and Suburbs*. New York: New American. (Paperback). How schools for non-white slums differ from those in suburbia; and what might be done about it.

Corbin, Richard and Crosby, Muriel, editors, *Language Programs for the Disadvantaged*. Champaign: National Council of Teachers of English, 1965.

Crosby, Muriel, *An Adventure in Human Relations*. Chicago: Follett, 1965. Description of program in Wilmington, Delaware.

Council on Interracial Books for Children, *Interracial Books for Children*. New York: The Council. A quarterly publication in newspaper format.

Darwin, Fred, Erman, Richard and Hanff, Helene, *Cities in Bondage*. New York: Parents', 1969. Three cities and their problems are studied in detail.

Davis, John P., *The American Negro Reference Book*. Englewood Cliffs: Prentice-Hall, 1966. A basic reference book.

DeKnight, Freda, *A Cook Book of American Negroes*. New York: Heritage.

Department of Public Instruction, Harrisburg, Pa., *Our Greatest Challenge, Human Relations: Guide to Intergroup Education in Schools*. Curriculum Development Series #6, 1962.

Detroit Public Schools, Division for Improvement of Instruction, *First Steps in Language Experiences for Preschool Children.* Publication 5-802TCH, 1966.

Detroit Public Schools, Division of Improvement of Instruction, *The Struggle for Freedom and Rights: Basic Facts About the Negro in American History.* Publication No. 5-216TXT, 1963.

Detroit Public Schools, Division for Improvement of Instruction., *The Negro in American History: A Guide for Teachers.* File No. 7397, 1965.

Deverell, A. Frederick, *Canadian Bibliography in Reading and Literature Instruction, 1760 to 1959.* Toronto: Copp, Clark, 1963. A comprehensive bibliography on the teaching of reading and literature, as well as books published in Canada.

Dodds, Barbara, *Negro Literature for High School Students.* Champaign: National Council of Teachers of English. Survey of Negro writers, works about Negroes.

ERIC on the Disadvantaged, *Social Class and the Socialization Process: A Review of Research.* by Edward Zigler. New York: ERIC, Teachers College, Columbia University, 1968. A monograph summarizing the research information stored on this subject by the information retrieval center.

ERIC on the Disadvantaged, *Language Development in Disadvantaged Children: An Annotated Bibliography.* New York: ERIC, Teachers College, Columbia University.

Feuer, Lewis S., *The Conflict of Generations.* New York: Basic, 1968. Intensive study of the student movement here and abroad.

Ford, David and Nicholson, Eunice, *Adult Basic Reading Instruction in the United States: An Annotated Bibliography.* Newark: International Reading, 1967. An excellent list of materials for students and instructors.

Franklin, John H., *The Emancipation Proclamation.* New York: Doubleday, 1963. Its impact and significance for later events.

Frost, Joe L. and Hawkes, Glenn R., editors, *The Disadvantaged Child.* Boston: Houghton Mifflin, 1966. A broad collection of background readings.

Gans, Herbert J. *The Urban Villagers: Group and Class in the Life of Italian-Americans.* New York: Free Press, 1965 (Paperback).

Golden, Ruth, *Improving Patterns of Language Usage.* Champaign: National Council of Teachers of English, 1960.

Gordon, Edmund W. and Wilkerson, Doxey A. *Compensatory Education for the Disadvantaged.* Princeton: College Entrance, 1966. A review of programs from preschool to college levels intended to offset the handicaps of educationally disadvantaged.

Grambs, Jean D. *Intergroup Education: Methods and Materials.* Englewood Cliffs: Prentice-Hall, 1968. Classroom suggestions, as well as an extensive bibliography of source materials for secondary teachers.

Greene, Mary F. and Ryan, Orletta, *The School Children: Growing Up in the Slums.* New York: Pantheon, 1965.

Grier, William H. and Cobbs, Price M. *Black Rage.* New York: Basic, 1968. An analysis by two psychiatrists of the Black's anger at his oppression.

Hansberry, Lorraine, *The Movement*: *Documentary of a Struggle for Equality*. New York: Simon and Schuster, R.L. 6-7. A visual documentary record of the Negro's plight.

Harrington, Michael, *The Other America*: *Poverty in the U.S.* New York: Macmillan, 1962 (Paperback.) A shocking presentation of the facts about America's 50 million poor.

Heller, G.S. *Mexican-American Youth*: *Forgotten Youth at the Crossroads*. New York: Random, 1966. Problems of Mexican-American male youths in the school, home and community.

Henderson, James L. *Education for World Understanding*. New York: Pergamon Press, 1968. Outlines a plan for educating for world cooperation and peace, extending in activities from elementary to secondary.

Hentoff, Nat, *The New Equality*. New York: Viking, 1964. A discussion of the contradictory attitudes of the middle class (including teachers).

Herndon, James, *The Way It Spozed to Be*. New York: Simon and Schuster, A teacher's story of his year in a Negro ghetto school.

Hickerson, Nathaniel, *Education for Alienation*. Englewood Cliffs: Prentice-Hall, 1966. An accusation of school practices which work toward producing failure for the economically deprived.

Hobart, L. *Mexican Mural*: *The Story of Mexico, Past and Present*. New York: Harcourt,1963. R.L. 9-10. Historical materials.

Hollingshead, August, *Elmtown's Youth*. New York: Wiley, 1949. R.L. 7-8. An analysis of the effects of class structure on the young people of a small midwestern town.

Huthmacher, J. Joseph, *A Nation of Newcomers*: *Ethnic Minority Groups in American History*. New York: Dell (Paperback). A narrative history of minority groups in America.

Huus, Helen, *Children's Books to Enrich the Social Studies*. Washington: National Council for the Social Studies, 1961. Extensively annotated.

Integrated School Books. New York: NAACP, 1967. Descriptive bibliography of almost 400 pre-school and school texts and trade books.

Intergroup Relations: *A Resource Handbook for Elementary School Teachers, Grades 4, 5, 6*. Publications Distribution Unit, Room 169, Education Building: University of State of New York, Albany, N.Y. 12200.

Jensen, J. Vernon, *Effects of Childhood Bilingualism*. Champaign: National Council of Teachers of English, 1962.

Josephy, Alvin M., Jr., *The Indian Heritage of America*. New York: Alfred A. Knopf, 1968. A technical but readable study of all Indian groups of the Western Hemisphere. See Appendices for many sources of materials on Indians.

Joyce, James A., *Decade of Development*: *The Challenge of the Underdeveloped Nations*. New York: Coward, 1966. R.L. 7-8. The successes and failures of the U.N. in the 60's.

Karls, John B., *Two Approaches to the Culturally Disadvantaged Student*. Champaign: National Council of Teachers of English, 1966.

Katz, Wm. L., editor, *Teacher's Guide to American Negro History*. Chicago: Quadrangle, 1968. Intensive discussion of materials and approaches.

Katz, Wm. L., *Eyewitness: The Negro in American History*. New York: Pitman. Offered as a supplement to American history courses or as a text in Afro-American history for secondary pupils.

Kaufman, Bel, *Up the Down Staircase*. Englewood Cliffs, N.J.: Prentice-Hall, 1965. Novel based on big-city school teaching.

Keating, Charlotte M., *Building Bridges of Understanding*. Tucson: Palo Verde. An annotated bibliography of 215 children's books which include ethnic-group representation.

Kelley, Douglas, *Introducing Children to Africa*. Athens, Ohio: Center for International Programs, 1964. Annotated list of 78 elementary books on Africa.

Kelley, Douglas C., *Africa in Paperbacks*. Ann Arbor: Michigan State University Press. An inclusive list of 200 paperbound books in print in 1960.

Kerber, August, and Bommarito, Barbara, editors, *The Schools and the Urban Crisis: A Book of Readings*. New York: Holt, 1967 (Paperback)

Koblitz, Minnie W., *The Negro in Schoolroom Literature*. New York: Center for Urban Education, 1968. Resource materials for K-VIth grade on the Negro-American heritage; annotates about 250 books.

Kvaraceus, William C., etal., *Negro Self-Concept: Implications for School and Citizenship*. New York: McGraw-Hill, 1965. The report of a conference sponsored by the Lincoln Filene Center for Citizenship and Public Affairs, Tufts University.

Letter Writing Committee of the People-to-People Program, Minnesota World Affairs Center, Minneapolis, Minnesota 55414.

Lewis, Oscar, *La Vida*. New York: Random, 1966. Written as the result of interviews with a large Puerto-Rican family, the book offers a very frank view of their customs and culture.

Lewis, Oscar, *Study in Slum Culture*. New York: Random, 1968.

Lewis, Oscar, *Five Families: Mexican Case Studies in the Culture of Poverty*. New York: Basic, 1959.

Lewis, Oscar, *Pedro Martinez: A Mexican Peasant and His Family*. New York: Random, 1964. A sociological study.

Lomax, Louis R., *The Negro Revolt*. New York: Harper, 1962. A journalist's report of the efforts toward equality and freedom.

Loretan, Joseph O. and Umans, Shelley, *Teaching the Disadvantaged Child: New Curriculum Approaches*. New York: Teachers College, 1966. Challenges many of the current assumptions regarding education of the disadvantaged.

Los Angeles City Schools, Council on Human Relations, *Improving Inter-Group Relations: A Handbook for Teachers*. Publication No. 4, 1965.

McGuire, Edna, *The Peace Corps: Kindlers of the Spark*. New York: Macmillan, 1966. The contribution of hope made by the Peace Corps.

Mackintosh, Helen, Gore, Lillian and Lewis, Gertrude M., *Disadvantaged Children Series*. U.S. Department of Health, Education and Welfare, Office of Education. Washington: U.S. Government Printing Office, 1965. A group of four brochures on disadvantaged children and the schools.

Millen, Jane, *Children's Games From Many Lands*. New York: Friendship, 1965. An anthology drawn from 64 countries.

Millender, Dharathula H., *Children's and Young People's Books about Negro Life and History*. Chicago: American Federation of Teachers.

Mills, C. W., Senior, Clarence and Goldsen, R.K., *The Puerto Rican Journey*. New York: Harper, 1950. R.L. 7-8. Based on interviews with Puerto Ricans who migrated to New York.

Milwaukee Public Schools, *Questions That Help in the Development of Reading Skills and Abilities: A Guide for Elementary Teachers*. 1965.

Milwaukee Public Schools, Division of Curriculum and Instruction, *Non-English Speaking Pupils: A Teacher's Guide*. 1963.

Minuchin, Salvador, et al., *Families of the Slums*. New York: Basic, 1967. A study of 12 delinquent and 10 nondelinquent families.

National Conference of Christians and Jews, *Books for Brotherhood*. New York: The Conference. A leaflet offering a list of carefully selected books for children and adults.

N.E.A., *The Negro American in Paperbacks*. Washington: National Education Association. A selected and annotated list for secondary students.

N.E.A. *School Programs for the Disadvantaged*. Educational Research Service Circular #1, 1965. Washington: National Education Association, 1965.

Negro Heritage Library. Yonkers: Educational Heritage, 1964-66. A ten-volume library offered as a basic reference set. Largely semi-fictionalized biographies. Some documentary materials and anthologies.

Negro Heroes of Emancipation. New York: NAACP, 1964. Profiles of 40 prominent Negroes.

New York City, Board of Education, *The Negro in American History*. Curriculum Bulletin. 1964-5 Series No. 4, 1964. Proposals for a K-12 Curriculum in History and the Social Sciences: A position paper for discussion and review.

New York City, Board of Education, *Puerto Rican Profiles: Resource Materials for Teachers*. Curriculum Bulletin, 1964-65 Series, No. 5, 1964.

Noar, Gertrude, *The Teacher and Integration*. Washington: National Education Association, 1966.

Ohannessian, Sirarpi, *The Study of the Problems of Teaching English to American Indians*. Champaign: National Council of Teachers of English, 1967.

One Hundred Years of Negro Freedom. Washington: Assn. for the Study of Negro Life and History, 1964. An adult bibliography. This association is also a source for picture material.

Pantell, Dora and Greenidge, *Blacklash*. New York: Dell, 1969 (Paperback). The Negro's problems in housing, education, employment and other areas.

Pennsylvania Department of Public Instruction, *Preschool-Primary Project for Culturally Disadvantaged Children*. Box 911, Harrisburg, Pa.: The Bureau of Research. A final report on the project.

Public Schools of the District of Columbia, Washington, *The Negro in*

American History: A Curriculum Resource Bulletin for Secondary Schools, 1964.

Rabe, Olive, *United Nations Day.* New York: Crowell, 1965. The purposes of the U.N. in fighting hunger and war are clearly outlined.

Rauch, Sidney J., compiler, *Handbook for the Volunteer Tutor.* Newark, Delaware: International Reading Assn., 1969. A rather complete guide for the paraprofessional aide.

Review of Educational Research. "Education for Socially Disadvantaged Children," 35, 5, December 1965. Review of the literature on the characteristics, language development, appraisal, learning disabilities and the programs for these children.

Riessman, Frank, *The Culturally Deprived Child.* New York: Harper, 1962. A scholarly analysis of the characteristics of culturally deprived children.

Rollins, Charlemae, *We Build Together.* Champaign: National Council of Teachers of English, 1967. An intercultural reading list ranging from preschool to ninth grade.

Rosen, Carl L. and Ortego, Philip D., compilers, *Issues in Language and Reading Instruction of Spanish-Speaking Children.* Newark, Delaware: International Reading, 1969. A frankly analytic bibliography of references.

Sanchez, George I., *Forgotten People: A Study of New Mexicans.* Albuquerque: Horn, 1967 (Paperback). Although written originally in 1940, the findings are relevant today. The education of Mexican-Americans in New Mexico has not materially changed.

San Francisco Unified School District, Division of Instructional Materials, *The Whole of Us: Selected Bibliographies on Human Relations,* 1963.

Scholes, William E., *Next Move for the Migrants.* New York: Friendship, 1966.

Schotta, Sarita G., *Teaching English as a Second Language.* Champaign: National Council of Teachers of English, 1966.

Sechrist, Elizabeth H. and Woolsey, Janette, *It's Time for Brotherhood.* New York: Macrae Smith, 1962. Description of persons and organizations fostering brotherhood.

Segal, Bernard E., editor, *Racial and Ethnic Relationships: Selected Readings.* New York: Crowell, 1966 (Paperback).

Selected Lists of Children's Books and Recordings. Children's Services Division American Library Association. Washington: Office of Economic Opportunity, printed by Government Printing Office, 1966. Annotated list of books and records for economically-deprived children and youth.

Silberman, Charles E., *Crisis in Black and White.* New York: Random, 1964. Every teacher should read Chapter IX, "The Negro and the School".

Southern Education Report. Nashville: Southern Education. A bimonthly factual survey of developments in education, with emphasis on programs for the culturally disadvantaged in the 17 Southern and border states.

Southwestern Cooperative Educational Laboratory, *SWCEL Newsletter.* 117 Richmond Drive, N.E. Albuquerque, New Mexico: The Laboratory.

A bimonthly containing, among other features, an abstract of developments in teaching various cultural groups.

Spache, George D., *Good Reading for Poor Readers.* Champaign: Garrard, 1970. (Paperback). Extensive lists, graded and annotated, of trade books, workbooks, games and texts, series books, magazines and newspapers, programmed materials and others suitable for use with poor readers of all ages.

Strom, Robert D. editor, *The Inner-City Classroom: Teacher Behaviors.* Columbus: Merrill, 1966. See particularly the articles by Paul H. Bowman and A. Harry Passow on teacher-pupil interaction.

Strom, Robert D., *Teaching in the Slum School.* Columbus: Merrill, 1965. A brief collection of comments and suggestions.

Swanton, John R., *The Indian Tribes of North America.* Washington: Government Printing Office, 1952. An official reference book.

Taba, Hilda, *Literature for Human Understanding.* Washington: National Council on Education, 1948. Ways of using literature in fostering better human relations.

Taba, Hilda, et al., *Curriculum in Intergroup Relations: Secondary Schools.* Washington: American Council on Education, 1950. Curricular suggestions for improving human relations. See parallel book on the elementary curriculum in the same area, from same source.

Taba, Hilda and Elkins, Deborah, *Teaching Strategies for the Culturally Disadvantaged.* Chicago: Rand, 1968. Suggestions on questioning, managing discussions and approaches, based on authors' research.

Taba, Hilda and Elkins, Deborah, *With Focus on Human Relations: The Story of an Eighth Grade.* Washington: American Council on Education, 1950. Day-by-day attempts to adapt the classroom procedures and curriculum to the better understanding of children.

Thomas, R. Murray, *Social Differences in the Classroom: Social, Class, Ethics and Religious Problems.* New York: McKay, 1965 (Paperback).

Three Lists of Recommended Books About Negroes or With Negro Characters. Los Angeles City School District's bulletin "Recommended Books on American Cultural Minority Groups" (resource).

Tucker, Sterling, *Why the Ghetto Must Go.* New York: Public Affairs. Mr. Tucker, director of the National Urban League, offers suggestions for eliminating ghettos.

Turner, Richard H., *A Letter to Teachers of America's Culture Victims,* Chicago: Follett, 1964.

U.S. Commission on Civil Rights, *Racial Isolation in the Public Schools.* Washington: Government Printing Office, 1967. A report on the facts of racial segregation in the schools.

Virginia Council on Human Relations, *A List of Intercultural Textbooks and Readers Available as of Spring 1966 in the Subject Areas of English and the Social Studies.* Richmond: The Council, 1966.

Walls, Esther J., editor, *African Encounter,* Chicago: American Library Association, 1963. A fine, selected bibliography of materials for promoting knowledge of Africa among young adults.

Ward, Betty A., *Literacy and Basic Elementary Education for Adults:
    A Selected, Annotated Bibliography*. Washington: Office of Education,
    Bulletin #9, 1961.

Warren, Virginia B., *How Adults Can Learn More—Faster*. Washington:
    National Association for Public Adult Education, 1961. A brochure of-
    fered as a handbook for adult literate students.

Webster, Staten W., *The Disadvantaged Learner*. San Francisco: Chand-
    ler, 1966. Available in three paperback sections: Knowing the Disad-
    vantaged; Understanding the Educational Problems of the Disadvantaged
    and Educating the Disadvantaged Learner.

CHAPTER XIX

Adult Literacy

The Problem: Although the world's rate of illiteracy declined from 44.3 percent to 39.3 percent during the decade from 1950-1960, the absolute number of illiterates increased from 700 million to 740 million. (17) Despite almost worldwide efforts, we are losing the battle due to the tremendous population growth. Even more pessimistic than this statistic, however, is the fact that the worldwide drop-out rate in primary school is averaging 21 per cent, with only 52 out of every hundred children that enter school staying in to reach the sixth grade. In Middle Africa the illiteracy rate is decreasing but it still approximates 70 per cent. Even in the United States, the portion of the adult population that has not attained functional literacy is about eleven per cent, and not much below five per cent in any of the 50 states. (4)

Olsen and many others (12) note the conflicting statistics on il- literacy in the United States owing to the confusions in definition of terms. The Office of Education, for example, claims that 11 million Americans are illiterate, while other sources place the figure as high as 40 million. From his own data, Olsen concludes that one in every twelve Americans is functionally illiterate.

Whatever the true extent of functional illiteracy in the United States is, it is obvious that this is a social, economic, and educational problem of the first magnitude. To some degree, at least, our government is reaching and supporting programs to reduce the number of illiterate adults. Under the Economic Opportunity Act of 1964, free schooling was offered to any person 18 years of age or older to improve his basic skills. During the period 1964-1966, $27 million were spent to set up adult education classes. These centers sprang up in churches, schools, factories, empty stores, vacant houses, and in every other available facility. In all, some 373,000 persons received instruction in basic educational skills. (3) During the next two years, successive appropriations of $40 and $60 millions have been set aside for this educational program. Included in this plan was the establishment of Job Corps centers for educationally disadvantaged youths.

Job Corps centers were often sponsored by business corporations with the basic purpose of offering basic and vocational training to the unemployable. Others, in rural areas, dealt only with basic literacy skills, after which the participants could transfer to urban centers for the vocational training of their choice.

The success of these various literacy programs varied greatly from one setting to another, as we shall point out later in our discussion of techniques and methods. In general, despite the massive nature of the effort, it touched only a small segment of the population for which it was intended. Only a small number of states entered into the program and three states accounted for over one-third of the 373,000 participants in the first year. If, as Olsen and Curry estimate, 8 million American adults need such training, only about two per cent were reached in the first year. At this rate, how long will it take to solve the literacy problem in the United States?

Definitions: How do we define adult literacy? When is an adult functionally literate? Some research in this country has indicated that fifth-grade reading ability seems to be the line of demarcation between economic dependence and self-sufficiency. Brooks (1) for example, concludes from a survey of able-bodied persons on public assistance in Cook County, Illinois that literacy programs should be divided into two levels—fifth grade and below, and above fifth grade. The Brooks study and others have shown, however, that there is little relationship between the present reading level of the individual and the grade of school completed. We cannot assume functional literacy simply because individuals once completed the fifth grade.

The fifth-grade level of reading ability is a significant point of division between illiterate and functionally literate for another reason. Surveys of adult reading ability made in the 1930's indicated that there is a tendency for reading ability to be maintained or even to improve among adults with more than five years of schooling. The reasons for this maintenance of reading skills were not ascertained, but probably reflect the greater opportunities for enjoyable and profitable reading for those who have reached this reading level.

The use of the fifth-grade level of reading ability to designate the lower level of functional literacy appears to be justified because of its obvious implications for economic self-sufficiency and maintenance of literacy.

The Goals: This concept of functional literacy has received worldwide acceptance. (17) Literacy is work-oriented and training programs as well as measures of reading ability should have this vocational orientation. Only when this emphasis is given to literacy efforts can they significantly contribute to economic and social development of the individual, as well as of nations.

The goals of a literacy program, then, are the preparation of the individual to a level of reading ability sufficient for vocational pursuits. Tests of literacy should therefore include not only the basic reading skills of rate, comprehension, and vocabulary, but also measures of writing, arithmetical, and, probably, vocational skills as needed for functional literacy. Such tests must obviously be built specifically for the adult population for which they are intended. Common school tests used with children lack these essential components. In fact, many of the current tests of basic education among adults also lack a true vocational orientation, and fail to recognize the dividing line between illiteracy and functional literacy. (2, 7, 15)

Varying levels of literacy may be required in countries which differ in levels of development, in intensity of communication, and in alphabet and writing script. For example, it requires more effort to become literate in Arabic or Chinese than in English, even for people who speak these languages as their mother tongues. The influence of a particular language upon literacy is manifest in the history of Turkey. In the 1920's, a new phonetic alphabet was totally substituted for the Arabic calligraphy. The illiteracy rate dropped from the then 93 per cent to 60 per cent in the 1960's, due certainly in part to the change in the written language. (6) The minimum literacy rate to be achieved, such as the 40 per cent level, is another factor to be considered in national literacy efforts. Perhaps the same percentage or the same level of reading ability may not be valid for all countries. More research is needed to test the belief that a particular level of literacy is necessary for industrial development and whether this minimum level should be similar in different parts of the world. Other research should be undertaken to determine the extent to which illiteracy should be regarded as a bottleneck to industry and a hindrance to foreign investment.

Instructional Problems: One problem continues to hinder literacy efforts both in this country and elsewhere. This is the failure to link literacy training directly to vocational application or even to other uses for reading. Few countries, including the United States, can offer a large group of appropriate materials for the individual who has achieved functional literacy. There is little of adult, contemporary nature for the functionally literate to read for pleasure or information. As a result, their reading skills tend to deteriorate and many mass literacy programs in the past have eventually failed simply because of this lack of materials in sufficient volume and variety to maintain literacy skills. Certainly the United States has the technical knowledge and resources to supply newspapers, magazines, books, and the like with adult appeal for undereducated adults. American educators have served as consultants to a number of governments of other countries to help produce such reading materials for these countries. Menefee (11), for example, tells of the growth in information and radio listening among Indian villagers when a simple weekly newsletter was made generally available. But no public or private agency in the United States has faced this problem or perhaps even admitted its existence.

Lack of adequate promotional work to arouse the motivation of the illiterate population, and to create a favorable climate for the project among the entire population as well as probable participants in it, has resulted in the failure of many programs. For example, in Florida a program offered on television called "Operation Alphabet" finished with less than five per cent of the viewers that began the program, perhaps because of the impersonal, unmotivating nature of the presentation medium. In other applications in classrooms this same program was much more successful.

Programs for Job Corpsmen (14) face an acute problem in terms of the motivation of their participants. Corpsmen are scholastic failures for economic and emotional reasons. For these same reasons, they are unable to compete in our society. In addition, they have experienced more violence, more sex, and more fantasy life than even much older citizens. As a group they have a strong sense of failure and a poor self-image in identity and self-assurance. Their rehabilitation is handicapped by short attention spans, barely-hidden hostilities, and substandard dialects.

Other motivational factors determine the success of literacy programs, such as the type of course itself, the teachers, the suitability of the classroom to adults, the problem of transportation to the center, and, even more significantly, the motives of the participants. The naive failure to provide instructional materials intended for and interesting to adults has vitiated many literacy attempts in the past.

The content of literacy programs is, of course, a central problem in their success. Since the program is intended to prepare adults for vocational success, there is the danger that the training may be too narrow and limit the participants' possible future choices. Content must necessarily be related to the occupations conceivably open to participants in providing the essential basic vocabulary and the language and the arithmetic skills with common values. But at the same time, extreme specialization or neutral courses which simply improve general reading ability will not achieve the basic goals. Considerably more research and trial with various variations of programs will be necessary both in this country and elsewhere to tailor them to the needs of different groups and nations.

Several other facets of literacy programs also need much further exploration. Research could help to determine the relationship between active participation of the adults and their tendency to persist in the program. Do illiterate adults respond favorably to an active or a passive role in the group? What is their self-concept in the beginning of the program, and how does this change as it progresses? Can we generalize about adult groups of various ethnic backgrounds or should our procedures differ for various groups?

The role of mass media such as the radio and television in promoting literacy, and in preparing illiterates to use other mass media, needs further research. This approach has been tried in the United States, Jamaica, Mexico, Algeria, and other countries. Some of the claimed advantages of these mass media programs are the relative cost per participant, the potential size of the audience, and the flexibility of the media. Disadvantages are present in the lack of teacher-pupil interaction, personal motivation, evaluation of student progress, and, as we have emphasized before, the failure to provide reading materials to maintain the skills obtained. Mass media programs must necessarily be general, emphasizing beginning reading skills rather than vocationally-oriented training. The obvious goal of preparing oneself for greater economic sufficiency may not be apparent to participants in these programs, nor may they find it simple to make direct use of their new skills in this direction without some guidance.

Dr. and Mrs. Lawrence Kasdon report on the results of television literacy programs in Mexico. (8) Of 1200 participants in one television series, 62.5 per cent completed the course, and two-thirds of those were awarded literacy certificates. In other words, 41 per cent of the viewers were successful in achieving the goal of functional literacy. In a second TV series, 27 per cent completed the course and 85 per cent of these were judged to be literate; that is, 23 per cent were successful. It is difficult, of course, to judge whether programs that are successful for 23 to 41 per cent of their audiences are really failures or successes. We know of no comparative data to indicate how many participants might have been successful if taught by other means. Nor do we know the ultimate outcomes of these Mexican programs in either continued literacy or improved vocational status. At this point, about all we do know is that mass media can be used to reach large numbers of illiterates, and that one or two of every five of these will be materially helped.

Types of Programs: Otto and Ford (13) attempted a national survey of adult basic education programs by collecting data from 367 programs in 36 states. Although many programs had been established prior to the enabling federal legislation, most were less than two years old. Older programs had probably been established largely to serve immigrants, and their clientele continued to be drawn mostly from this population. New programs catered to the marginally literate adult who had dropped out of school after the age of sixteen.

Despite the length of schooling, equivalent to ninth or tenth grade, the level of instruction in more than half the programs was below fourth grade. Teacher-made materials were prominent in 13 per cent of the programs and a substantial number admitted using materials prepared for elementary children. Commercial materials more or less intended for adult use formed the bulk of the instructional materials.

Scanty as they are, these data from Otto and Ford show the evolving nature of adult literacy programs in this country. Apparently the clientele, as well as the content and instructional materials, are in a developmental stage.

The adaptation of language laboratory techniques to literacy programs is recommended by Railsback. (14) Working with Job Corpsmen, Railsback used prerecorded audio tapes through which the student listened to a lesson and responded orally. The aural content is also available in printed form at this time. His written answers are corrected by the device immediately and a comparison of his oral responses with the teacher's voice is provided. The content of the program included phonic, word attack, and dictionary skills, and reading selections reflecting life at the Job Corps center. Railsback's results showed an average gain in one month of five months in vocabulary and six months in reading comprehension. However, the author wisely considered these results with caution because of the inappropriate achievement tests he used.

Many other types of programs are described in the literature: those teaching basic skills with basal readers written for children; those using linguistic materials emphasizing either a phonemic, sentence pattern, or word patterns based on spelling similarities rationale depending upon which linguistic school the authors espoused; those emphasizing audio-visual approaches with Language-Masters, tapes, records, films, and the like. A few make a real effort to fit the instructional materials to the age and interests of the group, to use or create materials directly related to vocational goals, to use such realistic matter as driver's manuals, shop manuals, basic English, shop arithmetic, safety rules, etc. (3, 5, 12, 16)

Strategies of Teaching: This variation in programs, content, and goals—or should we call it confusion—may justify the enunciation of basic principles which ought to guide adult literacy work. In our opinion, such programs should:

1. Begin with careful diagnosis of the participants' educational strengths and weaknesses. It is highly questionable whether tests standardized on school children are appropriate for this or any other testing.
2. Plan a program carefully structured to overcome deficiencies and promote obvious progress. The material should be sequenced to insure success with reasonable effort.
3. Establish short-range goals, expect relatively short attention span, and easy discouragement despite basic motivations.
4. Emphasize small group work, with special provision for individualized attention as needed. Insure frequent teacher-student contact.
5. Be certain that content of the program has a strong vocational component and realistically appeals to adult interests and experiences. Adults are pragmatic learners.
6. Employ reasonably experienced teachers in preference to adult novices or other paraprofessionals, if at all possible.
7. Keep exploring media and ways of learning for different students. Remember that many of these students failed in ordinary classrooms that used common methods.
8. Try to keep motivation high by discovering students' personal motives for entering the group and by trying to give direct help toward these goals. Relate to the group as adults joined in a common purpose, with your contribution being simply that of someone helping them toward their goals.
9. Help the group to improve in basic skills, not just to reach some particular academic grade level. The ways in which they can use their skills for their own purposes are significant; the exact level of those skills is not important.
10. Help participants to be aware of their progress, not necessarily by tests but by application of skills to their daily tasks.
11. Remember that the group is composed of adults, not children. The teacher's role is to stimulate and assist learning, not to maintain discipline, quiet, and order. Encourage interaction between students and small group work under a student leader or an advanced student helping others. Avoid lecturing or other types of whole-class instruction except for essential activities.

REFERENCES

1. Brooks, Deton J. *The Blackboard Curtain: A Study to Determine the Literacy Levels of Able-Bodied Persons Receiving Public Assistance.* Chicago: Science Research, 1963.
2. Burnett, Richard W. *Adult Basic Reading Inventory.* New York: Scholastic Testing Service, 1966.
3. Curry, Robert L. "Adult Literacy: Progress and Problems," pp. 236-39 in *Junior College and Adult Reading Programs*, George B. Schick and Merrill M. May, editors. Sixteenth Yearbook, National Reading Conference, 1967. Milwaukee: The Conference.
4. Gray, William S. "How Well Do Adults Read," p. 38 in *Adult Reading*, Fifty-fifth Yearbook, National Society for the Study of Education, Part II. Chicago: University of Chicago Press, 1956.
5. Greenleigh Associates Inc. *Field Test and Evaluation of Selected Adult Basic Education Systems.* New York: The Author, 1966.

6. Hunsaker, Herbert C. "Adult Education in Turkey," *Adult Leadership*, 13 (March 1965) 281-82.
7. Karlsen, Bjorn, Madden, Richard and Gardner, Eric F. *Adult Basic Learning Examination*. New York: Harcourt, Brace and World, 1967.
8. Kasdon, Lawrence M. and Kasdon, Nora S., "Television: Vehicle for Literary Training in Mexico," *Adult Leadership*, 16 (September 1967) 91-92.
9. Lanning, Frank W., and Many, Wesley A. *Basic Education for the Disadvantaged Adult: Theory and Practice*. Boston: Houghton Mifflin, 1966.
10. Mangano, Joseph A., editor. *Strategies for Adult Basic Education*. Newark: International Reading Assn., 1969.
11. Menefee, Selden and Menefee, Andree, "A Country Weekly Proves Itself in India," *Journalism Quarterly*, 44 (Spring 1967) 114-17.
12. Olsen, James, "Instruction Materials for Functionally Illiterate Adults," *Adult Leadership*, 13 (March 1965) 275-76.
13. Otto, Wayne and Ford, David, "Basic Literacy Programs for Adults: A National Survey," pp. 240-66 in *Junior College and Adult Reading Programs*. George B. Schick and Merrill M. May, editors. Sixteenth Yearbook, National Reading Conference, 1967. Milwaukee: The Conference.
14. Railsback, Lem, "Use of Automated Aural-Oral Techniques to Teach Functional Illiterates Who Are Upper Age Level Adolescents" in *The Psychology of Reading Behavior*, Eighteenth Yearbook, National Reading Conference, 1969. Milwaukee: The Conference.
15. Rasof, Elvin and Neff, Monroe C. *Adult Basic Education Survey*. Chicago: Follett, 1966.
16. Stanton, Paul E. "A Study of Systems for Teaching Adults Reading Skills," *Dissertation Abstracts*, (May 1967) 3738A-39A.
17. UNESCO, *Suggestions for Research in Adult Literacy*. Paris, December 4, 1968.

CHAPTER XX

Materials for Basic Education of Adult Illiterates and School Dropouts

Adair, J. B. and Curry, R. L., *Reading for a Purpose*. Chicago: Follett, 1965. One volume language arts program.

Adult Basic Education Series. New York: Noble, 1966. Set of three paperbacks for beginning instruction.

Allasina, T. A. and McLeod, N. N., *Beginning English for Men and Women, Part 1*. Seattle: Cascade Pacific, 1958. Primary level.

Anderson, Lorena and Dechant, Emerald, *Listen and Read*. Huntington, N.Y.: Educational Developmental Laboratories. Tapes for directed listening ranging from primary to secondary levels under various titles, as "Listen and Think", etc.

Arithmetic Skills Program. Huntington, N.Y.: Educational Developmental Laboratories. Visual memory drills, arithmetic fundamentals and problems for all grade levels.

Bamman, Henry and Whitehead, Robert, *World of Adventure Series*. Chicago: Benefic, 1964. Six adventure stories of primary reading difficulty.

Bauer, Josephine, *Communications*. Chicago: Follett, 1964. Three workbooks using linguistic patterns to teach beginning reading.

Beagle, S., *Elementary English Reader*. 1710 Broadway, New York: International Ladies Garment Workers Union, 1953. A simplified reader.

Berres, Frances, et al., *Deep Sea Adventure Series*. Chicago: Benefic, 1962. Action stories at primary level of reading.

Bright, E. L. and Mitchell, E. C., *Home and Family Life Series*. New London, Conn: Croft. Beginning readers for adults include simple paperback texts, workbooks and tests.

Canadian Citizenship Council, *Safety Education—Readings in Basic English*. 148 Lauria Ave. West, Ottawa, Ontario, Canada.

Caruso, Domenick and Krych, Robert, *You Can Read Better: Adult Approach to Better Reading*. New York: Cenco, 1966. Programmed lessons in a teaching machine.

Cass, Angelica W., *How We Live*. New York: Noble, 1949. Primary reading material. First year text for foreign born or bilingual.

Cass, Angelica W., *Live and Learn*. New York: Noble, 1962. Primary reading level on adult activities. Other titles available at intermediate grade reading levels.

Chapman, Byron E. and Schulz, Louis, *Mott Basic Language Skills Program*. Galien, Michigan: Allied Education Council, 1966. A tutorial, phonics-linguistic approach composed of several workbooks, teachers' manuals, dictionary, etc.

Clark, Ann N., et al., *Adult Education Series*. Washington: Bureau of Indian Affairs, Department of the Interior. Series of ten simple pamphlets for adults of limited education.

Dale, Edgar, *Stories for Today*. Washington: Superintendent of Documents, 1954-1964. One of series of U.S. Armed Forces Institute Materials in basic education. Other titles in series are *Men in Armed Forces*; *Servicemen Learn to Read*; *New Flights in Reading*.

Dialog I. Chester, Conn.: Chester Electronic Labs. Tapes, booklets and record forms for phonics training.

Dixson, Robert J., *USA—The Land and the People*. New York: Regents, 1959. History and geography in a limited vocabulary. Each section accompanied by various exercises. See catalog of Regents for other such books.

Ebony. 1630 S. Michigan St., Chicago, Ill. Magazine in the style of "Life", devoted to Negro life in America.

Federal Textbooks on Citizenship. Washington: Superintendent of Documents. Series of five books written for naturalization classes on our government, laws, rights, etc. Readily usable with other adults of limited reading ability. Parallel books at intermediate and higher levels also available.

Finding Your Job. 3350 Gorham Ave., Minneapolis: Finney Co. R.L. 3-4. Six units of 5 books each offering twelve simple job descriptions. Thus about 300 jobs are covered in a III-IV grade style.

Fitzhugh, Loren and Katheen, *Fitzhugh Plus Program*. Galien: Allied, 1966. Programmed materials for beginning readers.

Francis, Roger and Iftikhar, Sam, *How to Find a Job*. Syracuse: New Readers, 1959. At primary reading level.

Gillespie, George and Wanyee, George, *Why You Need Insurance*. Syracuse: New Readers, 1959. At primary level.

Gobles, Dorothy Y., editor, *California Migrant Ministry Series*. Los Angeles: California Migrant. A series of simple booklets on health, education, safety and related topics.

Goldberg, Herman R. and Brumber, Winifred T., *New Rochester Occupational Reading Series*. Chicago: Science Research, 1965. Texts and workbooks on finding and preparing for a vocation.

Gray, W. L. and Kohn, E., *Opening the Door to Reading*. Columbia, S.C.: State Department of Education, 1947. A simplified workbook-reader.

Grit. Williamsport, Pa.: Grit Publishing. A weekly newspaper for uneducated adults.

Guyton, M. L. and Kielty, M. E., *From Words to Stories*. New York: Noble and Noble, 1951. A workbook-reader of 144 word vocabulary.

Harding, Lowry M. and Burr, James B., *Men in the Armed Forces*.

MB001. Washington: Superintendent of Documents, 1956. Beginning reader, with service oriented content.

Harding, Lowry M. and Burr, James B., *Servicemen Learn to Read*. Practice Books I and II. MB001.2. Washington: Superintendent of Documents, 1956. Workbooks to accompany the reader.

Hardwick, Bettie L. *New Auditory—Visual Response Phonics*. Box 626, Shafter, Cal.: Polyphone. Tapes, text and worksheets for audio-visual phonics training.

Henderson, Ellen C. and Twila L., *Learning to Read and Write*. New York: Holt, 1965. Basic education skills for adults. Two beginning workbooks.

Henney, R. Lee, *System for Success, Book 1*. Chicago: Follett, 1964. A phonics approach to reading through phonogram groups. Also offers some material on arithmetic and English mechanics.

Henney, R. Lee, *System for Success, Book 2. A Complete Program*: *Reading, Writing, Spelling, Arithmetic, and English*. Chicago: Follett, 1965.

Horrocks, Edna M., *Word-Study Charts*. Boston: Ginn. Twenty illustrated charts for primary-intermediate levels.

Howard, Richard D., *Unemployed Uglies*. Phoenix, N.Y.: Richards, 1966. Cartoons and simple text—for group discussion.

Hudson, Margaret W. and Weaver, Ann A., *Getting Ready for Pay Day*. Phoenix, N.Y.: Richards, 1963. One of a series of short workbooks for adult illiterates and semi-literates. See catalog for other titles.

Hudson, Margaret W. and Weaver, Ann A., *Pacemaker Books*. Palo Alto: Fearon, 1966. Four workbooks in citizenship at second grade level.

Individual Reading Apparatus. 1601 South Michigan Ave. Chicago: School Material Co. A wide variety of boxed games for phonics and beginning reading.

Joe Wheeler Finds a Job and Learns about Social Security. Washington: Office of Education, Department of Health, Education and Welfare, 1964. Reader and workbook.

Kahn, Chas. H. and Hanna, J. Bradley, *Money Makes Sense*. Palo Alto: Fearon, 1964. Learning arithmetic through the use of money.

Kitchin, Aileen T. and Allen, Virginia F., *Reader's Digest Readings*. New York: Reader's Digest, 1953. Collections of articles in very simple style.

Know Your World. Middletown, Conn.: Wesleyan University. Newspaper on contemporary affairs written for young adults, at a primary readability level.

Kottmeyer, Wm. and Ware, Kay, *The Everyreader Series*. St. Louis: Webster. Twenty adapted classics in simplified style.

Laubach, Frank C., *Building Your Language Power, Book 1*. Morristown: Silver, Burdett, 1965. Programmed workbook; one of a series of six. Phonic approach to reading and handwriting.

Laubach, Frank C., *Charts and Stories*. Syracuse: New Readers Press, 1963. For adult beginners.

Laubach, Frank C., *New Streamlined English*. New York: Macmillan, 1966. A programmed approach to beginning reading based heavily on phonics.

Laubach, Frank C. and Hord, Pauline J., *A Door Opens*. New York: Macmillan, 1963. Primary reading text.

Laubach, Robert S., editor, *News for You*. Syracuse: Laubach Literacy. Weekly newspapers in two simplified editions, 3-4 grade, and 5-6 grade. For adults and adolescents of limited education.

Learning 100. Huntington, N.Y.: Educational Developmental Laboratories. A multi-media communication skills program for adults in listening, writing, reading and speaking.

Ling, S. and Mitchell, M. E., *Family Life Reader*. Atlanta: Allen James, 1936. A simple reader.

Loesel, W. G., *Help Yourself to Read, Write, and Spell, 1 and 2*. Boston: Ginn, 1965. Workbooks in basic education.

Lynn, K. D. and Whiting, H. A., *Everyday Living*. Atlanta: Allen James, 1949. A simplified reader.

McCall, Wm. A. and Crabbs, Lelah M., *Standard Test Lessons in Reading*. New York: Teachers College Press, 1961. Ranging from second to twelfth grade, these booklets provide drill in comprehension.

Milton, Bradley, *Reading Aids*. Springfield, Mass.: Milton Bradley, Inc. See catalog for a variety of seatwork games.

Mooney, Thomas J., *The Getting Along Series*. Phoenix, N.Y.: Frank E. Richards, 1963. A series of three simple readers to help school dropouts to adjust to life.

National Citizenship Education Program, *Literacy Readers*. Washington: Superintendent of Documents, 1943-44. Offers three simple readers written for naturalization programs.

New Reading Skill Builders. Pleasantville, N.Y.: Reader's Digest Services. Eight books in format of adult magazine, at primary reading levels. Accompanying workbooks.

Olson, Jim, *Step Up Your Reading Power, Book A*. New York: McGraw-Hill, 1966. Short reading selections on job hunting, hygiene, at 3-4 grade level.

Operation Alphabet. Washington: Nat'l Association of Public School Adult Educators, 1962. A workbook used to encourage adults to enroll in literacy programs. Offers 100 one page lessons.

Owens, A. A. and Sharlip, W., *Elementary Education for Adults*. Philadelphia: Holt, 1950. A text and workbook.

Parker, Don H. et al., *SRA Reading Laboratory*. Chicago: Science Research. A series of kits of reading selections planned for each grade, but ranging above and below the grade level.

Phonics. St. Paul: Visual Products Division, 3M Co. Color transparencies for Phonics training.

Photo-Phonics. Flossmoor, Illinois: Gifted Teachers Books. A language arts program including texts, workbooks, and film strips.

Rambeau, John and Nancy, *The Americans All Series*. San Francisco: Field. Eight easy reading books on racial and ethnic characters drawn from groups that contributed to American culture.

Rambeau, John and Nancy, *Morgan Bay Mysteries*. San Francisco: Field. Easy reading mystery stories. Eight titles.

Reader's Digest, *Adult Readers*. Pleasantville, New York.: Reader's Digest Services. Series of twelve paperbacks with adult level interest, and exercises in basic skills.

Reader's Digest, *Reading Skill Builders*. Pleasantville, N.Y.: Reader's Digest Services. Offers series of story collections in magazine format with exercises.

Reader's Digest, *Readings*. Pleasantville, N.Y.: Reader's Digest. Selections from the parent magazine for youth and adults of limited education.

Remedial Reading Program. Los Angeles: Rheem Califone. Kits of 130 to 250 tapes ranging from prereading to ninth grade level, with accompanying worksheets.

Richards, I. A. and Gibson, C. M., *English Through Pictures*. New York: Pocket Books, 1946. For beginning adult readers.

Richards, I. A. and Gibson, C. M., *Words on Paper*. Cambridge: English Language Research, 1943. For beginning adult readers.

Richards, I. A. and Gibson, C. M., *Learning the English Language*. Boston: Houghton, 1963. A series of three texts and accompanying workbooks intended for foreign-born but useful with native literacy programs.

Richards, I. A. and Gibson, C. M., *First Steps in Reading English*. New York: Washington Square, 1952. A simplified reader.

Richards, I. A. and Gibson, C. M., *A First Workbook in English*. Cambridge, Mass.: English Language Research, Inc., 1956. Workbook to accompany the above text.

Robertson, M. S., *Adult Reader*. Austin: Steck, 1964. Exercises of various types centered around the story of a family.

Rosenfeld, J. and Cass, A. W., *Write Your Own Letters*. New York: Noble, 1950. Basic instruction.

Smith, Edwin H. and Lutz, Florence R., *My Country*. Austin: Steck, 1956. Workbook in various reading skills.

Smith, Harley A. and King, Ida L., *How to Read Better*. Austin: Steck, 1966. Offered for adults beginning to read.

Smith, Harley A. and King, Ida L., *I Want to Learn English*. Austin: Steck, 1966. Slightly more advanced material for the beginning, adult reader.

Smith, Harley A. and King, Ida L., *I Want to Read and Write*. Austin: Steck, 1966. For the adult beginning to read and write.

Steps to Learning, Books 1 and 2. Austin: Steck, 1965. For adult beginners in reading, writing and arithmetic.

Stone, C. R. et al., *New Practice Readers*. St. Louis: Webster, 1962. R.L. 2-6. Each workbook offers many short selections followed by exercise material.

Strong Publications, *Young Americans*. 431 E. 57th St., New York, N.Y. 10022. A newspaper for young adults of limited education.

Sullivan Associates, *Programmed Reading for Adults*. New York: McGraw Hill, 1966. Five programmed workbooks with teachers' editions.

Thurstone, Thelma G., editor, *Reading for Understanding*. Chicago: Science Research. Reading kits for 3-8 and 5-12 in inferential reading.

Titus, Nicholas and Gebremarium, Negash, *Trouble and the Police*. Syracuse: New Readers, 1959. Young adult material at primary reading level.

Tripp, Fern, *Common Signs of Community Service and Safety*. The Author 2035 East Sierra Way, Dinuba, Calif. One hundred hand-size signs for reading practice.

Varnado, Jewel and Gearing, Philip J., *English Lessons for Adults*. New York: Harcourt, 1966. A three workbook series.

Weinhold, Clyde E., *English*. New York: Holt, 1962. Basic instruction in English—reading, writing, mechanics and vocabulary.

Wheel Transparencies. Boston: Cambosco Scientific. Transparencies on phonics.

Williams, Betty J., *Language Kit*. Haberfelde Bldg. Bakersfield, Cal.: The Author. A kit of interlocking pieces to practice forming sentences.

Woodcrafters Guild, *Syllabascope*. Washington: St. Alban's School. A wooden frame with shutters for practicing syllabication and word analysis.

Woolman, Myron, *Reading in High Gear*. Chicago: Science Research, 1964. A series of programmed workbooks extending, in all, through the eighth grade level.

Word Watching. Huntington, N.Y.: Educational Developmental Laboratories, 1964. A spelling program for grade 2 up involving tachistscopic training.

You and Your World. Columbus: American Education Publications. A weekly newspaper for individuals above 15, written at 3-5 grade level.

Author and Title Index

Title and Author Index

Presents for Johnny Jerome, Bell-Zano, Gina, 78

Problems of American Society, Leinwand, Gerald, 97

Profiles of Negro Womanhood (1619-1900), Dannett, Sylvia G. L., 38

Programmed Reading for Adults, Sullivan Associates, 136

The Progress of the Afro-American, Patrick, John J., 97

Project Cat, Burchardt, Nellie, 72

Prophets of Deceit, Lowenthal, Leo and Guterman, Norbert, 97

Proudly We Hail, Brown, Jack and Vashti, 93

Prudence Crandall: Woman of Courage, Yates, Elizabeth, 42

The Puerto Rican Journey, Mills, C. W. Senior, Clarence, and Goldsen, R. K., 120

Puerto Rican Profiles: Resource Materials for Teachers, Board of Education, New York City, 120

Puerto Rico, McGuire, Edna, 91

The Pup Who Became a Police Dog, Hays, Wilma P., 75

Puppy Named Gih, Machetanz, Sara, 69

The Pushcart War, Merrill, Jean, 75

A Question of Harmony, Sprague, Gretchen, 54

Questions That Help in the Development of Reading Skills and Abilities: A Guide for Elementary Teachers, Milwaukee Public Schools, 120

Quiet Boy, Waltrip, Lela and Rufus, 65

The Quiet Rebels, Sterling, Philip, 91

Quito Express, Bemelmans, Ludwig, 78

Race Riot, Lee, Alfred M. and Humphrey, Norman D., 107

Racial and Ethnic Relationships: Selected Readings, Segal, Bernard E., 121

Racial Isolation in the Public Schools, U.S. Commission on Civil Rights, 122

Raiders of the Mohawk, Miller, Hanson O., 60

Rain Boat, Kendall, Lace, 41

A Raisin in the Sun, Hansberry, Lorraine, 52

Ralph J. Bunche, Fighter for Peace, Kugelmass, J. A., 48

Ramon Makes a Trade: Los Cambios de Ramon, Ritchie, Barbara, 81

Ramona, Jackson, Helen H., 80

Raven's Cry, Harris, Christie, 106

Reach for a Star, Means, Florence, 53

Read About the Busman, Slobodkin, Louis, 95

Reader's Digest Readings, Kitchin, Aileen T. and Allen, Virginia F., 133

Reading Aids, Milton, Bradley, 134

Reading Development, Smith, Edwin H., 100

Reading for a Purpose, Adair, J. B. and Curry, R. L., 131

Reading for Understanding, Thurstone, Thelma G., 136

Reading Fundamentals for Teenagers: A Workbook of Basic Skill Building, Neufeld, Rose G., 100

Reading in High Gear, Woolman, Myron, 100, 136

Reading Ladders for Human Relations, American Council on Education, 115

Reading Programs and Evaluation of Materials for Basic and Continuing Adult Education, Berdrow, John R., 115

Reading Skill Builders, Reader's Digest, 135

Reading Success Series, American Education Publications, 100

Readings, Reader's Digest, 135

The Real Book About Alaska, Epstein, Samuel and Williams, Beryl, 68

The Rebel Trumpet, Shirreffs, Gordon D., 65

Red Cloud, Garst, Shannon, 59

Red Fox and His Canoe, Benchley, N., 63

Red Man, White Man, African Chief, Lerner, Marguerite R., 94

Reggie's No-Good Bird, Burchardt, Nellie, 47

The Reluctant African, Lomax, Louis, 104

Reluctant Reader Libraries, Scholastic Book Services, 100

Names and Addresses of Publishers

Abelard-Schuman, Ltd. 6 West 57th Street, New York, New York 10019

Abingdon Press, 201 Eighth Avenue S., Nashville, Tennessee 37202

Academic Press, Inc., 111 5th Avenue, New York, New York 10003

Addison-Wesley Publishing Co., 2725 Sand Hill Road, Menlo Park, California 94025

Adhere-O-Learning Aids, P.O. Box 32, Wilmette, Illinois 60091

African-American Institute, 345 E. 46th Street, New York, New York 10017

Afro-American Publishing Company, 1727 S. Indiana Street, Chicago, Illinois 60620

Air Age, Inc., 551 Fifth Avenue, New York, New York 10036

Dorothea Alcock, 107 North Elspeth Way, Covina, California 91722

Alexander Graham Bell Association for the Deaf, 1537 35th Street, Washington, D.C. 20007

Thomas Allen & Son, Ltd., 50 Prince Andrew Place, Don Mills, Ontario, Canada

Allied Education Council, P.O. Box 78, Galien, Michigan 49113

Allyn and Bacon, Inc., 47 Atlantic Avenue, Boston, Massachusetts 02210

Ambassador Books, Ltd., 10 Vulcan Street, Rexdale, Ontario, Canada

American Association for the Advancement of Science, 1515 Massachusetts Avenue, N.W., Washington, D.C. 20005

American Association of Colleges for Teacher Education (see National Education Association)

American Book Co., 450 W. 33 St., New York, New York 10001

American Council on Education, 1785 Massachusetts Avenue, N.W., Washington, D.C. 20036

American Education Publications, Education Center, 1250 Fairwood Avenue, Columbus, Ohio 43216

American Federation of Teachers, 716 N. Rust Street, Chicago, Illinois 60600

American Forestry Association, 919 17th Street, N.W., Washington, D.C. 20006

American Friends Service Committee, 160 N. 15th Street, Philadelphia, Pennsylvania 19102

American Guidance Services, Circle Pines, Minnesota 55014

American Heritage Publishing Co., 551 Fifth Avenue, New York, New York 10017

American Jewish Committee, 165 East 56th Street, New York, New York 10022

American Library Association, 50 East Huron Street, Chicago, Illinois 60611

American Museum of Natural History, Central Park West at 79th Street, New York, New York 10024

American National Red Cross, Washington, D.C. 20013

American Technical Society, 848 East 58th Street, Chicago, Illinois 60637

Americana Interstate Corp., 501 E. Lange St., Mundelein, Illinois 60060

Ann Arbor Publishers, 610 South Forest, Ann Arbor, Michigan 48104

Anti-Defamation League of B'nai B'rith, 29 East 10th Street, New York, New York 10022

Antioch Press, Box 148, Yellow Springs, Ohio 45387

Antof Educational Supplies, Route 2, Box 118, Medina, Ohio 44256

Appleton-Century-Crofts, 440 Park Avenue, South, New York, New York 10016

Ariel (see Holt, Rinehart and Winston)

Asia Society, 112 East 64th Street, New York, New York 10022

Associated Publishers, 1538 Ninth Street, N.W., Washington, D.C. 20001

Association for Childhood Education International, 3615 Wisconsin Avenue, N.W., Washington, D.C. 20016

Association for the Study of Negro Life and History, Inc., 1538 Ninth Street, N.W., Washington, D.C. 20001

Astra Corp., 31 Church Street, New London, Connecticut 06320

Atheneum Publishers, 122 East 42nd Street, New York, New York 10017

Atlantic Monthly Press, 8 Arlington Street, Boston, Massachusetts 02116

Australian Council for Educational Research, 369 Lonsdale Street, Melbourne, Cl, Victoria, Australia

Bantam Books Inc., 666 Fifth Ave., New York, New York 10019

Ella D. Barton and Myra F. Wyman, 607 Amherst Avenue, Columbia, South Carolina 29200

Basic Books Inc., 404 Park Avenue, South, New York, New York 10016

Beckley-Cardy Co., 1900 North Narragansett Avenue, Chicago, Illinois 60639

Behavioral Research Laboratories, Box 577, Palo Alto, California 94302

Benefic Press, 10300 West Roosevelt Road, Westchester, Illinois 60153

Benton Review Publishing Co., Fowler, Indiana 47944

Benziger Inc., 260 Park Ave. S., New York, New York 10010

Better Reading Foundation, Inc., 52 Vanderbilt Avenue, New York, New York 10017

Bobbs-Merrill Co., Box 558, 4300 W. 62 St., Indianapolis, Indiana 46268

Book-of-the-Month Club, 345 Hudson Street, New York, New York 10014

Boston Public Library, Copley Square, Boston, Massachusetts 02100

R. R. Bowker, Co., 1180 Avenue of the Americas, New York, New York 10036

Bowmar Publishing Corp., 622 Rodier Dr., Glendale, California 92101

Milton Bradley Co., Springfield, Massachusetts 01100

George Braziller, Inc., 1 Park Avenue, New York, New York 10016

Bremmer-Davis Phonics, 511 Fourth Street, Wilmette, Illinois 60091

British Book Service, Queenswood House, Ltd., 128 Bloor St. W., Toronto 5, Ontario, Canada

William C. Brown Co., 135 South Locust Street, Dubuque, Iowa 52001

Bureau of Educational Research, Ohio State University, Columbus, Ohio 43210

Burgess Publishing Co., 426 South Sixth Street, Minneapolis, Minnesota 55415

Burke Publishing Co., Ltd., (see Ambassador Books)

Burns and MacEachern, Ltd., 62 Railside Road, Don Mills, Ontario, Canada

Cadaco-Ellis Co., 1446 Merchandise Mart, Chicago, Illinois 60600

California Library Association, 1741 Solano Avenue, Berkeley, California 94707

California Migrant Ministry Services, 3330 West Adams Blvd., Los Angeles, California 93940
California Test Bureau, Del Monte Research Park, Monterey, California 93940
Cambosco Scientific Co., 342 Western Avenue, Boston, Massachusetts 02135
Cambridge University Press, 32 East 57th St., New York, New York 10022
Campbell and Hall, 989 Commonwealth Avenue, Boston, Massachusetts 02117
Canadian Audubon Society, 46 St. Clair Avenue, E., Toronto 7, Canada
Canadian Library Association, 63 Sparks Street, Ottawa, Ontario, Canada
Capital Area Development Assoc., State University College, Albany, New York 12200
Capitol Publishing Co., 850 Third Avenue, New York, New York 10022
Cascade Pacific Books, 5448 47th Street, S.W., Seattle, Washington 98100
Catholic Library Association, 461 W. Lancaster Avenue, Haverford, Pennsylvania 19041
Catholic University of America Press, 620 Michigan Avenue, N.E., Washington, D.C. 20017
Cenco Educational Aids, Carle Place, Long Island, New York 11010
Center for Programmed Instruction, Inc., Institute of Educational Technology, Teachers College, Columbia University, New York, New York 10025
Center for Urban Education, 33 West 42nd Street, New York, New York 10036
Century Consultants, Inc., 6363 Broadway, Chicago, Illinois 60626
Chandler Publishing Co., 124 Spear Street, San Francisco, California 94105
Chanticleer Press, Inc., 424 Madison Avenue, New York, New York 10017
Chicago Schools Journal, Chicago Teachers College, 6800 Stewart Avenue, Chicago, Illinois 60621
University of Chicago Press, 5750 Ellis Avenue, Chicago, Illinois 60637
Child Life, 3516 College Avenue North, Indianapolis, Indiana 46205
Child Study Association of America, 9 East 89th Street, New York, New York 10028
Children's Book Council, 175 Fifth Avenue, New York, New York 10010
Children's Playmate, 6529 Union Avenue, Cleveland, Ohio 44105
Children's Press, 1224 W. Van Buren St., Chicago, Illinois 60607
Children's Record Reviews, Box 192 Woodmere, New York 11598
Chilton Book Co., 401 Walnut Street, Philadelphia, Pennsylvania 19106
Citadel Press, Inc., 222 Park Avenue, South, New York, New York 10003
City College Educational Clinic, Remedial Reading Service, Convent Avenue and 136th Street, New York, New York 10027
Civic Education Service, 1733 K Street, N.W., Washington, D.C. 20006
College Entrance Book Co., 194 Fifth Avenue, New York, New York 10011
College Entrance Examination Board, Box 592, Princeton, New Jersey 08540
Wm. Collins Sons & Co., 100 Lesmill Rd., Don Mills, Ontario, Canada
Colorado Bibliographic Institute, Denver, Colorado 80200
Colorado Department of Education, Denver, Colorado 80200
Committee on Diagnostic Reading Tests, Mountain Home, North Carolina 28758
Conde Nast Publications, 420 Lexington Avenue, New York, New York 10017
Continental Press, Elizabethtown, Pennsylvania 17022
Copp Clark Publishing Co., 517 Wellington St., W., Toronto 2B, Canada

Coronet Instructional Films, 65 East South Water Street, Chicago, Illinois 60601

Council on Interracial Books for Children, 9 East 40th Street, New York, New York 10016

Coward-McCann, 200 Madison Avenue, New York, New York 10016

Criterion Books, Inc., 6 West 57th Street, New York, New York 10019

Croft Educational Services, 100 Garfield Avenue, New London, Connecticut 06320

Thomas Y. Crowell Co., 201 Park Avenue South, New York, New York 10003

Crowell Collier and Macmillan, Inc., 866 Third Avenue, New York, New York 10022

Crown Publishers, Inc., 419 Park Avenue, South, New York, New York 10016

Cupples and Leon Co., (see Platt and Munk) 1055 Bronx River Ave., Bronx, New York 10472

Curtis Publishing Co., Independence Square, Philadelphia, Pennsylvania 19105

The John Day Co., Inc., 62 W. 45th Street, New York, New York 10036

Stephen Daye Press, 131 East 23rd Street, New York, New York 10010

Delacorte (see Dell)

Dell Publishing Co., Inc., 750 Third Avenue, New York, New York 10017

T. S. Denison & Co., Inc., 5100 W. 82nd St., Minneapolis, Minnesota 55431

J. M. Dent & Sons, Ltd., 100 Scarsdale Road, Don Mills, Ontario, Canada

Devereaux Teaching Aids, Box 717, Devon, Pennsylvania 19333

Dial Press, Inc., 750 Third Avenue, New York, New York 10017

Dodd, Mead & Co., 79 Madison Avenue, New York, New York 10016

Doubleday and Co., Inc., Garden City, New York 11530

Dover Publications, Inc., 180 Varick Street, New York, New York 10014

Duell, Sloan and Pearce, 1716 Locust Street, Des Moines, Iowa 50303

E. P. Dutton and Co., Inc., 201 Park Avenue South, New York, New York 10003

E. R. A. Publishers, 2223 South Olive, Los Angeles, California 90000

The Economy Co., 1901 N. Walnut Ave., Oklahoma City, Oklahoma 73105

Ed-U-Cards Manufacturing Corp., 36 33rd Street, Long Island City, New York 11100

Education Engineering, 3810 Pacific Coast Highway, Torrance, California 90500

Educational Aids, 845 Wisteria Drive, Fremont, California 94538

Educational Cards, 8000 West Seven Mile Road, Detroit, Michigan 48200

Educational Developmental Laboratories, 284 Pulaski Road, Huntington, New York 11744

Educational Electronics Inc., 607 West Sheridan, Oklahoma City, Oklahoma 73100

Educational Heritage, Inc., 733 Yonkers Avenue, Yonkers, New York 10704

Educational Publications, Dublin, New Hampshire 03444

Educational Publishing Corp., (see Teachers Publishing Corp.)

Educational Service, Box 112, Benton Harbor, Michigan 49022

Educational Service Publications, Box 301 East Carolina College, Greenville, North Carolina 27834

Educational Test Bureau, Division of American Guidance Service, 720 Washington Avenue, S.E., Minneapolis, Minnesota 55414

Educational Visual Aids, East 64 Midland Ave., Paramus, New Jersey 07652

Educators Progress Service, Box 497, Randolph, Wisconsin 53956

Educators Publishing Service, 75 Moultan St., Cambridge, Massachusetts 02138

Elk Grove Press, 8112 Melrose Avenue, Los Angeles, California 90046

Encyclopaedia Britannica, Inc., 425 North Michigan Avenue, Chicago, Illinois 60611

ERIC, on the Disadvantaged, Teachers College, Columbia University, New York, New York 10027

Essex Publishing Co., Hapeville, Georgia 30054

Extending Horizons Books, Porter Sargent, Inc., 11 Beacon Street, Boston, Massachusetts 02108

Farrar, Straus and Giroux, Inc., 19 Union Square W., New York, New York 10003

Fawcett Publications, Inc., Fawcett Place, Greenwich, Connecticut 06830

F. W. Faxon Co., Inc., 15 Southwest Park, Westwood, Massachusetts 02090

Fearon Publishers, Inc., 2165 Park Boulevard, Palo Alto, California 94306

Fellowsville School, Newburg, West Virginia 26410

Field Educational Publications, Inc., 609 Mission Street, San Francisco, California 94105

Fleet Publishing Corp., 230 Park Avenue, New York, New York 10017

Follett Educational Corp., Box 5705, Chicago, Illinois 60680

Follett Library Book Co., 1018 West Washington Boulevard, Chicago, Illinois 60607

Ford's Wood Novelties, 4716 Second Street, N.W., Albuqerque, New Mexico 87100

Four Winds Press, 50 West 44th Street, New York, New York 10036

Friendship Press, 475 Riverside Drive, New York, New York 10027

Muriel Fuller, P.O. Box 193, Grand Central Station, New York, New York 10017

Funk and Wagnalls, 380 Madison Avenue, New York, New York 10017

Garrard Publishing Co., 1607 North Market Street, Champaign, Illinois 61820

General Education, 96 Mt. Auburn Street, Cambridge, Massachusetts 02138

Gifted Teachers Books, Flossmoor, Illinois 60422

Gilberton Co., 101 Fifth Avenue, New York, New York 10003

Ginn and Company, Statler Building, Back Bay P.O. Box 191, Boston, Massachusetts 02117

Girl Scouts of the USA, 830 Third Avenue, New York, New York, 10022

Globe Book Co., 175 Fifth Avenue, New York, New York 10010

Western Pub. Co., Golden Press, 850 Third Avenue, New York, New York 10022

Grit Publishing Company, 208 West 3rd Street, Williamsport, Pennsylvania 17701

Grosset and Dunlap, Inc., 51 Madison Ave., New York, New York 10010

E. M. Hale and Co., 1201 South Hastings Way, Eau Claire, Wisconsin 54701

Hall and McCreary Co. (see Schmitt, Hall and McCreary Company)

Hammond Inc., Maplewood, New Jersey 07040

Harcourt, Brace and World, Inc., 757 Third Avenue, New York, New York 10017

Harper and Row, 49 East 33rd Street, New York, New York 10016

Harr Wagner Co., (see Field)

Hart Publishing Co., 510 Avenue of the Americas, New York, New York 10011

Harvard University Press, Kittredge Hall, 79 Garden Street, Cambridge, Massachusetts 02138

Harvey House, Irvington-on-Hudson, New York 10533

Hastings House Publishers, Inc., 10 E. 40 St., New York, New York 10016

Hawthorn Books, Inc., 70 Fifth Avenue, New York, New York 10011

D. C. Heath and Co., 125 Spring St., Lexington, Massachusetts 02173

Highlights for Children, Inc., 2300 West Fifth Avenue, Columbus, Ohio 43216

Hill and Wang, Inc., 72 Fifth Avenue, New York, New York 10011

Hodder (see Musson)

Holiday House, Inc., 18 E. 56th St., New York, New York 10022

Holt, Rinehart and Winston, Inc., 383 Madison Avenue, New York, New York 10017

Honor Products, 50 Moulton Street, Cambridge, Massachusetts 02138

Calvin Horn, Box 4204, Albuquerque, New Mexico 87106

The Horn Book, Inc., 585 Boylston Street, Boston, Massachusetts 02116

Houghton Mifflin Co., 2 Park St., Boston, Massachusetts 02107

Hudson Bay Company, Winnipeg, Manitoba, Canada

Ideal School Supply Co., 8312 Birkhoff Avenue, Chicago, Illinois 60620

Independent Schools Education Board, Milton, Massachusetts 02186

Indiana State Teachers College, Division of Special Education, Terre Haute, Indiana 47801

Indianapolis Public Schools, Division of Curriculum and Supervision, 1644 Roosevelt Avenue, Indianapolis, Indiana 46200

Information Service, Inc., 1435 Randolph Street, Detroit, Michigan 48226

Inrad, P.O. Box 4456, Lubbock, Texas 79400

Institute of Educational Research, 2226 Wisconsin Avenue, N.W., Washington, D.C. 20007

Instructo Products, Philadelphia, Pennsylvania 19131

International Publishers, 381 Park Ave., S., New York, New York 10016

International Reading Assn., Six Tyre Avenue, Newark, Delaware 19711

International Visual Education Service, 300 South Racine Avenue, Chicago, Illinois 60607

Iroquois Publishing Co., 1300 Alum Creek Drive, Columbus, Ohio 43216

Johnson Publishing Co., 1820 South Michigan Ave., Chicago, Illinois 60616

Judy Co., 310 North Second Street, Minneapolis, Minnesota 55411

P. J. Kenedy and Sons, 866 Third Ave., New York, New York 10022

Kenworthy Educational Service, 138 Allen Street, Buffalo, New York 14205

Keystone Education Press, 71 Fifth Avenue, New York, New York 10003

King Co., 2414 West Lawrence, Chicago, Illinois 60625

Alfred A. Knopf, Inc., 201 E. 50th St., New York, New York 10022

John Knox Press, 801 East Main Street, Box 1176, Richmond, Virginia 23209

Juanita V. Kusner, 6294 North 15th Road, Arlington, Virginia 22200

Laidlaw Brothers, Thatcher and Madison Avenues, River Forest, Illinois 60305

Lane Book Co., Menlo Park, California 94025

Lantern Press Inc., 257 Park Avenue South, New York, New York 20010

Laubach Literacy, Inc., Box 131, Syracuse, New York 13210

Learning Inc., 131 East 6th Avenue, Scottsdale, Arizona 85251

Learning Materials Inc., 100 East Ohio Street, Chicago, Illinois 60611

Learning Through Seeing, Sunland, California 91040

Lerner Publications Co., 241 First Ave., N., Minneapolis, Minnesota 55401

Lexicon Press, Box 5963, Bethesda, Maryland 20014

Link Enterprises, Decatur, Alabama 35601

The Lion Press, 274 Madison Avenue, New York, New York 10016

J. B. Lippincott Co., East Washington Square, Philadelphia, Pennsylvania 19105

Little, Brown and Co., 34 Beacon Street, Boston, Massachusetts 02106

Liveright Publishing Corp., 386 Park Avenue South, New York, New York 10016

Barnell Loft, Ltd., 111 South Centre Avenue, Rockville Center, L.I., New York 11570

Longmans, Green (see David McKay)

Los Angeles City Schools, Division of Instructional Services, Library Division, Los Angeles, California 90000

Lothrop, Lee and Shepard Co., 381 Park Avenue South, New York, New York 10016

Robert B. Luce, Inc., 1244 19th Street, N.W., Washington, D.C. 20036

Lyons and Carnahan, 407 East 25th Street, Chicago, Illinois 60616

A. C. McClurg and Co., 2121 Landmeir Road, Elk Grove Village, Illinois 60007

Macrae Smith Co., 225 S. 15th Street, Philadelphia, Pennsylvania 19102

McClelland & Steward, Ltd., 25 Hollinger Road, Toronto 16, Ontario, Canada

McCormick-Mathers Publishing Co. Inc., 300 Pike St., Cincinnati, Ohio 45202

McGraw-Hill Book Co., 330 West 42nd Street, New York, New York 10036

David McKay Co., (see Ives Washburn)

McKinley Publishing Co., Brooklawn, New Jersey 08030

Macmillan Co., 866 Third Avenue, New York, New York 10022

Macmillan Company of Canada, Ltd., 70 Bond Street, Toronto 2, Ontario, Canada

C. N. McRae, Unadilla, New York 13849

Maxton Publishers (see Follett Publishing Company)

Melmont Publishers, 1224 West Van Buren St., Chicago, Illinois 60607

Mentor Books, New American Library of World Literature, 501 Madison Avenue, New York, New York 10022

Meredith Corp., 1716 Locust Street, Des Moines, Iowa 50303

G. and C. Merriam Company, 47 Federal Street, Springfield, Massachusetts 01101

Charles E. Merrill Publishing Co., 1300 Alum Creek Drive, Columbus, Ohio 43216

Julian Messner, 1 West 39th Street, New York, New York 10018

Bruce Miller, Box 369, Riverside, California 92501

University of Minnesota Press, 2037 University Avenue, S.E., Minneapolis, Minnesota 55455

Mission Press, Box 3943, Los Angeles, California 90000

William Morrow and Co. Inc., 105 Madison Ave., New York, New York 10016

The Musson Book Co., Ltd., 1037 Vanderhoff Avenue, Toronto 17, Ontario, Canada

NAACP, 1790 Broadway, New York, New York 10019

National Audubon Society, 1130 Fifth Avenue, New York, New York 10000

National Conference of Christians and Jews, 43 West 57th Street., New York, New York 10019

National Council for the Social Studies (see National Education Association)

National Council of Teachers of English, 508 South Sixth Street, Champaign, Illinois 61820

National Council of Teachers of Mathematics (see National Education Association)

National Education Association, 1201 16th Street, N.W., Washington, D.C. 20036

National Geographic Society, 17 & M. Sts., N.W., Washington, D.C. 20036

Natural History Press, American Museum of Natural History, Central Park W. at 79 St. New York, New York 10024

Negro Bibliographic and Research Centers, Inc., 117 R Street, Washington, D.C. 20002

Thomas Nelson and Sons, Copewood and Davis Streets, Camden, New Jersey 08103

Thomas Nelson and Sons, Ltd., 81 Curlew Drive, Don Mills, Ontario, Canada

New American Library, 1301 Avenue of the Americas, New York, New York 10019

New Dimensions in Education, Long Island House, Jericho, New York, 11753

New Readers Press, (see Laubach Literacy, Inc.)

New York Graphic Society, 140 Greenwich Avenue, Greenwich, Connecticut 06830

New York Public Library, 42nd Street and Fifth Avenue, New York, New York 10018

New York State Education Department, Bureau of Secondary Curriculum Development, 31 Washington Avenue, Albany, New York 12201

New York State Historical Society, Cooperstown, New York 13326

New York University Press, Washington Sq., New York, New York 10003

New York Zoological Society, 185th Street and Southern Boulevard, New York, New York 10468

Newsmap of the Week, 1512 Orleans Street, Chicago, Illinois 60610

Newsweek, Inc., 350 Denison Avenue, Dayton, Ohio 45401

Noble and Noble Inc., 750 Third Ave., New York, New York 10017

W. W. Norton Co., Inc., 55 Fifth Avenue, New York, New York 10003

Ivan Obolensky, Inc., 1114 First Avenue, New York, New York 10021

Oceana Publications, Inc., Dobbs Ferry, New York 10522

O'Connor Remedial Service, 1040 East Maple Road, Birmingham, Michigan 48008

Office of Education (Publications Distribution Unit), Washington, D.C. 20202

O'Henheimer Publishers, Inc., 1330 Registers Town Road, Pikesville, Maryland 21208

Ohio State University Press, Hitchcock Hall, Rm. 316—2070 Neil Ave. Columbus, Ohio 43210

F. A. Owen Publishing Co., Dansville, New York 14437

Oxford University Press, 200 Madison Avenue, New York, New York 10016

Pacific Books, Box 558, Palo Alto, California 94302

Palo Verde Publishing Company, P.O. Box 5783, Tucson, Arizona 85702

Pantheon Books Inc., 201 E. 50 St., New York, New York 10022

Parents' Magazine Enterprises, Inc., 52 Vanderbilt Avenue, New York, New York 10017

R. W. Parkinson, Urbana, Illinois 61801

Parnassus Press, 2422 Ashby Avenue, Berkeley, California 94705
Pergamon Press, Inc., Maxwell House, Fairview Park, Elmsford, New York 10523
Free Library of Philadelphia, Logan Circle, Philadelphia, Pennsylvania 19102
Philadelphia Yearly Meeting of Friends, 1515 Cherry Street, Philadelphia, Pennsylvania 19102
Miriam Piequet, P.O. Box 1251, Ontario, California 91761
Pitman's ita Publications, 20 East 46th Street, New York, New York 10017
Pitman Publishing Corp., 20 East 46th Street, New York, New York 10017
Phonovisual Products, P.O. Box 5625, Washington, D.C. 20016
Platt and Munk Co., 1055 Bronx River Ave., Bronx, New York 10472
Play'N Talk, P.O. Box 18804, Oklahoma City, Oklahoma 73118
Plays Inc., 8 Arlington Street, Boston, Massachusetts 02116
Pocket Books, 630 Fifth Avenue, New York, New York 10020
Polyphone, Box 626, Shafter, California 93263
Popular Mechanics Co., 575 Lexington Avenue, New York, New York 10022
Popular Science Publishing Co., 355 Lexington Avenue, New York, New York 10017
Edith Potter, 460 Cedar Avenue, Highland Park, Illinois 60035
Prentice-Hall, Englewood Cliffs, New Jersey 07632
Primary Playhouse, Sherwood, Oregon 97140
Programmed Records, Inc., 154 Nassau Street, New York, New York 10000
Public Affairs Committee, 23 East 38th Street, New York, New York 10016
Publishers Co., 1106 Connecticut Avenue, N.W., Washington, D.C. 20000
G. P. Putnam's Sons, 200 Madison Avenue, New York, New York 10016
Quadrangle Books, Inc., 12 E. Delaware Place, Chicago, Illinois 60611
Rand McNally and Co., P.O. Box 7600, Chicago, Illinois 60680
Random House, 201 E. 50 St., New York, New York 10022
Reader's Digest Educational Service, Pleasantville, New York 10570
Readers Press, c/o E. M. Cousins, 141 East 19th Street, Brooklyn, New York 11226
Regents Publishing Co., 200 Park Avenue, South, New York, New York 10003
Reilly and Lee Co., 114 West Illinois Street, Chicago, Illinois 60610
Remedial Education Center, 1321 West Hampshire Avenue, Washington, D.C. 20006
Research Concepts, 36176 Parkdale, Livonia, Michigan 48150
Fleming H. Revel/Co., Old Tappan, New Jersey 07675
Frank E. Richards Co., 215 Church Street, Phoenix, New York 13135
John F. Rider Publisher, 116 West 14th Street, New York, New York 10011
Rinehart and Co. (see Holt, Rinehart and Winston)
Ward Ritchie Press, 3044 Riverside Drive, Los Angeles, California 90039
Ronald Press Co., 79 Madison Ave., New York, New York 10016
Richard Rosen Press Inc., 29 East 21st Street, New York, New York 10010
Row, Peterson and Co. (see Harper and Row)
H. M. Rowe Co., 624 North Gilmor Street, Baltimore, Maryland 21217
Roy Publishers, 30 East 74th Street, New York, New York 10021
Russell Publishers, 30 East 74th Street, New York, New York 10021
    10017

Ryerson Press, 299 Queen Street W., Toronto 2B, Ontario, Canada
Sackett and Wilhelms Lithographing Corporation, 110 Old Country Road, Carle Place, L.I., New York 11514
St. Albans School, Mount St. Alban, Washington, D.C. 20016
St. John's School for the Deaf, Milwaukee, Wisconsin 53201
St. Martin's Press, 175 Fifth Avenue, New York, New York 10010
Gordon Salisbury and Robert Sheridan, P.O. Box 942, Riverside California 92501
Benjamin H. Sanborn and Co. (See L. W. Singer Company)
S. J. R. Saunders of Toronto, Ltd., 1885 Leslie Street, Don Mills, Ontario, Canada
W. B. Saunders Co., 218 West Washington Square, Philadelphia, Pennsylvania 19105
Scarecrow Press, Inc., 52 Liberty St, Metuchen, New Jersey 08840
Schmitt, Hall and McCreary Co., Park Avenue at Sixth, Minneapolis, Minnesota 55415
Schocken Books, Inc., 67 Park Avenue, New York, New York 10016
Scholastic Magazines, 904 Sylvan Avenue, Englewood Cliffs, New Jersey 07632
School Aids and Textbooks Publishing Co., 20 Densley Avenue, Toronto, 15 Ontario, Canada
School Material Co., 1801 S. Michigan Avenue, Chicago, Illinois 60616
Schutle Publishing, 80 Fourth Avenue, New York, New York 10003
Science Research Associates, 259 East Erie Street, Chicago, Illinois 60611
William R. Scott, Inc., 333 Avenue of the Americas, New York, New York 10014
Scott, Foresman and Co., 1900 East Lake Avenue, Glenview, Illinois 60025
Charles Scribner's Sons, 597 Fifth Avenue, New York, New York 10017
Seabury Press Inc., 815 Second Avenue, New York, New York 10017
Seventeen, 320 Park Avenue, New York, New York 10022
Simon and Schuster, 630 Fifth Avenue, New York, New York 10020
Silver Burdett Co., 460 South Northwest Highway, Park Ridge, Illinois 60068
L. W. Singer Co., (see Random House)
Sky Publishing Co., Harvard College Observatory, 49 Bay State Road, Cambridge, Massachusetts 02138
Slater's Book Store, Ann Arbor, Michigan 48103
Southern Education Reporting Service, P.O. Box 6156, Nashville, Tennessee 37312
Sporting News, 2018 Washington Avenue, St. Louis, Missouri 63166
Sports Illustrated, Time and Life Building, Rockefeller Center, New York, New York 10020
Stanford University Press, Stanford, California 94305
Stanwix House, 3020 Chartiers Avenue, Pittsburgh, Pennsylvania 15204
Steck-Vaughn Co., P.O. Box 2028, Austin, Texas 78767
Sterling Publishing Co., 419 Park Avenue, South, New York, New York 10016
Henry Stewart, Inc., 249 Bowen Road, East Aurora, New York 14052
Strong Publications, Inc., 431 East 57th Street, New York, New York 10022
Study Books, Inc., P.O. Box 21, East Rockaway, New Jersey 11518
Syracuse University Press, Box 8, 920 Irving Avenue, University Station, Syracuse, New York 13210

Systems for Education, Inc., 612 North Michigan Avenue, Chicago, Illinois 60611

Teachers Aids Institute, 12848 Weber Way, Hawthorne, California 90250

Teachers College Press, Columbia University, 525 West 120th Street, New York, New York 10027

Teachers National Information Service, 273 Williams Street, Longmeadow, Massachusetts 02155

Teachers Practical Press, 47 Frank Street, Valley Stream, New York 11580

Teachers Publishing Corp., 23 Leroy Avenue, Darien, Connecticut 06820

Tennessee Book Co., 123 Third Avenue, Nashville, Tennessee 37203

3M Co. Visual Products Division, Box 3344, St. Paul, Minnesota 55101

Time Inc., Book Division, Time and Life Building, Rockefeller Center, New York, New York 10020

TMI, Grolier Inc., 575 Lexington Avenue, New York, New York 10022

Toronto Public Library, College and St. George Streets, Toronto 2B, Ontario, Canada

Travel Magazine, Inc., Travel Building, Floral Park, New York 11001

Trend, Inc., 5959 Hollywood Boulevard, Los Angeles, California 90028

Trident Press (see Simon and Schuster)

Charles E. Tuttle Co., 28 South Main Street, Rutland, Vermont 05701

Twayne Publishers, 31 Union Square West, New York, New York 10003

UNESCO, Place de Fontenoy 75, Paris—7e, France

U.S. Committee for UNICEF, 331 East 38th Street, New York, New York 10016

U.S. Government Printing Office, Washington, D.C. 20402

Universal Electronics Laboratories, 510 Hudson Street, Hackensack, New Jersey 07601

University of North Carolina Press, Box 510, Chapel Hill, North Carolina 27514

University Publishing Co., 1126 Q Street, Lincoln, Nebraska 68501

Urban Educational Publications, Box 7191, North End Station, Detroit, Michigan 48220

Vanguard Press, 424 Madison Avenue, New York, New York 10017

Van Nostrand Reinhold Co., 450 W. 33 St., New York, New York 10001

Viking Press, 625 Madison Avenue, New York, New York 10022

Visual Education Association, 207 South Perry Street, Dayton, Ohio 45402

Wadsworth Publishing Co., Belmont, California 94002

George Wahr Publishing, 316 S. State Street, Ann Arbor, Michigan 48108

Henry Z. Walck, 19 Union Square West, New York, New York 10003

Walker & Co., 720 Fifth Avenue, New York, New York 10019

Frederick Warne and Co., 101 Fifth Avenue, New York, New York 10003

Ives Washburn Inc., 750 Third Avenue, New York, New York 10017

Washington Square Press, (see Simon and Schuster)

Franklin Watts, 575 Lexington Avenue, New York, New York 10022

Wayne State University Press, 5980 Cass, Detroit, Michigan 48202

Webster Publishing, Manchester Road, Manchester, Missouri 63011

The Press of Case Western Reserve University, 2029 Adelbert Road, Cleveland, Ohio 44106

Westminster Press, Witherspoon Building, Philadelphia, Pennsylvania 19107

Wheeler Publishing Co. (see Harper and Row)

David White Co., 60 East 55th Street, New York, New York 10022

Albert Whitman and Co., 560 West Lake Street, Chicago, Illinois 60606

Whittlesey House (see McGraw-Hill)

John Wiley and Sons, Inc., 605 Third Ave., New York, New York 10016

H. W. Wilson Co., 950 University Avenue, Bronx, New York 10452

John C. Winston Co. (see Holt, Rinehart and Winston)

Wisconsin Council of Teachers of English, Wisconsin State University, Oshkosh, Wisconsin 54901

Wonder Books (see Grosset)

World Book (see Harcourt Brace and World)

World Publishing Co., 110 E. 59 St., New York, New York 10022

Zenith Books (see Doubleday)

Ziff-Davis Publishing Co., One Park Avenue, New York, New York 10016